Cambridge IGCSE®
and International Certificate

Spanish
Foreign Language

Jacqueline López-Cascante
Judith O'Hare

Series Editor:
Mike Thacker

HODDER
EDUCATION
AN HACHETTE UK COMPANY

With thanks to Dr Lucila Makin for her help in developing the Student Book.

Hodder Education, an Hachette UK company, 338 Euston Road, London NW1 3BH

Orders
Bookpoint Ltd, 130 Milton Park, Abingdon, Oxfordshire, OX14 4SB
tel: 01235 827827
fax: 01235 400401
e-mail: education@bookpoint.co.uk

Lines are open 9.00 a.m.–5.00 p.m., Monday to Saturday, with a 24-hour message answering service. You can also order through the Hodder Education website: www.hoddereducation.co.uk

© Jacqueline López-Cascante and Judith O'Hare 2013

ISBN 978-1-4441-8100-5

First printed 2013
Impression number   5   4   3   2   1
Year   2017   2016   2015   2014   2013

This material is recommended by Cambridge International Examinations in the resource list for the Cambridge IGCSE® (0530) and International Level 1/Level 2 Certificate (0678) Spanish syllabuses as a valuable teaching resource for very able, well-motivated learners with a good level of English.

® IGCSE is the registered trademark of Cambridge International Examinations.

All efforts have been made to trace copyright on items used.

Illustrations by Emily Hunter and Jim Watson

Cover photo: Fotolia

Inside photographs are reproduced by permission of: Azucena Herrero (p. 109); César Ballestros (pp. 93 d, e, 113, 127 a, i and o); Chris Robinson (p. 93 g); Emily Hunter (pp. 12 (top), 93 f, 110, 127 h); Felix Absoram (p. 135 top); Fernando de Dios (p. 135 bottom); Francesca Streatfield (p. 81); Hannah Thacker (p. 96, 127 b); Image Library (p. 120); Ingram (p. 34); Mike Thacker (pp. 41, 64, 72, 76, 93 a, b, c, h, i, 97, 100, 127 c, d, e, f, g, j, k, l, m, n, 128, 131, 133); Sebastián Bianchi (p. 100 bottom right); TopFoto (pp. 25, 39, 46, 48, 49, 52, 98, 112, 136, 137); Theodore Liasi/Alamy (p. 47), Chris Fredriksson/Alamy (p. 105), dbimages/Alamy (p. 116), BE&W agencja fotograficzna Sp. z.o.o./Alamy (p. 117); Fotolia (pp. 12 (bottom), 88, 103, 146).

Typeset by Aptara, Inc.

Printed in Italy

Hachette UK's policy is to use papers that are natural, renewable and recyclable products and made from wood grown in sustainable forests. The logging and manufacturing processes are expected to conform to the environmental regulations of the country of origin.

PO2180

Contents

How to make the most of this book

This book provides all you need to prepare for your **Cambridge IGCSE® in Spanish** or **Level 1/Level 2 International Certificate in Spanish** qualification. It also teaches you about the way of life of the people in the Spanish-speaking world and about the language they speak.

Each of the five modules contains a sequence of texts and activities that enable you to discover the language and use it effectively. Each section includes the following features:

At the beginning of each section, a list of the unit's topic content and the main **grammar** items covered

Lots of **listening** activities to practise skills

Tasks to ensure effective **writing** in Spanish

Up-to-date **reading** passages based on life in Spanish-speaking countries

Varied activities to practise **speaking**

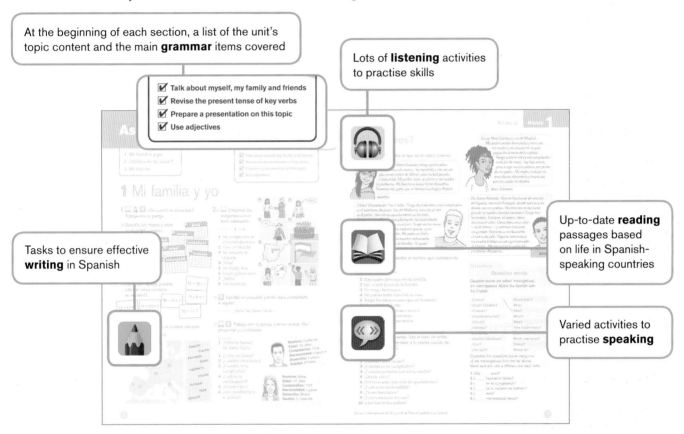

Watch out for these special features throughout the book too:

GRAMÁTICA These sections explain the key grammar points you need to know to communicate successfully in Spanish.

LENGUA CLAVE Under this heading, important language points (e.g. how to use certain phrases) are highlighted.

¡OJO! These sections offer tips on how to use and improve your Spanish.

CULTURA Items of interest relating to the culture and language of the Spanish-speaking world are included here.

At the end of each module you will find:

Exam Corner Specific preparation for the kind of tasks that you have to complete in the exams.

Vocabulario Lists of key vocabulary relating to the main topic areas covered in the module.

Towards the end of the book are:

Gramática A summary of all the grammar that you need to know with handy verb tables for quick reference.

Vocabulario A combined list of all the key vocabulary used in this book, in alphabetical order.

Enjoy the course!
Jacqueline López-Cascante   Judith O'Hare

About Exam Corner

The examinations

The **Cambridge IGCSE® Spanish** and **Cambridge International Level 1/Level 2 Certificate Spanish (UK schools)** qualifications are made up of four compulsory papers that test the four language skills. Each paper is taken at the end of the course. The content and questions are the same for both qualifications.

Exam Corners

At the end of each module are four Exam Corner pages that give specific advice and practice for the exam papers. Each Exam Corner covers all four skills: listening, reading, writing and speaking. The Exam Corners progress in difficulty throughout the book.

The following features appear in the Exam Corners:
- sample exam-style questions
- sample answers with commentary
- questions for further practice
- Tips for success
- Points to remember

Topics

You need to cover the topics listed below.

- **Area A**   Everyday activities
- **Area B**   Personal and social life
- **Area C**   The world around us
- **Area D**   The world of work
- **Area E**   The international world

Paper	Skill	Marks	Timing	Proportion of qualification
1	Listening	45 marks	Approx. 45 min	25%
2	Reading	45 marks	1 hour	25%
3	Speaking	100 marks	Approx. 15 min	25%
4	Writing	50 marks	1 hour	25%

 ## Paper 1: listening

Paper 1 is divided into three sections, each worth 15 marks. The extracts get longer as you work through the paper. **Section 1** recordings are mainly factual, **Section 2** requires listening for main points and identifying details and **Section 3** involves more detailed, longer recordings. You hear each recording twice. The instructions are written in Spanish. You must attempt to answer all three sections.

Paper 2: reading

Paper 2 is divided into three sections, each worth 15 marks. All instructions and questions are written in Spanish. **Section 1** has three questions, requiring you to read short pieces of text and answer the short questions. **Section 2** consists of questions on two texts, one short and the other longer. The longer text requires short answers in Spanish. **Section 3** includes two longer, more detailed texts with two questions that test general and specific comprehension. You must attempt to answer all three sections.

 # Paper 3: speaking

The speaking test is divided into three tests during a single interview.

Test 1 is a role play worth 30 marks that lasts approximately 5 minutes. You are given two role plays on a card in Spanish and have 15 minutes to prepare. Your teacher plays the part of the other person. You can keep the role-play card with you, but you must not make notes. The first role play is more straightforward than the second. Each role play consists of five tasks.

Test 2 is a presentation/conversation worth 30 marks and lasts approximately 5 minutes. You start by giving a 1–2 minute presentation on a topic of your choice, which you have prepared in advance. You are not allowed any notes. After your presentation, the teacher asks you spontaneous questions on the topic for a further 3 minutes.

Test 3 is a general conversation worth 30 marks and lasts approximately 5 minutes. This conversation takes place straight after your presentation conversation, but it is more general in nature. Your teacher tells you when this test is going to start. You may be asked some general questions about your everyday life and are expected to have a conversation about at least two of the topics areas A–E. To be awarded the highest marks you must use past and future tenses accurately.

The final 10 marks are awarded by the teacher for your overall performance, including pronunciation, intonation and fluency.

 # Paper 4: writing

Paper 4 is divided into two sections. All instructions and questions are written in Spanish.

Section 1 is worth 20 marks and has two questions. Question 1 is worth 5 marks and requires you to write single-word answers on a topic. Question 2 is a directed writing task worth 15 marks, of which 10 marks are available for communication and 5 marks for language.

Section 2 is worth 30 marks and offers a choice of three tasks from which you must select one to complete. For this longer writing task, 10 marks are available for communication, 8 marks for verbs and 12 marks for other linguistic features.

Así soy yo

1 **Mi familia y yo**
2 **¿Cómo es tu casa?**
3 **Mi barrio**

- ☑ Talk about myself, my family and friends
- ☑ Revise the present tense of key verbs
- ☑ Prepare a presentation on this topic
- ☑ Use adjectives

1 Mi familia y yo

1 📖 ✏️ 💬 **¿De cuánto te acuerdas?**
Trabaja con tu pareja.

a Descifra los meses y dilos en el orden correcto.

4 brial
3 erone
1 ijnuo
2 verbeniom
8 mebiderci
5 razom
6 ostago
7 amyo
12 brucote
9 boferre
10 luijo
11 remespetib

b ¿Con qué rapidez puedes calcular estos números en español?

65 + 40 = ?
25 × 4 = ?
90 − 11 = ?
15 + 12 = ?
21 + 34 = ?
50 − 7 = ?

c Empareja la letra con el nombre del pais.

Ejemplo: **a** — *Inglaterra*

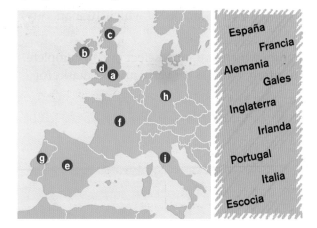

España
Francia
Alemania
Gales
Inglaterra
Irlanda
Portugal
Italia
Escocia

2a 📖 Empareja las imágenes con el texto adecuado.

Ana
15
Madrid

Ejemplo: **1 — d**

1 Mi cumpleaños es el veinte de enero.
2 Vivo en Madrid.
3 Me encanta el deporte.
4 ¡Hola!
5 Me llamo Ana.
6 Tengo quince años.
7 ¡Adiós!
8 Soy española.

b 💬 Escribe un pequeño párrafo para presentarte a alguien.

Ejemplo: *¡Hola! Me llamo Mark…*

c 📖 💬 Trabaja con tu pareja. Lee los textos. Haz preguntas y contéstalas.

Ejemplo:
1 *¿Cómo te llamas?*
Me llamo María.

1 ¿Cómo te llamas?
2 ¿Cuántos años tienes?
3 ¿Cuándo es tu cumpleaños?
4 ¿Cuál es tu nacionalidad?
5 ¿Dónde vives?
6 ¿Qué pasatiempos te gustan?

Nombre: Guillermo
Edad: 16 años
Cumpleaños: 31/4
Nacionalidad: mejicana
Domicilio: Cancún
Gustos: el fútbol

Nombre: Maria
Edad: 16 años
Cumpleaños: 12/7
Nacionalidad: inglesa
Domicilio: Bristol
Gustos: la natación

¿Quién eres?

3 🎧 📖 Escucha y lee lo que dicen estos jóvenes.

¡Hola! Me llamo Juanita y tengo quince años. Nací el once de marzo. Soy española y vivo en un piso en el centro de Bilbao, una ciudad grande e industrial. Mi padre, Juan, es médico y mi madre es profesora. Mi hermano Javier tiene doce años. Tenemos dos gatos que se llaman Lechuga y Pepino.

Juanita

¡Hola! ¡Encantado! Soy Carlos. Tengo dieciséis años y mi cumpleaños es el veintiuno de junio. Soy de Mallorca, una isla al este de España. Vivo en un apartamento en la costa. Es muy bonito. Desafortunadamente, las autoridades no nos permiten animales en el piso. Tengo un hermano y una hermana. Los dos son mayores que yo, pero nos llevamos todos muy bien. Mi padre es chef y mi madre trabaja con él en nuestro restaurante. En verano ayudamos toda la familia. ¡Es guay!

Carlos

Yo soy Mari Carmen y soy de Madrid. Mis padres están divorciados y vivo con mi madre y mi abuela en un piso pequeño al oeste de la cuidad. Tengo catorce años y mi cumpleaños es el dos de mayo. Soy hija única, pero tengo muchos primos por parte de mi padre. Mi madre trabaja en una oficina durante la semana así que me cuida mi abuela.

Mari Carmen

Me llamo Antonio. Vivo en Huelva en el suroeste de España, cerca de Portugal, donde nací yo y de donde son mis padres. Nuestro piso es bastante grande ¡y nuestra familia también! Tengo tres hermanos. Enrique, el mayor, tiene diecinueve años; Elena tiene once años — es la menor — y además está Juan, mi gemelo. Nacimos a medianoche el nueve de julio. Papá es mecánico y mi madre trabaja en un supermercado del barrio. Me encantan los animales y tenemos dos perros.

Antonio

a 🏫 ¿Qué dicen? Escribe el nombre que corresponde con cada frase.

Ejemplo: **1** — *Juanita*

1 Hay cuatro personas en mi familia.
2 Soy el más joven de la familia.
3 No tengo hermanos.
4 No puedo tener mascota en casa.
5 Tengo la misma edad que mi hermano.
6 Vivo al lado del mar.
7 Solo tengo un hermano menor.
8 Mi padre no vive conmigo.
9 Tengo una hermana menor.
10 No soy español.

b 🏫 Trabaja con tu pareja. Usa el texto de arriba para ayudarte a entrevistar a tu pareja usando las preguntas siguientes.

1 ¿Cómo te llamas?
2 ¿Cuántos años tienes?
3 ¿Cuándo es tu cumpleaños?
4 ¿Cuántas personas hay en tu familia?
5 ¿Dónde vives?
6 ¿Vives en una casa o en un apartamento?
7 ¿Cuál es tu nacionalidad?
8 ¿Tienes hermanos?
9 ¿Tienes mascota en casa?
10 ¿Qué hacen tus padres?

GRAMÁTICA

Question words

Question words are called 'interrogatives', *los interrogativos*. Match the Spanish with the English.

¿Cómo?	Where from?
¿Cuál? ¿Cuáles?	Who?
¿Cuándo?	How?
¿Cuánto/a/os/as?	When?
¿Dónde?	What?
¿Adónde?	How much/many?
¿De dónde?	Why?
¿Quién? ¿Quiénes?	Which one/ones?
¿Qué?	Where?
¿Por qué?	Where to?

Complete the questions below using one of the interrogatives from the list above. Make sure you use a different one each time.

1 ¿De _____ eres?
2 ¿ _____ hermanos tienes?
3 ¿ _____ es tu cumpleaños?
4 ¿ _____ es tu número de teléfono?
5 ¿ _____ eres?
6 ¿ _____ nacionalidad tienes?

4 🎧 Listen and then complete the table in English.

	A	B	C	D
Nombre				
Edad				
Cumpleaños				
Nacionalidad				
Domicilio				
Familia				
Mascotas				

abuelo   abuela

madre   padre   tía   tío

hijo   hija

5a 📖 Trabaja con tu pareja.

¿Qué significan estas palabras?
Usa el diccionario para ayudarte.

1 bisabuelo
2 primo segundo
3 cuñado
4 madrastra

5 novia
6 nuera
7 suegro
8 hermanastra

b ✏️ Escoge una palabra del recuadro para completar cada frase.

tía   primo   hermano   marido   madrastra   hija   mujer   abuela

Ejemplo: La madre de mi padre es mi **abuela**.

1 La madre de mi padre es mi _____ .
2 La hermana de mi madre es mi _____ .
3 El hijo de mi tío es mi _____ .
4 La segunda mujer de mi padre es mi _____ .
5 Mi madre es la _____ de mi padre.
6 Mi padre es el _____ de mi madre.
7 El hijo de mi madre es mi _____ .
8 Mi hermana es la _____ de mi madre.

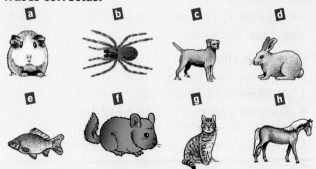
4

6 ¿Cuál es tu opinión? Adapta cada frase para ti.

Ejemplo: *1 Me parezco a mi madre o*
No me parezco a mi madre.

1 Me parezco a mi madre.
2 Me llevo bien con mi padre.
3 No me llevo bien con mi hermano.
4 Mi abuela me trata como a un adulto.
5 Mi hermana mayor me trata como a un niño.
6 Mis padres son bastante estrictos.
7 Me molesta mi hermano menor.
8 Discuto mucho con mi hermana.
9 Mi hermano y yo somos muy parecidos.
10 No me parezco físicamente a los demás de mi familia.

¡OJO!

Remember to use connectives to make what you say and write more interesting.

y	and	porque	because
que	that, which, who	si	if
también	also	cuando	when
además	besides	ni…ni	neither…nor
pero	but	sin embargo	however
o	or	siempre	always

Escoge una palabra de la lista arriba para formar una frase más larga.

Ejemplo: *1 Tengo un hermano. No tengo hermanas.*
> Tengo un hermano, pero no tengo hermanas.

1 Tengo un hermano. No tengo hermanas.
2 Mi padre tiene el pelo moreno. Mi padre tiene los ojos azules.
3 Tenemos muy buenos amigos. Se llaman Maite y Ramón.
4 No me gusta jugar al fútbol. No me gusta jugar al rugby.
5 Soy alto y delgado. Mi hermana es alta y delgada.
6 Mi hermana menor me molesta. Me coge todas mis cosas personales. En general es una chica buena.
7 Me encantan los animales. No nos permiten tener un animal en el piso.
8 Soy muy deportista. Los lunes juego al tenis. Los jueves monto en bicicleta.
9 Hablo portugués. Mi madre es portuguesa. Hablamos portugués en casa.
10 Mi abuelo es muy alto. Tiene el pelo gris. Es alegre. Resulta gracioso.

7 Listen to what Ana says about her family. Answer the questions in English.

1 How old is Ana?
2 Where is she from?
3 What does she say about the English language?
4 How many people are there in her family?
5 What does she say about her mother?
6 What does she say about her father?
7 What does she tell you about her brother and her sisters?

GRAMÁTICA

The present tense of four key verbs

When talking about yourself and your family the following key verbs are used. Learn them well.

1 *llamarse* (to be called)
me llamo
te llamas
se llama
nos llamamos
os llamáis
se llaman

2 *tener* (to have)
tengo
tienes
tiene
tenemos
tenéis
tienen

3 *vivir* (to live)
vivo
vives
vive
vivimos
vivís
viven

4 *ser* (to be)
soy
eres
es
somos
sois
son

¡Atención! In Spanish, when giving your age you say 'I **have** X years.'
***Tengo** catorce años.*

Completa las frases siguientes usando el verbo y la persona correctos.

Ejemplo: *1 Mis hermanos **se llaman** Juan y Martín.*

1 Mis hermanos _____ Juan y Martín.
2 Mis padres y yo _____ en Madrid.
3 ¿De dónde _____ tú?
4 Mi padre _____ cuarenta años.
5 Mi mejor amiga _____ Ana.
6 Pablo y Juan _____ mis hermanos.
7 ¿Dónde _____ tu madre?
8 ¡Hola! _____ Juanita, ¿y tú?
9 Mis padres _____ muchos amigos.
10 En mi familia _____ cuatro personas.

8a 🎧 ¿En qué trabajan sus padres? Escribe las palabras adecuadas en la tabla.

1
cocinero

2
enfermera

3
profesora

4
ingeniero

5
mecánica

6
ama de casa

7
peluquero

8
auxiliar de vuelos

9
dentista

10
dependienta

11
hombre de negocios

12
bombero

13
taxista

14
recepcionista

15
periodista

16
cartero

17
electricista

18
granjeros

19
fotógrafa

20
secretaria

Madre	Padre
Ejemplo: secretaria (20)	*hombre de negocios (11)*

¡OJO!

The indefinite article *un, una* is omitted in Spanish before an unqualified noun indicating nationality, rank or occupation, used after **ser** (to be). For example:

Es italiano. — He is Italian.
Mi hermano es profesor. — My brother is a teacher.

If you cannot remember the Spanish for a job, you could describe it by saying where a person works:

Trabaja en una oficina. — He/She works in an office.
Trabaja en un colegio. — He/She works in a school.
Trabaja con enfermos. — He/She works with sick people.
Trabaja con niños. — He/She works with children.

b 💬 ✏️ Pregunta a tus compañeros de clase en qué trabajan sus padres. Escribe un pequeño párrafo para explicar tus resultados usando las siguientes frases para ayudarte.

Haz la pregunta siguiente a X personas:
¿En qué trabajan tus padres?

Aquí están los resultados de mi encuesta:
- X trabajan en el sector empresarial (work in business).
- X trabajan desde casa (work from home).
- X están en el paro/no trabajan (are unemployed/don't work).
- En el futuro me gustaría trabajar _____ porque _____ .

9 📖 ✏️ Escribe una respuesta al correo electrónico siguiente.

Fichero Edición Inserción Formato Instrumentos Mensaje

¡Hola!

Me llamo Salvador. Tengo quince años y nací el ocho de agosto. Soy estadounidense y vivo en Florida en Estados Unidos. ¿Y tú? En mi familia hay cuatro personas. Tengo un hermano que se llama Tobi. Vivimos en un piso grande. Tengo un perro y un gato y ¡nada más!

¡Hasta luego!

Salvador

10 💬 Ahora prepara una breve presentación de ti mismo y de tu familia. Menciona lo siguiente:
- nombre
- edad
- cumpleaños
- nacionalidad
- domicilio
- familia
- mascotas

¿Cómo eres?

11a 📖 Lee el texto. Empareja cada persona con la descripción adecuada.

Ejemplo: 1 — e

1 Soy alta y delgada con ojos azules y el pelo largo, rubio y rizado.
2 No soy ni alto ni bajo. Tengo ojos azules y el pelo corto y pelirrojo.
3 Llevo gafas. Tengo el pelo corto y castaño.
4 Soy muy baja con el pelo largo, liso y negro.
5 Tengo ojos azules y pecas. Tengo el pelo medianamente largo y castaño.
6 Tengo el pelo gris y llevo barba. Tengo los ojos marrones.
7 Soy muy alta con el pelo ondulado y largo. Tengo los ojos marrones.
8 Soy calvo y tengo bigote.

b 💬 Trabaja con tu pareja. Descríbete a ti mismo y a los miembros de tu familia. Describe también a algunos de tus amigos.

Ejemplo: ¿Cómo es tu madre?
Mi madre es alta y delgada. Tiene el pelo largo y castaño y los ojos azules.

12 🎧 Carolina and Miguel are talking about their families. Answer the following questions in English.

1 In what way are both families similar?
2 How well does Carolina get on with her elder sister?
3 Explain Miguel's relationship with his sisters.
4 What does Miguel have to say about his mother?
5 What do they both have to say about their fathers?

LENGUA CLAVE

¿Cómo eres?	(no) soy	alto/a
	(no) es	bajo/a
¿Cómo es tu...?		de talla media
		ni alto/a ni bajo/a
¿Cómo es tu pelo?	tengo el pelo	corto
		largo
		rizado
		ondulado
		liso
		rubio
		castaño
		negro
	soy	calvo/a pelirrojo/a
¿De qué color son tus ojos?	tengo los ojos	azules
		marrones
		verdes
		grises
		negros
¿Llevas gafas?	llevo gafas	

Adjectives

Adjectives have to agree with the noun they describe and are generally positioned after rather than before the noun as in English.

Masculine singular	Masculine plural	Feminine singular	Feminine plural
alto	altos	alta	altas
largo	largos	larga	largas
negro	negros	negra	negras

Ejemplo: Mi herman**a** es alt**a**, tiene el pel**o** larg**o** y negr**o**.

Adjectives that end in a consonant or with the letter –e only change in the plural form.

Masculine singular	Masculine plural	Feminine singular	Feminine plural
azul	azules	azul	azules
verde	verdes	verde	verdes
gris	grises	gris	grises

Ejemplo: Mi madre tiene el pelo **gris** y los ojos **azules**.

Piensa bien en cómo terminan estos adjetivos y completa las frases siguientes.

1 Me llamo Ana. Tengo los ojos azul… y soy pelirroj… . Soy alt… .
2 Soy Pepe. Mi pelo es cort… y negr… y mis ojos son marron… .
3 Mi hermana es baj… y gord… . Tiene el pelo larg… y rubi… .
4 Mi mejor amigo se llama Jaime. No es ni alt… ni baj… . Tiene el pelo castañ… y los ojos gris… .
5 Soy hija únic… . Tengo el pelo cort… y los ojos marron… .
6 Mi amiga Belén no es ni alt… ni baj… . Es una persona muy simpátic… .
7 Me llevo bien con mi tía Rosa porque es muy sincer… .
8 Tengo un gato grand… con pelo negr… . Desafortunadamente mi hermano es alérgic… al pelo de los gatos.
9 Mis padres están divorciad…, pero son supersimpátic… y me llevo bien con ellos.
10 Mi familia es bastante pequeñ… .

13 🎧 ✏️ Escucha lo que dicen. Completa la tabla con los detalles que faltan.

Nombre	Talla	Ojos	Pelo	Otros
Ejemplo: Ana	baja	azules	negro largo	16 años española
Sandra				
Enrique				
Catalina				
José				
Sara				

14a 📖 ¿Cómo eres? Mira las imágenes. Emparéjalas con las palabras del recuadro.

Ejemplo: **a** — deportivo

antipático   simpático   deportivo   inteligente
trabajador   un poco loco   amable   tonto
perezoso   divertido   tímido   aburrido

8

b  ¿Qué dicen estos jóvenes de sus amigos?
Completa la tabla con los detalles que faltan.

Nombre	Carácter
Ejemplo: Marco	*simpático y divertido*
Yésica	
Juan	
Marta	
Paco	
Susi	

15 📖 Lee lo siguiente.

¿Eres como tu nombre?

En los países hispanohablantes la mayoría de la
gente tiene uno o dos nombres y dos apellidos.
El primer apellido es en general el primer apellido
de la familia del padre, mientras el segundo es el
primer apellido de la madre. Las chicas normalmente
no cambian sus apellidos al casarse. Por ejemplo,
si Juan López García se casa con María Arollo Cruz,
los dos mantendrán sus apellidos. Entonces digamos
que tienen un hijo llamado Felipe, su nombre
completo sería Felipe López Arollo. Los nombres
de pila* son a menudo gracias a algún santo,
aunque también pueden ser de planetas o estaciones.
Si buscas los orígenes de los apellidos en tu familia,
es muy probable que tenga relación con el lugar
donde vivía o con la profesión que tenía la mayoría.
¿Pero sabías que hay conexiones entre nombres
españoles y la personalidad? ¡Además pasa con
los colores! Mira esto:

Nombre	Carácter	Color	Carácter
Ana	simpático	azul	valiente
Jorge	generoso	verde	animado
Dolores	triste	negro	obediente
Pilar	honesto	marrón	sencillo
Santi	hablador	rojo	romántico
Begoña	cariñoso	amarillo	extrovertido
Rosario	ambicioso	blanco	tranquilo
Antonio	inteligente	gris	tímido
Felipe	paciente	naranja	deportivo

*first name

a 📖 ¿Verdad o mentira? Indica si las
frases son verdaderas (V) o falsas (F).

1 Todos los españoles tienen cuatro nombres.
2 Los apellidos españoles vienen de los dos padres.
3 Las mujeres cambian sus apellidos cuando
se casan.
4 La mayoría de los nombres son nombres
de planetas.
5 Los apellidos a menudo tienen que ver con
un trabajo.

b ✏️ ¡A adivinar! Trabaja con tu pareja. ¿Cuántos
adjetivos conoces? Haz una lista. Usa un
diccionario para ayudarte.

16 💬 Trabaja con tu pareja. Haz preguntas sobre los diferentes miembros de su familia. ¡No te olvides de contestarlas!

Ejemplo:
A: ¿Cómo se llama tu hermano menor?
B: Mi hermano menor se llama Tomás.
A: ¿Cuántos años tiene?
B: Tiene doce años.
A: ¿Cuándo es su cumpleaños?
B: Su cumpleaños es el once de enero.
A: ¿Cómo es?
B: Es alto y delgado. Tiene el pelo corto y negro
y los ojos azules.
A: ¿Cómo es su carácter?
B: Es muy travieso, pero también es cariñoso.

2 ¿Cómo es tu casa?

1a 🎧 Escucha las descripciones para cada persona que habla. Apunta las letras que corresponden.

Ejemplo: **1** *Begoña* — *h, i*

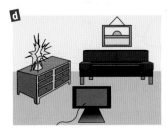
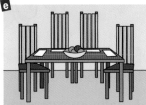

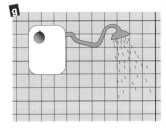
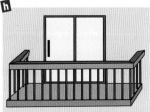
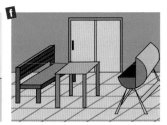

b 🎧 📖 ¿Qué dicen? Escribe el nombre de la persona correcta.

Ejemplo: **1** — *Juan*

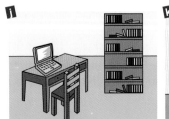

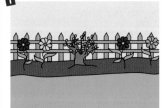

1 Vive en una casa.
2 Vive en un piso.
3 Nació donde vive.
4 Vive en la costa.
5 Comparte su dormitorio.
6 Vive en un sitio tranquilo.
7 No tiene jardín.
8 Vive en el campo.
9 Acaba de mudarse.

CULTURA

Look at these addresses:

C/ Sepúlveda 28 1° B, 28045 Madrid

Carrer Gardel 32, Barrio Montes, Barranquilla, Colombia

For addresses in Spanish-speaking countries the C/ stands for *Calle* (road or street), although in countries like Colombia the word *Carrer* may also be used. You might also see *Av*, which stands for *Avenida*. In most cases the number of the building comes after the road name and there is always some form of postcode. The postcode indicates in which part of the city or town an address is located.

2a Escucha lo que dicen. Rellena la tabla con los detalles que faltan.

	Ejemplo	1	2
Domicilio	casa		
Habitaciones	5		
Arriba	2 dormitorios y baño		
Abajo	cocina/salón-comedor/aseo		
Afuera	nada		
Otros detalles	pequeño comparto con hermana		

b Trabaja con tu pareja. Usa los apuntes de la actividad anterior. Haz preguntas y contéstalas.

1 ¿Vives en una casa o en un piso?
2 ¿Cuántas habitaciones tiene?
3 ¿Qué hay arriba/abajo/afuera?

c Usa esta tabla para ayudarte a escribir una descripción de tu casa. Intenta usar adjetivos y conectores para hacerla más interesante.

Ejemplo: Vivo en una casa grande en las afueras de Santander, cerca de la costa. Arriba tenemos cuatro dormitorios y un baño. Abajo hay salón, comedor y cocina. Afuera hay un jardín pequeño. También tenemos garaje.

vivo en	un piso un apartamento una casa una granja un chalet	grande pequeño/a	en el centro de en las afueras de cerca de en la primera/segunda planta de en el campo en la costa
arriba/abajo hay	... dormitorios un cuarto de baño un aseo una ducha un salón un comedor una cocina un despacho		
afuera hay	balcón patio terraza jardín garaje		

d Rellena los espacios con los verbos de encuadro. ¡Ojo! Hay tres verbos de más.

vamos   van   juega   trabaja   pongo   estudia   viven   echa

1 Mis padres _____ en Buenos Aires desde hace 35 años.
2 Mi hermana mayor _____ español desde hace mucho tiempo.
3 Mi padre _____ como contable desde hace 20 años.
4 Isabel y yo _____ al colegio británico desde hace nueve meses.
5 Mi amigo Sebastián _____ al golf desde hace poco.

GRAMÁTICA

How long?

To say you how long you have been doing something, use *desde hace* + a verb in the present tense.

Example: I've been living in my house for 2 years.
Vivo en mi casa desde hace dos años.

Rellena los espacios con la forma correcta del verbo entre paréntesis.
1 _____ el francés desde hace 3 años. (*yo, aprender*)
2 _____ en España desde hace 2 años. (*nosotros, vivir*)
3 Está _____ sus deberes desde hace 2 horas. (*hacer*)
4 _____ en este hotel desde hace 6 meses. (*ellos, trabajar*)
5 _____ sus CDs desde hace 10 años. (*ella, comprar*)

3a  What do Carla and Rafael say about their dream home? Answer the questions in English.

1 Where would Carla like to live?
2 Why?
3 How does she describe her dream home?
4 Where would Rafael like to live?
5 Why?
6 Describe Rafael's dream home.

b Describe tu casa ideal.

Ejemplo: Mi casa ideal es una casa grande…

4 Lee la carta de Darío y contesta las preguntas.

> Lima, 8 de enero
>
> Querido amigo,
>
> ¿Qué tal? Como ya sabes, acabamos de mudarnos de casa. Antes vivía en el campo cerca de Trujillo, pero desde el mes pasado, vivimos en un piso en el centro de la ciudad de Lima. El piso no es grande, así que tengo que compartir mi habitación con mi hermano menor. Éste me molesta mucho, sobre todo por la tarde cuando él quiere jugar con el ordenador mientras yo estoy estudiando. Sin embargo el piso es práctico y a solo diez minutos andando del colegio y del polideportivo.
>
> Estamos en la tercera planta de un bloque moderno. Hay una entrada pequeña y a la izquierda una cocina. El salón-comedor es enorme. Está a la derecha, enfrente del cuarto de baño. Al final del pasillo hay tres dormitorios. También hay un balcón que da al jardín y es muy tranquilo. No tenemos animales. Las autoridades no los permiten. Además a mi padre le irritan mucho el ruido y el olor. ¿Y tú? ¿Cómo es donde vives? ¿Vives en una casa o en un piso?
>
> Un saludo,
>
> Darío

1 ¿Desde cuándo vive Darío en Lima?
2 ¿Por qué le molesta compartir su habitación con su hermano?
3 ¿Por qué le gusta el piso? Menciona dos razones.
4 ¿Por qué Darío no tiene mascota? Menciona dos razones.

5 📖 Mira la imagen. Indica si las frases son verdaderas (V) o falsas (F).

Ejemplo: En mi dormitorio hay dos camas — V

1 Hay una lámpara en la cama.

2 La estantería está encima de la mesa.

3 El armario está al lado de la puerta.

4 Hay una mesilla entre las camas.

5 Nuestra habitación está muy ordenada.

6 Hay una silla delante de la mesa.

7 En las paredes hay muchos pósters.

6 🎧 Añade los cuartos usando palabras del recuadro, según la descripción.

Ejemplo: 8 — la entrada

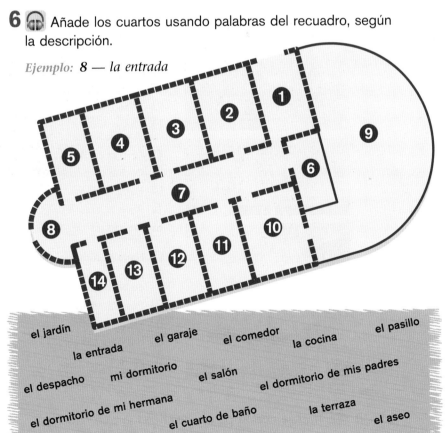

el jardín

la entrada

el despacho   mi dormitorio

el garaje   el comedor   la cocina   el pasillo

el salón

el dormitorio de mi hermana   el cuarto de baño   la terraza   el dormitorio de mis padres   el aseo

GRAMÁTICA

Using prepositions

Learn the following prepositions:

entre	between
sobre	on top of/above
encima de	on
detrás de	behind
delante de	in front of
a la derecha de	to the right of
al lado de	beside/next to
debajo de	under
enfrente de	opposite
contra	against
cerca de	near
a la izquierda de	to the left of

Some of these prepositions are followed by **de**. Remember that **de + el = del**

Example: La cama está al lado del armario.
The bed is beside the wardrobe.

Las tareas de casa

7a Busca estas palabras en el diccionario. ¿En qué habitación se encuentran? Completa la tabla.

- el lavaplatos
- la cama
- el sofá
- la bañera
- la mesa
- el retrete
- el televisor
- la silla
- el armario
- la nevera
- el horno
- la estantería
- el sillón
- la lavadora
- la cómoda
- el aparador
- el congelador
- el fregadero

Habitación	
la sala de estar	el sofá, el televisor...
el comedor	
la cocina	
el cuarto de baño	
el dormitorio	

b Trabaja con tu pareja. Describe y compara los cuartos en tu casa.

Ejemplo:

A: *Vivo en una casa grande y moderna.*
B: *Yo también vivo en una casa pero no es grande.*
A: *En mi dormitorio hay dos camas.*
B: *En mi dormitorio solo hay una cama.*
A: *El salón está al lado del comedor.*
B: *El salón de mi casa no está al lado del comedor. Está enfrente del comedor.*

8 Prepara una breve presentación sobre tu casa.

Usa estos apuntes para ayudarte:
- Dónde vives.
- Con quién vives.
- Cuánto tiempo llevas viviendo allí.
- Qué habitaciones hay en la casa.
- Dónde están las habitaciones.
- Cómo es tu dormitorio.

9a Escucha y empareja las imágenes con el texto.

Ejemplo: **1** — *c*

1. Friego los platos.
2. Pongo la mesa.
3. Paseo con el perro.
4. Lavo el coche.
5. Cocino un poco.
6. Hago mi cama.
7. Saco la basura.
8. Arreglo mi dormitorio.
9. Hago la compra.
10. Hago un poco de bricolaje.
11. Paso la aspiradora.
12. Plancho la ropa.
13. Hago de canguro.
14. Vacío el lavavajillas.

b Trabaja con tu pareja. Averigua lo que hace y lo que no hace para ayudar en casa.

10 🎧 La familia de Maite tiene un hotel. ¿Qué dice de las tareas de casa? Completa la tabla con los detalles que faltan.

Persona	Actividad 1	Frecuencia	Actividad 2	Frecuencia
Ejemplo: padre	*basura*	*cada mañana*	*bricolaje*	*de vez en cuando*
madre				
Juan (hermano)				
Maite				

11a 📖 💬 Trabaja con tu pareja. Lee lo que dicen estos jóvenes ¿Estás de acuerdo con ellos? ¿Por qué (no)?

Ejemplo: *Estoy de acuerdo con Maribel. Su hermano debería ayudar.*

No sé porque Ramón no está contento. Tiene que arreglar su dormitorio, pero le gusta tener las cosas en su sitio.

Tengo que arreglar mi dormitorio todos los días. Me gusta tener las cosas en su sitio. Pero mi hermana menor deja sus cosas por todas partes y mis padres no dicen nada. No sé por qué. No estoy nada contento.

Ramón

Mis padres pagan a mi hermana por hacer tareas domésticas mientras que yo ayudo siempre sin cobrar. Hago mi cama y todo. No me dan nada y no estoy contento.

Alberto

Mi hermana y yo tenemos que quitar la mesa y fregar los platos después de cada comida. No creo que sea justo porque mi hermano no hace nada. Sale del salón después de comer y se sienta enfrente del ordenador.

Maribel

b 📝 Escribe sobre lo que pasa en tu casa.

Los sábados por la tarde mi padre y mi hermano mayor van al estadio de fútbol. Mi madre y yo tenemos que hacer las compras y limpiar la casa. No me gusta ayudar y estoy harta.

Carla

Asking questions

For people you know well, use the second person singular (*tú/tu*):

¿Qué hace tu padre?
¿Qué quieres ser?

Also, use a variety of questions and phrases such as:

¿Quién?; ¿Cuándo?; ¿Cómo? etc.,
el lunes; por la tarde/mañana;
siempre/nunca/a menudo.

How many questions and answers can you make?

Example: ¿Ayudas en casa?
Sí, ayudo. Lavo los platos y hago mi cama. ¿Y tú?
Siempre lavo los platos pero nunca hago mi cama.

LENGUA CLAVE

Los adverbios siguientes te ayudarán a hacer tus respuestas más interesantes:

siempre	always
a menudo	often
mucho	a lot
muy poco	very little
nunca	never
a veces	sometimes
cada día/todos los días	each/every day
por la mañana/tarde	in the morning/afternoon
los fines de semana	at the weekends
el lunes	on Mondays

El dinero

12a 🎧 Mira las imágenes. Escucha lo que dicen los jóvenes. ¿En qué gastan su dinero?

Ejemplo: 1 — c

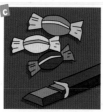

b 📖 🏫 ¿Cuánto dinero reciben? Lee el texto y completa la tabla con los detalles que faltan.

Según una encuesta hecha recientemente parece ser que no todos los jóvenes están contentos con la cantidad de dinero que reciben. Preguntamos a nuestros lectores. Debajo hay una selección de sus respuestas. ¿Qué piensas tú? Mándanos tus opiniones.

> A mí me dan 80€ al mes. Si necesito más para algo como salir con mis amigos o para comprar un regalo especial, le ayudo a mi padre en su empresa para ganar un poco de dinero extra. Eso me parece muy bien. Muchos de mis amigos trabajan cada fin de semana pero no quiero hacer eso porque tengo que estudiar también.
>
> **Conchita (16 años)**

> Mis padres no me dan nada de dinero. Así que tengo que trabajar en un restaurante los fines de semana, limpiando mesas y fregando. No es justo, pero por lo menos el dinero es mío para gastar como quiera.
>
> **Paco (17 años)**

> Mis padres me dan 8 pesos cada día y aparte de eso me pagan todo como mi ropa. El problema es que no siempre puedo hacer lo que quiero. Pero no está mal del todo.
>
> **Ana (15 años)**

> Recibo unos 20€ cada semana. Eso es mucho menos que mis amigos.
>
> **Eduardo (14 años)**

> Mis padres me dan 25 colones los sábados. No está mal porque trabajo también. Creo que los padres deberían pagar más a sus hijos, pero solo si hacen cosas en casa para ayudar.
>
> **Maite (15 años)**

Nombre	Cantidad	Frecuencia	Opinión
Ejemplo: Eduardo	*20€*	*cada semana*	*menos que sus amigos*

c 💬 Trabaja con tu pareja. Contesta las preguntas.

1 ¿Te dan dinero tus padres?
2 ¿Cuánto dinero recibes?
3 ¿Cuándo recibes tu dinero?
4 ¿Trabajas para ganar dinero?
5 ¿En qué te gastas tu dinero?
6 ¿Estás contento con el dinero que recibes?
7 ¿Por qué (no)?

¡OJO!

Mi(s) padre/madre/padres me da(n)......? por día /semana /mes.

Mi(s) padre/madre/padres no me da(n)...... .

Trabajo los fines de semana/el sábado/durante las vacaciones.

Mi(s) padre/madre/padres paga(n) mi ropa

Gasto mi dinero en ....

En mi opinión (no) es suficiente.

La rutina diaria

13a 🎧 📖 Según lo que oyes y lees, empareja las imágenes con las frases correctas.

Ejemplo: **1** — *d*

1 Durante la semana siempre me despierto a las siete.
2 Normalmente regreso a casa a las cuatro y media.
3 Después de la cena me relajo enfrente de la televisión.
4 Siempre me ducho por la mañana.
5 Me peino y me lavo los dientes en el cuarto de baño.
6 Tomo la cena a las ocho.
7 A las seis de la tarde hago mis deberes. Tengo mucho que hacer.
8 Me visto.
9 Desayuno cereales y café.
10 Normalmente me acuesto a las diez y media.
11 A las ocho y media salgo de la casa para ir al instituto.
12 Me levanto a las siete y cuarto o así.
13 Antes de acostarme me baño.

b 💬 Trabaja con tu pareja. Haz preguntas como las de abajo y contesta. ¿Puedes añadir unas cuantas más?

1 ¿A qué hora te despiertas?
2 ¿Te duchas por la mañana?
3 ¿Desayunas?
4 ¿Cuándo regresas a casa por la tarde?
5 ¿Qué haces por la tarde?
6 ¿A qué hora te acuestas?

c 🎧 📖 Escucha a Mari Vi. Lee las frases e indica si son verdaderas (V) o falsas (F).

Ejemplo: **1** — *F*

1 *Se levanta a las seis de la mañana.*
2 Le gusta bañarse por las mañanas.
3 No desayuna.
4 Vive bastante cerca de su colegio.
5 El día de colegio es bastante largo.
6 Normalmente se baña antes de cenar.
7 Se acuesta tarde los fines de semana.

d ✏️ Escribe un pequeño párrafo para describir tu propia rutina.

Por la mañana, me despierto...

GRAMÁTICA

Reflexive verbs

In Spanish, most reflexive verbs are used to describe actions you do to yourself every day or that involve a change of some sort, for example getting up, sitting down or becoming angry. In Spanish, the 'self' word is a reflexive pronoun and appears in front of the verb, except in the infinitive. Here is an example:

levantar**se**	to get (**oneself**) up
me levanto	I get up
te levantas	you get up
se levanta	he/she/it gets up
nos levantamos	we get up
os levantáis	you get up
se levantan	they get up

Can you recognise these common reflexive verbs? If you are unsure, use a dictionary to help you.

acostarse	irse	ponerse
afeitarse	lavarse	quitarse
bañarse	levantarse	secarse
despertarse	llamarse	sentarse
dormirse	limpiarse	vestirse
ducharse	maquillarse	
enfadarse	pasearse	

A lot of the reflexive verbs in the activity above are not reflexive in English (i.e. they don't use the 'self' word), for example *acostarse* is 'to go to bed'. Can you find some others?

3 Mi barrio

1 ¿Qué hay en tu barrio? Pon los dibujos en el orden correcto según la lista a la derecha.

Ejemplo: **1** — *f*

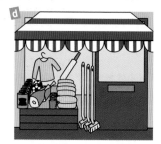

1	un banco
2	una discoteca
3	un instituto
4	una biblioteca
5	un teatro
6	un museo
7	Correos
8	una tienda
9	una piscina
10	una playa
11	una pista de hielo
12	un castillo
13	un parque
14	un polideportivo
15	un mercado
16	un cine
17	una iglesia

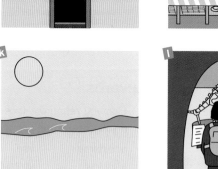

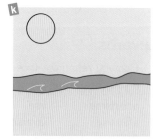

2 🎧 📖 Escucha y lee lo que dicen estos jóvenes. Indica si cada frase es verdadera (V) o falsa (F).

Ejemplo: Ana vive en el campo — V

1 Ana vive en un sitio grande.
2 Cree que es entretenido.
3 Enrique se ha mudado mucho.
4 Dice que donde vive es civilizado.
5 Donde vive Luci hay mucho que hacer para los jóvenes.
6 No es muy limpio.
7 Patrick está contento donde vive.
8 Vive en un sitio de vacaciones.
9 Su barrio es muy animado.

> ¡Hola! Me llamo Ana y vivo en un pequeño pueblo en el campo en el norte de España. Aquí no está mal. Es limpio y no hay mucho tráfico. Lo malo es que no hay mucho que hacer para los jóvenes, así que me aburro bastante.

Ana

> Me llamo Enrique. He vivido en varias ciudades pero ahora vivo en una ciudad pequeña y tranquila en el oeste de España. Creo que es mucho más agradable vivir aquí. Hay muchas diversiones como cines y discotecas. Sin embargo, no hay mucho vandalismo o graffiti como en otras ciudades más grandes. Prefiero ésta.

Enrique

> ¡Hola! Soy Luci. Vivo en una ciudad muy grande e industrial en el centro de España. Llevamos un mes viviendo aquí. Las atracciones son fantásticas y hay mucho para los jóvenes. Lo malo es que también hay muchos problemas. Por ejemplo, es una ciudad bastante ruidosa y con mucha polución y hay mucho tráfico. Además, hay basura por las calles. Cuando era joven vivíamos en un pueblo y lo prefería.

Luci

> Yo me llamo Patrick. Soy de Irlanda y me mudé aquí hace ocho años con mis padres. Vivimos en una ciudad pequeña pero turística, en el sur de España. Verdaderamente me encanta aquí. Hay mucho para los jóvenes pero a veces me parece que hay demasiados turistas en el verano.

Patrick

3 🎧 What do these people say about where they live? Answer the questions in English.

1 Why doesn't Antonio like his town? Give three reasons.
2 What is there for young people to do in Marisol's town? Give two ideas.
3 What does Yolanda see as the advantages of living in the country? Give three ideas.
4 Why is Carlos concerned about living in an industrial town?
5 What is the biggest advantage of living in Ana's town?

4a 💬 Habla con tu pareja. Describe tu pueblo.

Vivo en	Madrid Bilbao Londres Cardiff Bristol	una cuidad un pueblo una aldea	grande pequeño/a	y/e	industrial histórico/a turístico/a importante

Está situado/a en	el norte el sur el este el oeste	de España de Inglaterra de Escocia de Irlanda de Gales

Está cerca de…	
Está a…kilómetros de…	
Hay más o menos…habitantes.	

En…hay Cerca de…hay Para los jóvenes hay	un banco una discoteca un instituto una biblioteca un teatro un museo Correos una tienda una piscina una playa una pista de hielo un castillo un parque un polideportivo un mercado un cine una iglesia

b 💬 Trabaja con tu pareja. Pregúntale lo siguiente.

1 ¿Dónde vives?
2 ¿Dónde está tu cuidad/pueblo/aldea?
3 ¿Cómo es tu cuidad/pueblo/aldea?
4 ¿Qué hay en tu cuidad/pueblo/aldea?

c ✏️ Escribe una descripción del lugar donde vives.

Vivo en…

Lo bueno y lo malo

5 📖 🏛 Lee lo que dice esta gente de donde viven. Escoge los adjetivos que mejor describan lo que piensan del recuadro de abajo. Escríbelos en la columna adecuada de la tabla.

Ejemplo: No hay ruido aquí, pero tampoco hay mucho que hacer.

3 El tiempo es fantástico pero ¡hay tanta basura!

1 Es un pueblo en la costa que está muy concurrido en el verano, pero cuesta mucho vivir.

4 Mi pueblo está en el norte. Hay muchas fábricas, lo que afecta el medio ambiente.

2 Hay mucho que hacer aquí, pero con todos los coches no te puedes entender.

5 Tenemos muchos castillos y museos aquí. Es de verdad pintoresco. Pero prefiero las ciudades grandes.
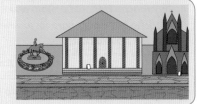

aburrido	animado	caluroso	caro
contaminado	histórico	industrial	pequeño
ruidoso	sucio	tranquilo	turístico

	Lo bueno	Lo malo
Ejemplo:	*tranquilo*	*aburrido*
1		

GRAMÁTICA

Ser, estar, hay

There are two verbs meaning 'to be': *ser* and *estar*. *Ser* is used when things are permanent and do not change, for example:

*Mi ciudad **es** grande.* My town is large.

Estar is used for things that might change or to say where something is, for example:

De momento la ciudad At the moment the town
***está** sucia pero…* is dirty but…

*Caracas **está** en el* Caracas is in the
norte de Venezuela. north of Venezuela.

ser	estar
soy	estoy
eres	estás
es	está
somos	estamos
sois	estáis
son	están

To say '**there is**' or '**there are**', use *hay*. For example:

*En mi pueblo **hay*** In my village there is
mucho tráfico. a lot of traffic.

Completa las frases utilizando la forma correcta de **ser** o **estar**, o **hay**, según convenga.

1 En la capital _____ muchos edificios y monumentos.
2 Normalmente la plaza mayor _____ en el centro de la ciudad.
3 Mi familia y yo _____ de Barcelona.
4 En mi pueblo _____ un polideportivo nuevo.
5 Aquí las casas _____ muy bonitas.
6 Mi barrio _____ en el norte de la región.
7 Aquí _____ una pista de hielo donde puedes patinar.
8 Para ir al centro _____ mejor coger el metro.
9 En el verano _____ fiestas en el pueblo.
10 La primavera _____ una estación agradable.

6 🎧 Unos jóvenes están hablando de donde viven. Lee las frases con cuidado. Hay algo que no corresponde con lo que oyes. Corrige las palabras destacadas.

Ejemplo: Mi cuidad es **grande,** pero no hay nada que **ver.**

Mi cuidad es <u>bonita</u>, pero no hay nada que <u>hacer</u>.

1 Hay muchas tiendas en mi pueblo, pero está muy lejos.

Hay muchas _____ en mi pueblo, pero está muy _____ .

2 Me encanta ir de paseo, pero no me gusta el clima.

Me encanta ir de _____ , pero no me gusta el _____ .

3 Vivo cerca de la costa, pero hay demasiados jóvenes aquí en el verano.

Vivo cerca de la _____ , pero hay demasiados _____ aquí en verano.

4 Hay excursiones para los jóvenes. En mi opinión son muy baratos.

Hay _____ para los jóvenes. En mi opinión son muy _____ .

LENGUA CLAVE

Lo bueno/malo es/son
Lo bueno es/son… — the good thing(s) is/are…
Lo malo es/son… — the bad thing(s) is/are…

These can be used with a noun:
Lo bueno es la playa.
The good thing is the beach.

Lo malo son los turistas.
The bad thing is the tourists.

They can also be used with another verb or *hay* by adding 'es que':
Lo bueno es que está cerca de las tiendas.
The good thing is it's near the shops.

Lo bueno es que hay mucho que hacer.
The good thing is there's a lot to do.

Lo malo es que son caros.
The bad thing is they're expensive.

Lo malo es que no hay aparcamiento.
The bad thing is there isn't anywhere to park.

7 🎧 📖 Escucha esta entrevista. Llena los huecos añadiendo las palabras que faltan.

Entrevistador: Hola Francina, ¿Me puedes contar algo sobre donde vives?
Francina: Vivo en Mallorca — es la isla más _____ de España y está situada en el mar Mediterráneo. Es una de las Islas Baleares.

E: ¿Y cuánto tiempo has vivido allí?
F: Llevo _____ años viviendo allí.

E: ¿Y dónde vivías antes?
F: Antes vivía en Bilbao — una ciudad grande e _____ en el _____ de España.

E: ¿Y dónde exactamente vives en Mallorca?
F: Vivo en Palma, la capital de la isla. También es la capital de las Islas Baleares.

E: ¿Y qué tipo de ciudad es Palma, Francina?
F: Como puedes imaginar, la industria principal es el turismo. De hecho, ¡es casi la única industria!

E: ¿Y cómo es la isla?
F: Es muy bonita con _____ , una gran variedad de _____ y por supuesto el clima es _____ .

E: ¿Y cómo se llega a Mallorca?
F: Eso es fácil. Hay un _____ grande en Palma y también se puede llegar en _____ .

E: ¿Qué es lo bueno de Mallorca?
F: Hay mucho que hacer, incluso en invierno. Hay muchos clubs y restaurantes.

E: ¿Y lo malo?
F: Lo malo es que la isla tiene demasiados turistas. Durante el verano, especialmente en _____ no es fácil encontrar un hotel o alquilar un _____ . También es difícil encontrar un sitio donde extender tu toalla en la _____ .

8 💬 Trabaja con tu pareja. Habla de tu ciudad. Usa y adapta las preguntas de arriba.

9a 🎧 Escucha y pon los dibujos en el orden correcto. Indica la dirección con una de las señales.

Siga todo recto 🔼 Tuerza a la izquierda ◀️

Tuerza a la derecha ▶️

Ejemplo: ¿Por dónde se va a la estación, por favor?
Sigue todo recto — a 🔼

la estación de trenes

la piscina

el mercado

El Centro Comercial
el centro comercial

el ayuntamiento

el teatro

H
el hospital

la parada de autobús

el puerto

la plaza mayor

el aparcamiento

Oficina de turismo
ⓘ
la oficina de turismo

b 💬 Habla con tu pareja.
Haz preguntas y contéstalas.

¿Dónde está	el puerto? la iglesia?
¿Por dónde se va	al puerto? a la iglesia?
¿Está lejos/cerca?	

¡Atención! — a + el = al

Many shops in Spanish come from the name of the product they principally sell. While the addition of some other letters beforehand varies, generally the shop will end in *–ía*.

Mira estos sustantivos y conviértelos en tiendas. Usa un diccionario para ayudarte.

	Cosa	Tienda
	pan	*panadería*
	fruta	
	carne	
	pastel	
	flor	
	pescado	
	libro	
	zapato	
	papel	
	café	

Another way to make the name of a shop is to use the following: *tienda de…*

Mira estos sustantivos y conviértelos en tiendas. Usa un diccionario para ayudarte.

	Cosa	Tienda
	ropa	*tienda de ropa*
	discos	
	deportes	
	disfraces	
	caramelos	
	bricolaje	
	videojuegos	

¡Atención! — a book shop is **una librería** and a library is **una biblioteca**.

10a ¿Sabes orientarte por el laberinto?
Mira el plano. Lee las indicaciones.
Para cada persona indica su destino.

Ejemplo: **1** *e — tienda de discos*

Key:	d supermercado	h carnicería
a zapatería	e tienda de discos	i panadería
b pastelería	f papelería	j cine
c frutería	g tienda de ropa	k cafetería

Dentro del centro comercial

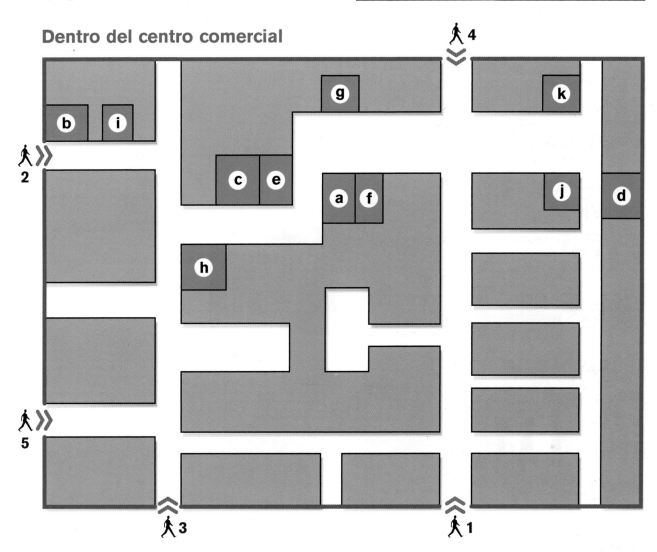

1 Cuando entres, tuerce en el primer pasillo a la izquierda. Sigue por él y coge el primero a la derecha. En la segunda esquina a la derecha verás la carnicería. Coge ese pasillo y es la tienda que hace esquina a la izquierda.

2 Sigue por este pasillo, gira a la derecha y a continuación a la izquierda. En este pasillo, al fondo está la tienda, en la esquina opuesta a la tienda de discos y enfrente de la tienda de ropa.

3 Si coges el primer pasillo a la derecha, sigues por él hasta que puedas girar a la izquierda. Una vez en ese pasillo tuerces la segunda esquina a la izquierda y en esa calle, en el lado izquierdo justo antes de la zapatería que hay en la esquina, tienes la tienda que buscas.

4 Es muy fácil. Tuerces ahí la primera a la izquierda, al fondo verás una cafetería en la esquina de la izquierda, en la de la derecha está lo que buscas, pero la entrada es por la otra calle, frente al supermercado.

5 Tuerces la primera a la izquierda, sigues hasta la segunda a la izquierda y en ese pasillo, a la derecha pasas la panadería y a ese mismo lado, justo antes de la salida, ahí tienes.

b Trabaja con tu pareja.
Practica orientándote alrededor del centro comercial.

Cuando era pequeño

11a 🎧 ¿Quién habla?

Escribe el nombre que corresponda con cada imágen.

Ejemplo: ***a** — Paco*

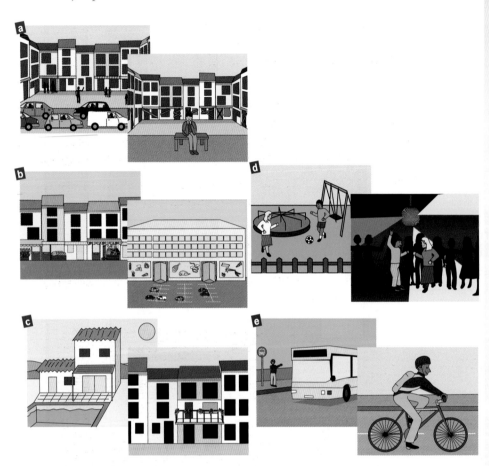

b 🔺 Termina los verbos en estas frases con la forma correcta del imperfecto.

1 Cuando mis primos venían, íb____ a la piscina todos los días.

2 Cuando vivíamos en Bogotá, viaj____ al colegio en autobús.

3 Cuando era pequeño, me gust____ mucho jugar con los niños de nuestros vecinos.

4 En el verano nosotros sal____ todas las noches a tomar una copa.

5 Mi madre trabaj____ como profesora mientras vivíamos en Asunción.

GRAMÁTICA

The imperfect tense

To describe what used to happen, what was happening or what happened habitually/frequently at some time in the past, we use the imperfect tense.

To form the imperfect tense look at the box below.

-ar verbs	-er/-ir verbs
trabajaba	vivía
trabajabas	vivías
trabajaba	vivía
trabajábamos	vivíamos
trabajabais	vivíais
trabajaban	vivían

There are three irregular verbs in the imperfect tense

ser	ir	ver
era	iba	veía
eras	ibas	veías
era	iba	veía
éramos	íbamos	veíamos
erais	ibais	veíais
eran	iban	veían

The verb *soler* can also be used with the infinitive to replace the imperfect tense:

Solía ir a clase de baile todos los días.
I used to go to a dance class every day.

Copia y completa las frases con la forma correcta del pretérito imperfecto.

1 Cuando (*ser*) joven mi familia y yo (*vivir*) en la costa.

2 (*ir*) al colegio a pie con mi hermano.

3 Antes mi madre (*ser*) profesora.

4 ¡Mis amigos (*ser*) todos españoles!

5 Mi padre (*trabajar*) en una fábrica.

12 🎧 Escucha a esta gente hablando de su juventud. ¿Qué hacían y con qué frecuencia? Rellena la tabla.

Actividad	Cuando
Ejemplo: deberes	*antes de salir con amigos*
1	

13 📷 Habla con tus padres y con otra gente para acordarte de lo que hacías antes.
Escribe un pequeño párrafo sobre ello. Indica con qué frecuencia hacías las cosas.

14a 📖 📷 Lee el texto sobre Guatemala. Copia las frases en negrita y encuentra sus significados entre las frases en inglés en la lista.

- it is worth a visit
- everything is beginning to change now
- it is the third biggest nation in Central America
- there is a great variety...
- they tend to wear traditional clothes
- they say that...
- live close to each other
- what you are going to become

b Contesta las preguntas.

1 Menciona dos rasgos geográficos de Guatemala.
2 ¿Por qué han disminuido las costumbres tradicionales en la capital?
3 ¿Qué tipo de traje lleva la gente del campo?
4 ¿Qué se aprende de los padres de familia guatemaltecas?
5 ¿Cómo cuida la familia a los mayores?
6 ¿Por qué cambia todo ahora?

Guatemala

Guatemala, una república de Centroamérica, es una tierra escabrosa de montañas y volcanes, lagos preciosos y fauna fértil. **Es la tercera nación más grande de Centroamérica.** Es muy bonita y desde luego **vale la pena visitarla.**

Hay una gran variedad de modos de vivir en Guatemala. En la capital, por ejemplo, la cultura y la moda europea dominan. Cine, música, cultura y moda — incluso la comida rápida — han dejado su marca, lo cual ha hecho disminuir hasta cierto punto las costumbres tradicionales hispánicas.

Fuera de la capital — en el campo — siguen todavía las maneras antiguas. En los pueblos, por ejemplo, **tienden a llevar ropa tradicional** de colores vivos y destacados.

Para la gente guatemalteca la familia es muy importante. **Dicen que** los padres son *espejos* y que a través de ellos aprendes quién eres y **en qué te vas a convertir.** Los niños reciben de sus padres consejos y ayuda a lo largo la vida.

Los miembros de las familias tienden a **vivir el uno cerca del otro**, y una familia típica consta de padres, hijos solteros y casados, y todos sus respectivos niños. La familia cuida bien a los mayores, y los padrinos son muy importantes en la vida de los pequeños. Sin embargo, **todo empieza a cambiar ahora** con la adopción de valores occidentales.

Paper 1: listening

These questions test understanding of individual words and short statements that should be familiar.

Ejercicio 1, preguntas 1–4

Vas a oír una serie de observaciones o diálogos cortos que podrías oír en países donde se habla español.

Para cada pregunta indica tu respuesta escribiendo una X en la casilla correcta.

Estás hablando con tu amigo de su familia y de su pueblo.

1 Tu amigo dice algo sobre su familia:

¿Cuántas personas hay en la familia de tu amigo?

A		3 personas
B		4 personas
C		5 personas
D		6 personas

Tips for success

- Read all the questions carefully before you begin.
- Think about the words you know rather than the ones you do not know.
- Remember it is always worth having a guess if you are unsure.
- If you make a mistake, cross it out carefully.

[1]

2 Le preguntas a tu amigo dónde vive. Te responde:

¿Dónde vive tu amigo?

A	
B	
C	
D	

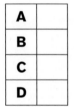 A  B 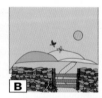 C  D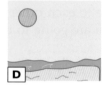

[1]

3 Le preguntas a tu amigo si tiene una mascota. Te responde:

¿Tiene mascota?

A	
B	
C	
D	

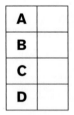 A 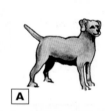 B  C  D

[1]

4 Quieres saber cómo llegar a su casa. Te responde:

¿Dónde está su casa?

A	
B	
C	
D	

A   B

C   D

X
Estás aquí

[1]

[Total: 4]

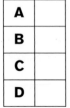

Paper 2: reading

This next question tests your ability to pick out the main points and some details in a short text, in this instance, an e-mail. Again the language should be familiar to you.

Lee el texto con cuidado. Para cada pregunta indica tu respuesta escribiendo una X en la casilla correcta.

¡Hola!

Me llamo Rodrigo y tengo catorce años. Soy de Colombia, pero ahora vivo en España – en Barcelona – con mis padres y mi hermana Sofía. Estudio en un instituto y soy modesto y tímido. Tengo amigos, pero no salgo mucho. Prefiero quedarme en casa. Me gusta más leer o estudiar que ver la tele. Como mis padres trabajan, tengo que ayudar en casa. Odio fregar los platos, pero lo bueno es que si los friego, mis padres me dan la paga. No soy ni alto ni bajo. Tengo los ojos marrones y el pelo corto, negro y rizado. Soy bastante moreno. ¡Mi familia dice que soy guapo!

Some parts of this text have been highlighted. What do these items mean? Work with a partner. What strategies did you use to find the solutions?

1 Rodrigo vive con… From the list of possible answers, think about the words you know. Are these referred to in the text?

| **A** | su familia. | **B** | sus tíos. | **C** | sus amigos. | **[1]** |

2 Prefiere… To answer this question think about the verbs related to each possible activity.

| **A** | la lectura. | **B** | la televisión. | **C** | la informática. | **[1]** |

3 Para ganar dinero, Rodrigo…

| **A** | trabaja. | **B** | viaja. | **C** | ayuda. | **[1]** |

4 Es de talla … The possible answers here should help you to understand the meaning of this word.

| **A** | grande. | **B** | mediana. | **C** | pequeña. | **[1]** |

5 Su pelo es… Understanding this word is key to finding the answer.

| **A** | negro. | **B** | moreno. | **C** | castaño. | **[1]** |

Tips for success

- The questions always follow the order of the text.
- You will be successful in this question if you read carefully, picking up the links between the question and the passage (e.g. in question 4), if you know the adjectives used to describe height, you will be sure to make the right connections and answer correctly.

Paper 3: speaking

In part 1 of the speaking exam you have to do two role plays, A and B. You are given a card containing the two role-play situations and have 15 minutes to prepare your answers. The role plays last no more than about 5 minutes. Below is a sample role play A.

A

Estudiante: tú mismo/a

Profesor(a): amigo/a español(a)

Hablas por primera vez con tu nuevo/a amigo/a por correspondencia español(a).

E **(i)** Saluda a tu amigo/a por correspondencia; **y**

   (ii) Pregúntale si está bien.

E Escucha lo que te dice y dile algo sobre tu familia.

E Explícale dónde vives.

E Dile cómo vas a ir a casa.

E **(i)** Escucha lo que te dice, dale las gracias; **y**

   (ii) Pregúntale si quiere conocer a tus amigos.

Points to remember

- Read through the task carefully.
- Think about the answers you can give to each point.
- Remember to listen carefully to what your partner says, as you need to respond to any further questions you are asked.
- Make sure you answer everything on your list.
- In some sections you need to give more than one detail.

🎧 Listen to and then read through this example dialogue. The student's answers are short. Can you expand on the items that have been highlighted? Practise the role play with your partner.

P Me llamo Alicia y soy tu amiga por correspondencia.

E ¡Hola Alicia! ¿Qué tal?

P Muy bien, gracias. ¿Cuántas personas hay en tu familia?

E Hay cinco.   Can you say *who* these people are?

P ¿Vives cerca de aquí?

E Sí, muy cerca.   Can you mention the directions or the address?

P Tengo mucho equipaje. ¿Cómo vamos a ir a casa?

E En autobús.   Can you say where the bus stop is or the time it leaves?

P Tengo unos regalos para tu familia.

E Gracias. ¿Quieres que te presente a mis amigos?

P Sí. Me encantaría. Vamos.

What questions would you ask a new friend about their home and their family? Make up a dialogue of your own and work with a partner to complete it.

Paper 4: writing

In the task below, you have to write a list of eight items in Spanish, all related to the topic of places of interest.

1 Estás pasando tiempo en una ciudad española. Haz una lista de
8 lugares de interés **en español**.   **[Total: 5]**

Ejemplo: catedral

Points to remember

- Think carefully about your spelling.

- Read the words back to yourself. Does what you have written match the sound of each word?

- If you do not remember the words for the pictures, think of other places you might find in a town.

Read this second task carefully.

2 Acabas de mudarte de casa. Escribes en tu blog.

Menciona:

(a) dónde está tu casa

(b) las habitaciones que hay y lo que haces para ayudar

(c) lo que hay para los jóvenes en tu barrio

(d) si te gusta o no la casa y por qué

Debes escribir 80–90 palabras **en español**.   **[Total: 15]**

Points to remember

In this type of exercise, you should aim to:

- cover *all* the points as listed in (a)–(d)

- demonstrate that you can write simple, accurate and full sentences

- use a range of vocabulary, verbs and structures

- express simple opinions

Vocabulario

Family

el **abuelo**   grandfather
la **abuela**   grandmother
el/la **bebé**   baby
el **bisabuelo**   great-grandfather
la **bisabuela**   great-grandmother
el **cuñado**   brother-in-law
la **cuñada**   sister-in-law
el **esposo**, el **marido**   husband
la **esposa**, la **mujer**   wife
el **hermano**   brother
la **hermana**   sister
el **hermanastro**   stepbrother
la **hermanastra**   stepsister
el **hijo**   son
la **hija**   daughter
el **hijastro**   stepson
la **hijastra**   stepdaughter
el/la **hijo**/a **único**/a   only child
la **madrastra**   stepmother
la **madre**   mother
el **nieto**   grandson
la **nieta**   granddaughter
el **novio**   boyfriend
la **novia**   girlfriend
el **padrastro**   stepfather
el **padre**   father
los **padres**   parents
los **parientes**   relatives
el/la **primo**/a   cousin
el **tío**   uncle
la **tía**   aunt
el **sobrino**   nephew
la **sobrina**   niece

Personal descriptions

¿Cómo eres/es?   What do/does you/he/ she look like?
Soy/Es…   I am/He/She is…
   alto/a   tall
   bajo/a   short
   bonito/a   pretty
   calvo/a   bald
   delgado/a   slim
   feo/a   ugly
   gordo/a   fat
   guapo/a   good-looking
   ni alto/a ni bajo/a   neither tall nor short
   pelirrojo/a   red-haired
Tengo/Tiene…   I/He/She have/has… .
   los ojos azules   blue eyes
   los ojos grises   grey eyes
   los ojos marrones   brown eyes
   los ojos negros   dark eyes
   los ojos verdes   green eyes
Llevo/Lleva gafas.   I/He/She wear/wears glasses.
Tengo/Tiene…   I/He/She have/has…
   el pelo castaño   light-brown hair
   el pelo corto   short hair

el pelo largo   long hair
el pelo liso   straight hair
el pelo negro   black hair
el pelo ondulado   wavy hair
el pelo rubio   blond hair
el pelo rizado   curly hair
Tengo/Tiene bigote.   I have/He has a moustache.
Tengo/Tiene barba.   I have/He has a beard.

Adjectives

activo/a   active
agradable   pleasant
alegre   cheerful
amable   nice
ambicioso/a   ambitious
antipático/a   unpleasant
cariñoso/a   affectionate
casado/a   married
comprensivo/a   understanding
contaminado/a   polluted
divorciado/a   divorced
egoísta   selfish
extrovertido/a   outgoing
generoso/a   generous
gracioso/a   funny
grande   big
hablador/a   talkative
histórico/a   historic
honrado/a   honest
impaciente   impatient
industrial   industrial
inteligente   intelligent
joven   young
jubilado/a   retired
limpio/a   clean
orgulloso/a   proud
paciente   patient
peligroso/a   dangerous
perezoso/a   lazy
pequeño/a   small
responsable   responsible
ruidoso/a   noisy
rural   rural
sensible   sensitive
separado/a   separated
serio/a   serious
severo/a   strict
simpático/a   nice, friendly
sincero/a   sincere
sucio/a   dirty
tímido/a   timid
tonto/a   stupid, crazy
trabajador/a   hardworking
tranquilo/a   quiet
triste   sad
turístico/a   tourist
viejo/a   old
viudo/a   widowed

My home

el **apartamento**   apartment
el **ático**   attic
el **balcón**   balcony
la **casa**   house
el **chalet**   bungalow, house, cottage
la **cocina**   kitchen
el **comedor**   dining room
el **cuarto de baño**   bathroom
el **despacho**   office, study
el **dormitorio**   bedroom
la **ducha**   shower
el **garaje**   garage
la **granja**   farm
el **jardín**   garden
el **piso**   flat
el **salón**   lounge, living room
el **sótano**   cellar
la **terraza**   terrace

Furniture

el **aparador**   sideboard
el **armario**   wardrobe; cupboard
la **bañera**   bath, bathtub
la **cama**   bed
la **cómoda**   chest of drawers
el **congelador**   freezer
la **estantería**   bookcase
el **fregadero**   kitchen sink
el **horno**   oven
la **lavadora**   washing machine
el **lavaplatos**   dishwasher
la **mesa**   table
el **microondas**   microwave
la **nevera**   fridge
el **retrete**   toilet
la **silla**   chair
el **sofá**   sofa
el **sillón**   armchair
el **televisor**   television

My town and my area

norte   north
sur   south
este   east
oeste   west
el **aeropuerto**   airport
la **aldea**   village
el **aparcamiento**   car park
el **ayuntamiento**   town hall
el **barrio**   neighbourhood
la **biblioteca**   library
la **cafetería**   café
el **castillo**   castle
la **catedral**   cathedral
el **centro**   centre
el **centro comercial**   shopping centre
el **cine**   cinema
la **ciudad**   town; city
Correos   post office

la **comisaría**   police station
la **discoteca**   disco
la **estación** de **trenes/autobuses**   train/
bus station
el **estadio**   stadium
la **fábrica**   factory
la **fuente**   fountain
la **gente**   people
el **hospital**   hospital
el **hotel**   hotel
la **iglesia**   church
las **instalaciónes**   facilities
los **jardines**   gardens
el **lago**   lake
el **mercado**   market
el **museo**   museum
la **oficina de turismo**   tourist office
la **parada de autobús**   bus stop
el **parque de atracciones**   amusement
park
la **piscina**   swimming pool
la **plaza**   square
la **plaza de toros**   bullring
el **polideportivo**   sports centre
el **pueblo**   small town; village
el **puerto**   port
el **restaurante**   restaurant
el **río**   river
el **supermercado**   supermarket
el **teatro**   theatre
el **valle**   valley
el **videoclub**   video-rental shop
el **zoo**   zoo

Jobs

el **empleo**   job
estar en el paro   to be unemployed
el/la **amo/a de casa**   housewife/husband
el/la **arqueólogo/a**   archaeologist
el/la **camarero/a**   waiter/waitress
el/la **canguro**   childminder, babysitter
el/la **cantante**   singer
el/la **carpintero/a**   carpenter, joiner
el/la **cocinero/a**   cook, chef
el/la **contable**   accountant
el/la **dependiente/a**   shop assistant
el/la **deportista**   sportsman/woman
el/la **diseñador/a**   designer
el/la **economista**   economist
el/la **electricista**   electrician
el/la **empleado/a**   employee
el/la **enfermero/a**   nurse
el/la **farmacéutico/a**   chemist,
pharmacist
el/la **granjero/a**   farmer
el/la **hombre/mujer de negocios**
businessman/woman
el/la **jefe/a**   boss
el/la **peluquero/a**   hairdresser
el/la **recepcionista**   receptionist

la **oficina**   office
los **grandes almacenes**   department store
trabajar   to work
la **empresa**   company
la **compañía**   company
el **departamento**   department

Animals

la **araña**   spider
el **caballo**   horse
el **canario**   canary
la **chinchilla**   chinchilla
la **cobaya**   guinea pig
el **conejo**   rabbit
el **gato**   cat
el **jerbo**, el **gerbo**   gerbil
el **hámster**   hamster
el **lagarto**   lizard
la **lagartija**   small lizard
el **papagayo**, el **loro**   parrot
el **perico**   parakeet
el **perro**   dog
el **pez**   fish
la **rana**   frog
la **rata**   rat
el **ratón**   mouse
la **serpiente**   snake
la **tortuga**   tortoise

Daily routine

acostarse   to go to bed
afeitarse   to shave
bañarse   to bathe
despertarse   to wake up
desayunar   to have breakfast
dormirse   to go to sleep
ducharse   to shower
hacer los deberes   to do your homework
lavarse   to wash
levantarse   to get up
peinarse   to comb one's hair
regresar a casa   to go home
salir de casa   to leave the house
ver la televisión   to watch television
vestirse   to get dressed

Household chores

ayudar   to help
barrer el suelo   to sweep the floor
cocinar   to cook
dar de comer a las mascotas   to feed
the pets
fregar los platos   to do the washing-up
hacer la cama   to make the bed
hacer la compra   to do the shopping
lavar el coche   to wash the car
lavar la ropa   to do the washing
limpiar los cristales   to clean the windows
limpiar el polvo   to do the dusting
pasar la aspiradora   to vacuum
pasear al perro   to walk the dog

planchar   to iron
poner la mesa   to lay the table
quitar la mesa   to clear the table
regar las plantas   to water the plants
sacar la basura   to take the rubbish out

Prepositions

a   to
al final de   at the end of
al lado de   next to
a la derecha de   to the right of
a la izquierda de   to the left of
alrededor de   around
antes de   before
bajo   below/under
cerca de   near
con   with
contra   against
debajo de   below, under, underneath
delante de   in front of
desde   since
después de   after
durante   during
en   in, on
encima de   on top of
entre   between
excepto   except
fuera de   outside (of)
lejos de   far from
por   by
sobre   on top of

Adverbs

abajo   downstairs; below
afuera   outside
antes   beforehand
arriba   upstairs, above
debajo   below
desde hace mucho tiempo   for a long
time
después   afterwards
encima   on top, above
inmediatamente   immediately
luego   then
más   more
mucho   a lot
muy   very
muy poco   very little
nunca   never
recientemente   recently
siempre   always
sin embargo   however
sobre todo   above all

Conjunctions

o   or
pero   but
porque   because
y   and

Gente joven

1 El tiempo libre
2 ¿Cómo te enteras?
3 ¿A quién admiras?

☑ Say what I like to do in my free time
☑ Arrange to go out
☑ Use the present and past tenses

1 El tiempo libre

1a 📖✏️ Mira los dibujos y descifra las frases.

Ejemplo: **1** *jugar al fútbol*

1 garuj la túfobl

2 rev al veleótinsi

3 ri al a yalpa

4 hucersac scamúi

5 crato le napio

6 rele brilso

7 alibar

8 tramon a balacol

9 srali ocn gomsia

10 ri a la spicani

11 rujag al netis

12 chare teroped

13 rapinat

14 chear frundriws

15 ri ed scrampo

b 📖✏️ ¿Qué les gusta hacer? Completa la tabla con los detalles que faltan.

> Me gusta mucho salir con amigos, pero no me gusta nada bailar.
> Cristina

> Lo que más me gusta es ir al cine. No me gusta mucho hacer deporte.
> Ana

> En mi tiempo libre me gusta leer libros y revistas. No me gusta ver la televisión.
> Pablo

> Me divierte estar al aire libre así que me encanta ir de paseo en el campo. No me interesa tanto escuchar música.
> Loli

> En mi opinión los videojuegos son para niños. Prefiero ser activo. Soy aficionado a todos los deportes de equipo, el baloncesto por ejemplo. ¡Es fantástico!
> Juan

> Mis pasatiempos favoritos son la natación y la vela. Odio el fútbol.
> Eduardo

	☺	☹
Ejemplo: Cristina	*salir con amigos*	*bailar*
Pablo		
Ana		
Eduardo		
Loli		
Juan		

The present tense

The present tense is used to describe actions that are happening now, usually happen or those which are true at the moment.

The present tense of regular verbs

Regular present tense verbs, as you already know, are formed as follows:

	escuchar	leer	escribir
yo	escucho	leo	escribo
tú	escuchas	lees	escribes
él/ella/usted	escucha	lee	escribe
nosotros/as	escuchamos	leemos	escribimos
vosotros/as	escucháis	leéis	escribís
ellos/as/ustedes	escuchan	leen	escriben

Look at these examples:
Escucho música todos los días.
I listen to music every day.

¿Lees mucho, Pablo? Sí, leo el periódico cada día.
Do you read much, Pablo? Yes, I read the paper every day.

María siempre escribe cartas por correo electrónico.
María always writes email letters.

The present tense of stem-changing or radical-changing verbs

Many verbs change their stem in the present when the stress is on the stem:
1 *e – ie*
2 *u – ue*
3 *o – ue*
4 (sometimes) *e – i*

You met some of these verbs in Module 1. You need to learn them. Look at the examples below.

1 *cerrar* (to close)
cierro
cierras
cierra
cerramos
cerráis
cierran

The following verbs follow the same pattern: *pensar* (to think), *empezar* (to begin/start), *entender* (to understand), *perder* (to lose), *preferir* (to prefer) and *querer* (to want to).

2 *jugar* (to play)
juego
juegas
juega
jugamos
jugáis
juegan

3 *encontrar* (to find)
encuentro
encuentras
encuentra
encontramos
encontráis
encuentran

The following verbs follow the same pattern: *recordar* (to remember), *contar* (to tell (a story)/to count), *poder* (to be able to), *dormir* (to sleep) and *volver* (to return/to come back).

4 *pedir* (to ask for)
pido
pides
pide
pedimos
pedís
piden

Servir (to serve) follows the same pattern.

Some radical-changing verbs are also reflexive. You met these verbs in Module 1.

- *despertarse* (to wake up):
  e → ie
- *acostarse* (to go to bed):
  o → ue
- *vestirse* (to get dressed):
  e → i

Pon un verbo en la forma correcta en cada espacio.

¡Hola amigo!

Te (escribir) sobre lo que hago en mi tiempo libre. Me gusta ir al club juvenil con mis amigos. Los lunes y los jueves (**jugar**) al fútbol pero en verano yo (**preferir**) ir a la playa. Mis padres no (**ser**) nada deportistas. En casa mi padre (**poner**) la televisión y luego (**dormirse**). Mi madre (**pasar**) todo su tiempo en la cocina. (**Cocinar**) y (**escuchar**) la radio. Mi hermana y yo (**ser**) miembros de la orquesta del colegio. Yo (**tocar**) el violín y mi hermana (**tocar**) el saxofón. Es muy divertido. Los sábados mis amigos y yo (**ir**) juntos a la discoteca del barrio. Siempre (**empezar**) a las nueve. (**Bailar**) y (**cantar**) hasta medianoche. Los domingos (**levantarse**) tarde. (**Leer**) o (**charlar**) con amigos por teléfono. Y tú, ¿Qué (**hacer**)? ¿(**Practicar**) algún deporte?

¡Hasta luego!

Teo

c  ¿Qué te gusta hacer en tu tiempo libre? Completa las frases siguientes.

1 Para mí lo ideal es…
2 Me encanta…
3 Mi pasatiempo favorito es…

4 No me gusta tanto…
5 Lo que más me gusta es…
6 En mi opinión lo mejor es…

d Trabaja con tu pareja. Pregunta y contesta lo siguiente.

Ejemplo: ***A:*** *¿Qué es lo que más te gusta hacer en tu tiempo libre?*
B: *Lo que más me gusta hacer en mi tiempo libre es ir a la discoteca con mis amigos.*
A: *¿Cuál es tu pasatiempo favorito?*
B: *Mi pasatiempo favorito es hacer deporte — por ejemplo fútbol o baloncesto.*

2a Escucha la grabación. Antes de contestar las preguntas, haz una lista de las actividades de Julián en su tiempo libre. Si hay algunas que no conozcas, búscalas en el diccionario.

b Escucha la grabación otra vez y contesta las preguntas.

1 ¿Qué deporte prefiere Julián?
2 ¿Le gustan otros deportes? ¿Cuáles?
3 ¿Qué deportes no le gustan?
4 ¿Qué más le gusta hacer en su tiempo libre? Menciona 4 cosas.
5 ¿Qué le parecen los videojuegos?

¡OJO!

el tenis — jugar al tenis
el cine — ir al cine

3 Escribe un correo electrónico a un(a) amigo/a español(a) de 100 palabras para contarle tus gustos. Menciona:

- los deportes que te gustan y por qué
- los deportes que no te gustan y por qué
- lo que te gusta hacer el fin de semana
- pregúntale qué le gusta hacer en su tiempo libre

¡No te olvides de saludar y despedir a tu amigo/a!

4 Escucha la grabación. Completa la tabla con los detalles que faltan.

Nombre	Lo que le gusta hacer	Razones	Lo que no le gusta hacer	Razones
Ejemplo: Juanita	*salir con amigos*	*divertido*	*ir de compras*	*aburrido*
Federico				
Emma				
Pablo				
Isabel				

LENGUA CLAVE

Saying what you like or do not like doing

Use for example, *me gusta* + the infinitive of the verb. Use the table below to help you.

(no) me gusta me encanta prefiero detesto	bailar escuchar hacer jugar ir leer montar salir tocar ver	la televisión música deporte al fútbol la guitarra en la discoteca a caballo revistas al cine con amigos

En el club juvenil

5 📖🖊️ Lee esta información. Apunta los detalles.

a 📖 Algunas palabras del texto están en negrita.
Escríbelas y lo que significan en inglés.
Usa un diccionario para ayudarte.

b 📖 Indica si las frases siguientes son
verdaderas (V) o falsas (F). Si son falsas, escribe
una frase en español para corregirlas.

Ejemplo: El club se llama Campamento
La Hermita. — V

1 Solo hay dos sesiones cada semana para
los niños de ocho años.
2 Hay clases de baile para todas las edades.
3 El club cuesta más para gente joven.
4 Hay clases cada tarde de la semana.
5 Se puede ir de excursión.
6 La cafetería sirve solo comida rápida.
7 Solo hay cierta cantidad de plazas
en excursiones.

c 📖 Busca la palabra intrusa.
Explica por qué.

1 me gusta   me divierto   prefiero   odio
2 lunes   martes   jueves   domingo
3 fútbol   tenis   badminton   squash
4 karate   natación   judo   baloncesto
5 playa   campo   parque   piscina

Campamento La Hermita
Programación mes de julio
Los martes: 8–15 años (de 17:30 a 19:30)
Por solo 10€: natación, snooker, gimnasia, ping pong,
club de ajedrez, acceso internet, **esgrima**.
Los miércoles: 13 años+ (de 19:00 a 21:00)
Por 12€: snooker, natación, ping pong, club de
dibujo, actividades deportivas (fútbol, **tiro con
arco** o baloncesto).
Los jueves: 8 a 12 años (de 18:00 a 20:00)
Por 12€: **juegos de equipo**; futbolín, tenis de
mesa, natación, snooker, **artesanía y bricolaje**,
clases de baile, tarde de cine, **pesas**, club de música,
judo, fútbol, atletismo.
Camping
Cafetería (con amplia gama de raciones sanas)
Horario fin de semana: sábados de 9:00 a 17:00
Parque de atracciones:
• 26€ sin límite de atracciones
• 19€ con tres atracciones
• 15€ con dos atracciones
Excursión marítima 21€ comida incluida.
• Paintball
• Escalona libre 10€   • **Vela** 25€
Plazas limitadas — no te lo pierdas!   • Windsurf 20€

6a 🎧 ¿A qué hora? Empareja lo que oyes
con la hora correcta.

Ejemplo: **1 — c**

a 14:15 **b** 21:45 **c** 10:00 **d** 11:05 **e** 12:00
f 18:30 **g** 09:10 **h** 17:20 **i** 15:00

b 💬 Mira los relojes del ejercicio de arriba. Trabaja con tu
pareja. ¿Cuándo quedáis?

Ejemplo: **A:** *¿A qué hora nos vemos?*
B: *Nos vemos mañana a las dos y cuarto.*

¡ojo!

Spelling changes affect nouns
as well as verbs. For example:

e → ie: *ventana* (window)
— *viento* (wind)

o → ue: *volar* (to fly)
— *vuelo* (flight)

u → ue: *jugar* (to play)
— *juego* (game)

The stems of verbs and their
endings can help you to work
out the meaning of nouns.
For example:

comer (to eat) — *comida* (food/meal)

beber (to drink) — *bebida* (drink)

7a 📖 Mira las imágenes. Emparéjalas con las frases.

Ejemplo: **a** — *en el bar*

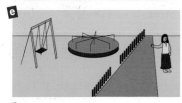 

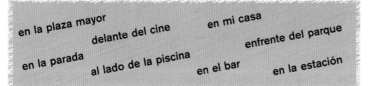

en la plaza mayor
delante del cine   en mi casa
enfrente del parque
en la parada   al lado de la piscina
en el bar   en la estación

b 💬 Observa las imágenes de la actividad anterior. Trabaja con tu pareja. ¿Dónde vais a quedar?

Ejemplo: **A:** *¿Dónde nos vemos?*
B: *Nos vemos en el bar.*

8a 🎧 Escucha la grabación. Completa la tabla con los detalles que faltan.

	Actividad	Día	Hora	Lugar
Ejemplo:	*tenis*	*mañana*	*2:30*	*en el parque*
1				
2				
3				
4				

b 💬 Trabaja con tu pareja. Usa la información en la tabla arriba para ayudarte con tu propio diálogo.

9a 🎧 📖 Escucha la grabación y sigue la conversación. Elige las palabras del recuadro que faltan y llena los huecos.

> te apetece
> estoy segura
> a las ocho   bien   ponen
> tu casa   hasta luego   me interesan

A: ¡Hola! Soy Adelina ¿_____ ir al cine conmigo esta tarde?

B: ¡Quizás! ¿Qué _____?

A: No _____ de los títulos, pero sé que echan una comedia romántica.

B: No _____ las películas románticas, incluso si son graciosas. ¿Por qué simplemente no vemos una película en la tele?

A: Si quieres. Me parece _____ ¿Qué echan?

B: Hay una película de ciencia-ficción _____ esta tarde si te apetece.

A: ¡Guay! Me encantan las películas de ciencia-ficción. Llegaré a _____ a las siete y media.

B: Vale ¡_____!

b 💬 Trabaja con tu pareja y adapta el diálogo según las imágenes abajo.

A: *Hola Javier, soy Adelina. ¿Te apetece ir al cine conmigo esta noche?*

B: *Depende. ¿Qué echan?*

A: *Echan dibujos animados esta tarde.*

B: *¡No seas boba! Odio los dibujos animados. Son muy aburridos.*

10a 🎧 📖 Escucha a estos jóvenes hacer planes para el fin de semana. Lee la conversación.

Paco:	¡Hola Sonia! ¿Tienes las entradas para el sábado?
Sonia:	¡Todavía no! ¡Ahora llamo! *(Saca su móvil)*
Paco:	Vale.
Recepcionista:	¡Dígame!
Sonia:	¡Oiga! Sí. Hola. Quisiera reservar unas entradas para el concierto el sábado.
Recepcionista:	¿Qué fecha?
Sonia:	El veinticuatro de noviembre.
Recepcionista:	¿Y para qué concierto?
Sonia:	El concierto de Nacen de las Cenizas.
Recepcionista:	¿De pie o sentado?
Sonia:	De pie, por favor.
Recepcionista:	¿Cuántas entradas quiere?
Sonia:	Seis.
Recepcionista:	Sí, quedan entradas.
Sonia:	¿Cuánto cuesta?
Recepcionista:	Son trescientos euros. Le puedo guardar las entradas hasta las ocho esta tarde. ¿Cuál es su nombre?
Sonia:	Sonia Delgado.
Recepcionista:	De acuerdo. Le esperamos hasta las ocho.
Sonia:	Muchas gracias. Adiós. *(Cuelga)* ¡Ya está! ¡Hay que ir al teatro antes de las ocho!

b 💬 Ahora practica el juego de rol con tu compañero, sustituyendo la información según las imágenes.

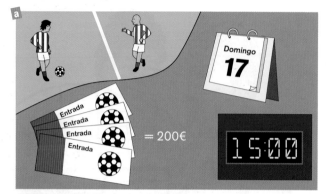

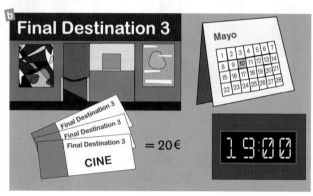

11 📖 🎨 ¿Qué actividades son? Completa las definiciones eligiendo la palabra adecuada del recuadro de abajo.

Ejemplo: **1** — *nadar*

ir de compras	jugar al ping pong
jugar al tenis	ir al cine
esquiar	nadar
jugar al ajedrez	ir a un concierto
hacer equitación	ir a la discoteca

1 Esto se hace en el agua.
2 Esto se puede hacer en el centro de la ciudad.
3 Para hacer esto necesitas una raqueta.
4 Para hacer esto, ¡hace falta un caballo!
5 Esto se juega en una mesa.
6 Se va la gente aquí para ver todo tipo de películas.
7 Se hace esta actividad en la nieve.
8 Esto es un juego de tabla.
9 Se va aquí para bailar.
10 Aquí es adonde se va para escuchar música en vivo.

12 🎧 ¿Qué haces? Escucha lo que dicen estos jóvenes de qué hacen en su tiempo libre y apunta las actividades que nombran.

Ejemplo: **1** — *b*

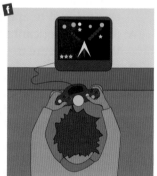

13a 🎧 📖 ✏️ Escucha otra vez el texto 12 y léelo. Haz una lista de todos los verbos mencionados por los chicos. ¿Puedes identificar todos?

Entrevistador: Carmen, ¿qué haces en tu tiempo libre?

Carmen: Yo veo bastante la tele. Me relaja mucho.

E: ¿Y tú, Carlos? ¿Ves la tele?

Carlos: Sí, a veces, pero normalmente juego con mi PSP u otros juegos electrónicos.

E: ¿Y qué haces tú, Leticia?

Leticia: En mi tiempo libre salgo con mis amigos y paseo al perro. ¡Qué divertido!

E: ¿Qué dices, Nacho?

Nacho: Yo no salgo mucho y ¡no tengo perro! Sin embargo, practico mi guitarra y la trompeta. ¡Quiero ser famoso!

E: Y tú, ¿practicas la guitarra, Alberto?

Alberto: Sí. Todo el rato. Soy miembro de un grupo y ensayamos tres veces a la semana.

E: ¿Qué haces tú en tu tiempo libre, Susana?

Susana: Yo soy muy deportista y juego al fútbol o al baloncesto. A veces juego al tenis también. También escucho música.

E: ¿Practicas algún deporte, Luis?

Luis: Vivo en una granja en las afueras de la ciudad y tenemos muchos caballos. Así que durante la mayoría de mi tiempo libre hago equitación. Me encanta y es buen ejercicio para mí y para el caballo.

E: ¿Y tú, Leonor? ¿Qué haces?

Leonor: ¿Yo? Err. Normalmente en mi tiempo libre hago natación. Me gusta mucho nadar y soy bastante fuerte. También hago dibujos animados y tal. ¡Soy artista!

b 💬 Habla con tu compañero/a de lo que los verbos mencionados tienen en común. Piensa en el tiempo y en la terminación de los verbos.

c 📖 ✏️ Pon un verbo en la forma correcta en cada espacio. Escoge entre los verbos del recuadro de abajo.

La ciudad de Méjico ____ una de las ciudades más grandes del mundo y se ____ considerar la ciudad más rica y poblada del país. En el centro de la ciudad ____ la catedral Metropolitana y el palacio Nacional. ____ unos de los monumentos más importantes de toda América. La ciudad ____ también una gran variedad de museos, actividades y diversiones. Si ____ hacer algo diferente, solo ____ que alquilar alguno de los barcos en los canales de Xochimilco. La aventura ____ cada día a las once. Conocer todos los rincones de la Ciudad de Méjico es una tarea imposible. Si ____ a ir a Méjico de vacaciones, ¿por qué no ____ unos días en la capital? ¡____ la pena visitar!

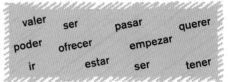

valer   ser   pasar   querer   poder   ofrecer   empezar   ir   estar   ser   tener

---

GRAMÁTICA

The present tense of irregular verbs

Some common verbs are irregular in the *yo* form only, as follows:

dar (to give) – *doy* (I give)

decir (to say) – *digo* (I say)

hacer (to do/make) – *hago* (I do/make)

poner (to put) – *pongo* (I put)

salir (to go out) – *salgo* (I go out)

ver (to see/watch) – *veo* (I see/watch)

Look at these examples:

Salgo de casa a las ocho.	I leave home at 8.
Siempre **hago** mis deberes en la cocina.	I always do my homework in the kitchen.

The following verbs are very irregular and need to be learned carefully. You met some of these verbs in Module 1.

	estar	ir	ser	tener	venir
yo	estoy	voy	soy	tengo	vengo
tú	estás	vas	eres	tienes	vienes
él/ella/usted	está	va	es	tiene	viene
nosotros/as	estamos	vamos	somos	tenemos	venimos
vosotros/as	estáis	vais	sois	tenéis	venís
ellos/as/ustedes	están	van	son	tienen	vienen

Look at these examples:

Vamos a la piscina los domingos.	We go to the swimming pool on Sundays.
¿*Vienes* a la playa con nosotros?	Are you coming to the beach with us?

¿Qué hiciste el fin de semana pasado?

14a 📖 Antes de escuchar la grabación, lee las frases siguientes e intenta comprenderlas. Presta atención a la forma del los verbos.

- El fin de semana Marta salió con sus amigos.
- Pedro se quedó en casa. Hizo sus deberes y vio la televisión.
- Marta jugó al tenis con sus amigos y fue a la discoteca. El domingo tomó el sol en la playa y fue a una fiesta.
- Alberto leyó una revista en el jardín y navegó por Internet.

b 🎧 Escucha la grabación. Empareja los dibujos con Marta o Alberto y escribe lo que dijo.

Ejemplo: **a** *Alberto — vi la television*

c 🗒️ Escribe cinco frases que cuenten lo que hiciste el fin de semana pasado, utilizando el pretérito.

Ejemplo: Fui a la casa de mi abuela.

The preterite tense

When talking about free time, it is important to use a variety of tenses. To talk about what you did yesterday, last week, last month, last year, use the preterite tense. Look at the tables below. They represent the most common verbs you will want to use. Learn these carefully.

The preterite tense of **regular** verbs

Regular present tense verbs are formed as follows:

	hablar	comer	vivir
yo	hablé	comí	viví
tú	hablaste	comiste	viviste
él/ella/usted	habló	comió	vivió
nosotros/as	hablamos	comimos	vivimos
vosotros/as	hablasteis	comisteis	vivisteis
ellos/as/ustedes	hablaron	comieron	vivieron

Look at these examples:
- **Hablé** *con Andrés por teléfono*
  I spoke to Andrés on the telephone.

- *¿Dónde **comiste** anoche, Juan?*
  Where did you eat last night, Juan?

- **Comí** *en un restaurante italiano.*
  I ate at an Italian restaurant.

Be very careful with the *yo* part of the following two verbs:
jugar: jugué (I played) but: *jugó* (he played)

navegar: Navegué por Internet toda la noche but: *María navegó por Internet ayer.*

The preterite tense of the three most frequently used **irregular** verbs:

	ir	ser	hacer
yo	fui	fui	hice
tú	fuiste	fuiste	hiciste
él/ella/usted	fue	fue	hizo
nosotros/as	fuimos	fuimos	hicimos
vosotros/as	fuisteis	fuisteis	hicisteis
ellos/as/ustedes	fueron	fueron	hicieron

You will notice that *ir* and *ser* share the same preterite form. Look at this example:
- **Fui** *al colegio a las ocho. El día fue muy aburrido*
  I went to school at 8. It was a very boring day.

The preterite form of *hay* (there is/are) is *hubo*:
- **Hubo** *tormenta anoche.*
  There was a storm last night.

15 Los sábados, Raúl siempre hace las mismas cosas. ¿Qué hizo el sábado pasado? Cambia los verbos al pretérito.

Ejemplo: Se levantó a las ocho…

Me levanto a las ocho, **me ducho**, **desayuno** y entonces **salgo** de casa a las diez. **Llego** a casa de mi amigo Martín a las diez y media. **Jugamos** con los videojuegos hasta mediodía, luego **vamos** al polideportivo donde **nadamos** en la piscina y **vamos** al gimnasio. Yo **hago** una sesión con el entrenador y Martín **hace** las pesas. A las dos, **volvemos** al centro donde **tomamos** algo de comida en una cafetería. Por la tarde **nos reunimos** con otros amigos y entonces **compramos** las entradas para ir al cine. A las diez, **vuelvo** a casa. **Veo** la televisión y **escucho** música. Por fin, **me acuesto** a las once.

16 Ana habla de su fin de semana. Escucha la grabación y contesta las preguntas.

1 ¿Adónde fue Ana el fin de semana pasado? ¿Por qué?
2 ¿Qué dice del viaje?
3 ¿Dónde se alojó?
4 ¿Qué hizo durante la visita?
5 ¿Qué tal lo pasó? ¿Por qué?

LENGUA CLAVE

Frases útiles
Match the Spanish words with the English ones.

hoy	in the evening
esta mañana	last night
esta tarde	last week
por la noche	today
ayer	this morning
anoche	a week ago
anteayer	this afternoon
hace una semana	the day before yesterday
la semana pasada	yesterday

17 Usando lo que sabes ya de como se habla del tiempo libre, haz la pareja adecuada español–inglés.

*Ejemplo: **a — 1***

Español
a Cada tarde escucho música.
b Ayer jugué al tenis con mi hermano.
c Los lunes veo la tele o escucho música.
d El sábado pasado salí con mis amigos.
e Jugué al fútbol el viernes.
f El verano pasado practiqué la natación todos los días.
g Normalmente voy al cine los martes.
h El miércoles paseé el perro de mi vecina.
i A veces hago equitación.

Inglés
1 I listen to music each afternoon
2 I usually go to the cinema on Tuesdays.
3 Sometimes I go horseriding.
4 Yesterday I played tennis with my brother.
5 On Mondays I watch TV or listen to music.
6 Last Saturday I went out with my friends.
▌ I played football on Friday.
8 Last summer I went swimming every day.
9 On Wednesday I took my neighbour's dog for a walk.

18 Ahora escribe por lo menos seis frases sobre lo que haces tú en tu tiempo libre. Incluye alguna información en el pasado. Explícaselo a tu pareja.

Ejemplo: Me gusta mucho nadar y siempre voy a la piscina el martes y el jueves. Ayer fui a la playa por la tarde y nadé en el mar.

19 Copia estas preguntas y prepara tus respuestas. Pregunta a tres personas lo que hacen en su tiempo libre. ¡No te olvides del pasado!

1 ¿Qué haces normalmente en tu tiempo libre después del colegio?
2 ¿Qué haces los fines de semana?
3 ¿Qué hiciste ayer?
4 ¿Qué hiciste el sábado pasado?
5 ¿Qué hiciste el verano pasado?

2 ¿Cómo te enteras?

Say what types of media I prefer

Give opinions and reasons

Use impersonal verbs and infinitives

1a Escribe la palabra adecuada al lado de cada imagen.

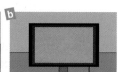
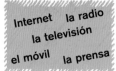

Internet   la radio
la televisión
el móvil   la prensa

b Lee las palabras en el recuadro abajo. Empareja cada palabra con la imagen que corresponde. Haz una lista.

*Ejemplo: correo electrónico — **a***

correo electrónico	cadena	antena	oyente
noticias	periódico	documental	ring tone
película	dibujo animado	presentador	teclado
mensaje	lector	periodista	espectador
carta	página web	chat room	artículo

2 Escucha la grabación. Completa el cuadro con las palabras adecuadas.

	Medio de comunicación	☺	☹	Razones
Ejemplo: **1**	Internet	✓		fácil/interesante
	televisión		✓	un rollo
2				
3				
4				

3 Habla con tu pareja de los medios de comunicación.

Ejemplo: **A:** *¿Qué te parece Internet?*
B: *Me entusiasma Internet porque es divertido.*

4 Escribe un pequeño párrafo explicando qué medio(s) prefieres y por qué.

GRAMÁTICA

Expressing an opinion

Pay special attention when expressing an opinion. It is what you have an opinion about that tells you the ending to use. Look at the table below:

me	gusta/n
te	chifla/n
le	gusta/n mucho
a usted le	encanta/n
nos	inspira/n
os	entusiasma/n
les	
a ustedes les	

Look at these examples:
- *Me encanta ver la televisión. Pienso que los anuncios son muy divertidos.*
- *A Manuel le encantan las películas de acción.*
- *A mis padres les gustan los documentales.*

Adapta las frases siguientes. Usa algunos de los verbos en la tabla arriba.

Ejemplo: Mi amigo Juan compra muchas revistas.
A Juan le gusta mucho leer revistas.

1 Marta siempre surfea Internet.
2 Escuchamos la radio a veces.
3 Mis hermanos no leen los periódicos.
4 ¿Qué opinas de los anuncios?
5 Creo que ir al cine es muy aburrido.

5 📖 Empareja los verbos con las imágenes. ¿Qué tienen las frases en común? Explícaselo a tu pareja.

1 No entiendo muy bien. ¿Me puedes **explicar**?

2 ¿Cuál es el número? Quiero **telefonear**.

Ejemplo: **1 — e**

3 Mis amigos acaban de **llegar**.

4 ¿Te gusta **viajar** en tren? Yo prefiero **viajar** en coche.

5 A mi hermano le encanta **leer** tebeos.

6 Hay que **estudiar** para **sacar** buenas notas.

7 No puedo **salir** esta noche. Tengo que **ayudar** a mis padres.

8 Voy a **jugar** al baloncesto esta tarde.

9 No deseo **tener** más hermanos.

10 ¿Sabes **esquiar**?

a
b
c
d
e

f
g
h
i
j

LENGUA CLAVE

Preguntas	Positivos/negativos	¿Por qué?
¿Te gusta.../¿Qué te parece... ...la televisión? ...la radio? ...Internet? ...el cine?	A mí me gusta... Me chifla... Me gusta mucho... Me encanta... Me inspira... Me entusiasma... No me gusta (nada)... Lo/la odio... Lo/la detesto...	porque es/creo que es/pienso que es... ...importante. ...interesante. ...educativo/a. ...divertido/a. ...fácil. ...genial. ...útil. ...un rollo. ...inútil. ...aburrido/a. ...una pérdida de tiempo.
¿Te gustan.../¿Qué te parecen... ...las películas? ...los periódicos? ...las revistas? ...las noticias? ...los anuncios? ...los documentales? ...las cartas?	A mi me gustan... Me chiflan... Me gustan mucho... Me encantan... Me inspiran... Me entusiasman... No me gustan (nada)... Los/las odio... Los/las detesto...	Creo que son/pienso que son... ...importantes. ...interesantes. ...educativos/as. ...divertidos/as. ...fáciles. ...geniales. ...útiles. ...inútiles. ...aburridos/as.

Cambridge IGCSE® Spanish ● International Certificate in Spanish

---

GRAMÁTICA

Using infinitives

The infinitive is the form of the verb that hasn't had any ending added to it. It is the only form of the verb you will find listed in a dictionary.

In English, the infinitive is usually shown with the word **to**:

● *cantar* – **to** sing

Be careful when translating the English *–ing* form. This is often an infinitive in Spanish:

● *Me encanta **comer** pizza.* I love eating pizza.

The second verb used in any sentence is always in the infinitive form:

● *Me encanta **hablar** con mis amigos* I love talking to my friends.

● *Prefiero **escuchar** música pop.* I prefer listening to pop music

Escribe la forma del infinitivo de estos verbos. Usa un diccionario para ayudarte.

● dibujó
● salgo
● anduviste
● saltamos
● se sienta
● corrieron
● pongan
● pagué
● volvió
● abren
● compramos
● cae
● venimos
● recuerde
● evitamos
● decidieron

6 📖 Read the article. Answer the questions in English.

¿Qué es Facebook?

Facebook es un sitio web de redes sociales. Fue creado originalmente para estudiantes de la Universidad de Harvard, pero ha sido abierto a cualquier persona que tenga una cuenta de correo electrónico. Los usuarios pueden participar en una o más redes sociales en relación con su situación académica, su lugar de trabajo o región geográfica.

¿Por qué utilizar las redes sociales?

La vida es más alegre si se puede compartir y los problemas parecen más sencillos contados a otra persona. Por eso principalmente se ha hecho tan popular el uso de redes sociales como Facebook o su equivalente español, Tuenti. Ofrecen contactos que también sirven en los negocios y es un foro excelente para anunciarse y así, vender. Además, para muchas organizaciones y empresas, es una manera de encontrar información sobre ti – así que ¡ojo! ¡Nunca sabes quién te está observando!

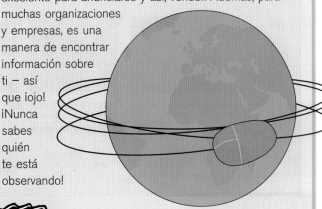

¿Y qué piensan nuestros lectores?

A mi madre le encanta Facebook porque es una forma de localizar a amigos con quienes perdió el contacto.

Idoya

Para mí es la mejor manera de hacer nuevos amigos con quienes puedo intercambiar fotos y mensajes. También se pueden reunir personas con intereses comunes.

Héctor

Sé que a la gente las redes sociales le parecen una maravilla, pero yo creo que son una pérdida de tiempo. Prefiero leer periódicos y revistas y sobre todo, ¡mi Kindle!

Olinda

No me interesa mucho la vida de otra gente — en realidad hay demasiado de ese tipo en la tele. No sé si quiero que cualquiera sepa algo sobre mi vida privada.

Antolín

Oí de alguien que perdió su trabajo por usar Facebook en la oficina. Eso es lógico. La gente debería ser responsable y usar esos medios en su propio tiempo. ¡No se puede usar Facebook en mi cole!

Óscar

1 What exactly is Facebook?
2 Who is Facebook for?
3 Name two advantages of social networking sites.
4 Name two advantages of Facebook mentioned.

5 What is the majority opinion of the readers? Are they for or against social networking sites?
6 From what these young people say, how should Facebook and equivalents be used responsibly?

7 📖 Lee esta información. Empareja las imágenes con la hora de los programas.

*Ejemplo: **a** — 11.30*

Programación televisiva
Lunes el 24 de mayo

TVE 1

06:00	Noticias 24 horas
11:30	Entrevista
14:00	Oliver y Benji (dibujo animado)
15:00	Piratas y corsarios (ciencia-ficción)
15:55	El tiempo
16:00	La naturaleza en África (documental)
16:50	Destilando amor (telenovela)
17:50	La viuda de blanco (Película de suspense)
18:20	Millonario (concurso)
20:00	Fútbol: Copa del Mundo
22:00	Siete vidas (comedia)
23:00	Ópera desde Sydney

8a 🎧 ¿Qué deciden ver estos jóvenes? ¿Por qué razones? Pon una X en la casilla adecuada.

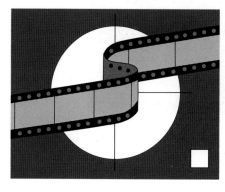

b 🔺 ¿Por qué eligen esa idea? Da cuatro razones en español.

9 💬 Trabaja con tu pareja. Habla de lo que te gustaría ver en la tele.

Ejemplo: **A:** *Me gustaría ver una película esta tarde.*
B: *¿Qué tipo de película?*
A: *Es una película de risa. Se llama* Los Simpsons. *Lo echan a las cuatro.*
B: *La verdad es que no me apetece ésa. Prefiero ver un programa de música. MTV internacional, por ejemplo.*
A: *Vale. ¿A qué hora es?*
B: *Empieza a las cinco de la tarde.*

¿Qué opinas?

10 Lee lo siguiente. Decide si las frases son positivas o negativas. Escribe tus respuestas en la tabla.

No me gustó la película porque...

Me gustó la película porque...

Anoche fui a ver *El caballero oscuro: La leyenda renace*. La verdad es que no me gustó mucho la película y había gente que hablaba todo el rato — ¡cosa que me molesta un montón! Para mí no era nada interesante. En realidad no es mi tipo de entretenimiento, ¡aunque tengo que admitir que el protagonista era superguapo! No sé qué pasaba en el cine, pero no se oía bien, ni siquiera la música. ¡Creo que tenían algún problema! En fin, la verdad es que no creo que valga la pena.

1 La historia era increíblemente aburrida.
2 El actor principal era muy guapo.
3 La música era demasiado alta.
4 Fue bastante entretenida.
5 Valía la pena verla.
6 Había muchas distracciones.
7 Las entradas eran muy caras.
8 Había mucha acción.
9 Daba demasiado miedo para mi gusto.
10 Los efectos especiales eran fantásticos.
11 El paisaje era alucinante.
12 No era mi tipo de película.

11 Recibes este mensaje electrónico. Escribe una respuesta.

¡Hola!

¿Qué te pareció la peli de anoche? Estoy deseando saber lo que piensas.

Hasta pronto.

Óscar

GRAMÁTICA

Negatives

Negative statements are ones in which we say 'no' or deny something or disagree.

No tengo las entradas.　　I haven't got the tickets.

No voy nunca al cine./Nunca voy al cine.　　I never go to the cinema

Notice that a negative expression, with the exception of *no*, meaning 'not', can consist of one word or two words, as in the second example. When the negative is one word, it is always placed before the verb. When the negative is two words, *no* goes before the verb and the second word goes after the verb.

Other important negative expressions are:

no...nada	nothing
no...nadie	nobody
no...ni...ni	neither...nor
no...ninguno	no
no...tampoco	neither

Look at the reading text again and make a list of the negative expressions you find.

Positivas	Negativas
Ejemplo: 2 El actor principal era muy guapo.	*Ejemplo: 1 La historia era increíblemente aburrida.*

¡OJO!

With adjectives ending in –o or –a an easy way to add emphasis in Spanish is to take off the final vowel and add –ísimo/–ísima, as appropriate. For example, *bueno* (good) becomes *buenísimo* (very good); *mala* (bad) becomes *malísima* (very bad) etc. Most adjectives ending in other vowels, or consonants, have to rely on the use of *muy* or *mucho* before them, for example, *trabajador — muy trabajador* (hardworking — very hardworking) or *emocionante — muy emocionante* (moving/exciting — very moving/exciting).

Use some in your writing to make it more authentic.

12a 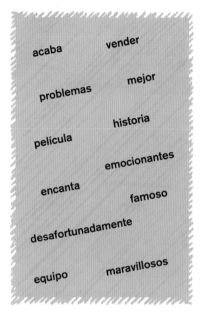 Lee estas palabras y después lee la carta. Decide en cada caso qué palabra falta. Usa un diccionario para ayudarte.

Ejemplo: **1** — *historia*

> acaba   vender
>
> problemas   mejor
>
> película   historia
>
> emocionantes
>
> encanta   famoso
>
> desafortunadamente
>
> equipo   maravillosos

b 📝 Usa la carta para ayudarte a escribir tu propia carta a un amigo contándole sobre una película que has visto últimamente.

¿Qué hay?

¡Hola David!

Acabo de ver una película fantástica llamada Flying Start y como me impresionó muchísimo, decidí escribirte para contártelo.

Es la ___(1)___ de un mecánico de coches de carrera. Le ___(2)___ conducir y un día le hace caso el director del equipo — un tal Nerón.

Nerón es celoso y le da envidia el talento de Sabi así que le mete en un ___(3)___ malo para impedir su éxito. Pero Sabi es tan bueno que gana de todas formas. Se hace ___(4)___ y gana todo. Se enamora de una azafata guapísima y se casa con ella.

Más que nada es un hombre casado y contento. Tiene una casa preciosa, dos hijos ___(5)___ y una carrera de ensueño.

___(6)___ su vida ideal se transforma cuando tiene un accidente grave que le deja sin poder conducir más. No tiene más remedio que ___(7)___ todo y mudarse a un barrio pobre.

La película trata principalmente de su pelea para conseguir de nuevo todo lo que perdió. ¡No te voy a contar cómo ___(8)___!

Es una ___(9)___ magnífica que desde luego vale la pena ver. Tiene música preciosa y las escenas de las carreras de coches son verdaderamente ___(10)___. Me hizo reír y llorar.

Flying Start demuestra como es mejor enfrentarse a sus ___(11)___ y no hay que ignorar las cosas esperando que se mejoren sin ningún esfuerzo.

Esa es la ___(12)___ película que he visto este año.

Por favor, escríbeme para contarme sobre la última peli que has visto.

Besos,

Luis

CULTURA

¿Ya sabes?

Guillermo del Toro es uno de los cineastas más célebres de México que ha tenido mucho éxito en el mundo del cine no hispanohablante también.

Nacido el 9 de octubre de 1964, empezó haciendo un aprendizaje con el maquillista cinematográfico, Dick Smith, pasó casi una década supervisando el maquillaje cinematográfico, y entonces formó su propia empresa.

Su éxito cinematográfico comenzó en 1993 con su película *Cronos* que ganó nueve premios en México. Su primer éxito conocido fuera de México fue *Mimic* (1997). Diez años más tarde, hizo la película célebre *El laberinto del faunio* (2006). Esas películas muestran su interés por la fantasía, la ciencia ficción y lo sobrenatural. A Guillermo le encanta usar espacios subterráneos, oscuros o encerrados, en sus películas.

Es, sin duda, una personalidad imprescindible en el panorama cultural español e internacional.

¿Conoces otras de sus películas? ¿Cómo se llaman? ¡Haz una investigación!

Visitando Correos

13 🎧 Empareja lo que oyes con la imagen apropiada.

Ejemplo: **1** — *d*

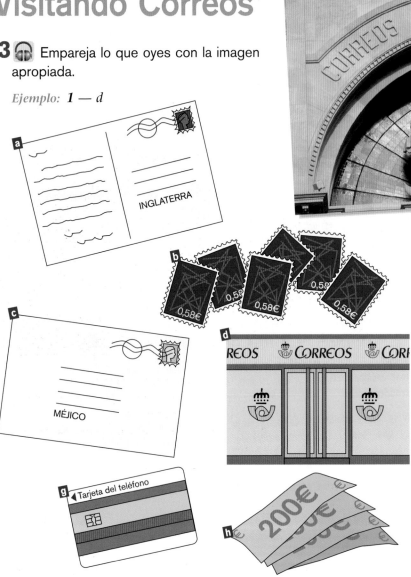

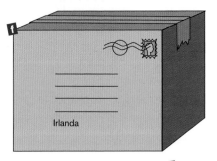

14 💬 Trabaja con tu pareja. Practica los diálogos.
Te ayudarán las palabras en la caja.

Ejemplo: **A:** *Buenos días señor. ¿Qué desea?*
B: *¿Cuánto cuesta enviar una carta a Inglaterra, por favor?*
A: *Cuesta 58 céntimos*
B: *Gracias. Quisiera dos sellos de 58 céntimos por favor.*
A: *Aquí tiene. ¿Algo más?*
B: *Sí, un billete de la lotería de la Cruz Roja, por favor.*

¿Dónde está	Correos?		
Hay	un buzón de correo	por aquí/cerca de aquí?	
¿Cuánto cuesta ¿Puedo	enviar mandar cambiar comprar	un paquete una carta dinero un sello	a Inglaterra? a España? a Cuba a Costa Rica
Quisiera	una tarjeta móvil		

15a 📖 Lee este artículo de una revista española y contesta las preguntas.

¿Estás enchufado?

¿Sabías que hoy en día cinco de cada seis jóvenes tienen teléfono móvil? ¡Y que la mayoría de ellos mandan unos 100 mensajes de texto por día!

Los que venden los móviles justifican esa cifra diciendo que con la tecnología de ahora nuestra juventud disfruta también del acceso a Internet, con lo cual pueden recibir todo tipo de información y enterarse de lo que está pasando en el mundo. Los que están en contra piensan que son peligrosos — dañan la salud, y también provocan atracos. Sin hablar de como distraen a los chicos de sus estudios y de lo que les cuestan a sus padres.

Marta, una joven entusiasta de Valladolid dice:- 'Yo soy adicta! No puedo sobrevivir ahora sin mi móvil. Me hace sentirme segura y así mantengo contacto con mi familia y mis amigos. ¿Por qué estar sola?'

Hicimos una encuesta para saber cómo los jóvenes prefieren enterarse de las noticias. Como se ve en el gráfico, la mayoría escucha las noticias en la tele, mientras 224 consiguen esa información de Internet. Sorprendentemente, más de 300 personas escuchan la radio. ¿Quién ha dicho que la generación de la radio ya no existe?

Otros medios
Libros electrónicos
Periódicos
Radio
Televisión
Internet

Muy pocos compran y leen periódicos. Dicen que son incómodos y sucios y que otros medios son preferibles. Una cifra pequeña usa otros medios de comunicación, como hablar con el móvil y usarlo. Graciosamente, ninguno admitió que no lee ni escucha las noticias en absoluto.

Muchos de los chicos con quienes hablamos afirman que saber lo que pasa es importante, pero que quieren un método rápido y fácil — como hoy en día no hay tiempo para nada — y en este respecto la tecnología es una maravilla.

Un porcentaje muy pequeño cree que hay demasiada tecnología y que se sienten controlados por el Gran Hermano de Orwell. No importa si los odias o los crees imprescindibles, los medios de comunicación siguen desarrollándose y ya no hay excusa para no saber lo que pasa en el mundo. Muchos están de acuerdo con que el mundo ahora es mucho más pequeño y asequible gracias a los logros de la tecnología.

¿Y tú? Tienes móvil? ¿Cuántas horas pasas al día hablando por teléfono o mandando mensajes? ¿Y usas Internet? ¿Para qué?

Queremos oír lo que opinas tú. Mándanos un correo electrónico explicándonos todo.

1 Según el artículo, ¿qué ventajas tienen los móviles? Menciona dos ventajas.

2 ¿Qué desventajas hay para algunos?

3 ¿Por qué muchos jóvenes no leen periódicos?

4 ¿Por qué el mundo parece más pequeño hoy día?

5 ¿Qué quiere el periodista que haga el lector?

b Ahora escribe un correo electrónico a la revista contestando todas las preguntas del recuadro. No te olvides de dar razones de tus opiniones y hábitos.

Señor,
He leído su artículo en la revista *Prima* y quisiera comunicarle lo que pienso yo de los medios de comunicación…

3 ¿A quién admiras?

☑ Practise using *ser* and *tener* to describe people

☑ Practise talking about people I admire

☑ Practise extended writing

☑ Use adverbs and adjectives

☑ Use the perfect tense

☑ Use the superlative

1 Mira la lista de adjetivos siguientes. Pon cada uno en la categoría apropiada.

interesante	feo	horrible	trabajador	feliz
aburrido	bueno	estupendo	nervioso	cortés
antipático	bonito	tímido	contento	agradable
divertido	emocionante	simpático		
perezoso	malo	abierto		
orgulloso	inteligente	honesto		

Positivo	Negativo
trabajador	

2 Trabaja en pareja. ¿Cómo es tu amigo/a?

¿Cómo es tu amigo?	¿Cómo es tu amiga?
Creo que el amigo ideal es (no es)/está (no está)…	**Creo que la amiga ideal es (no es)/está (no está)…**
de buen humor ○	de buen humor ○
de moda ○	de moda ○
relajado ○	relajada ○
abierto ○	abierta ○
honesto ○	honesta ○
simpático ○	simpática ○
pensativo ○	pensativa ○
cariñoso ○	cariñosa ○
bien educado ○	bien educada ○
perezoso ○	perezosa ○
egoísta ○	egoísta ○
tranquilo ○	tranquila ○
un poco loco ○	un poco loca ○
menos hablador que yo ○	menos habladora que yo ○
tan inteligente como yo ○	tan inteligente como yo ○

3 💬 Trabaja con tu pareja. Pregunta y contesta las preguntas siguientes sobre la encuesta.

1 ¿Cómo es tu mejor amigo/a?
2 Mi mejor amigo/a es un(a) chico/a...
3 ¿Qué rasgos no te gustan en un amigo/a?
4 No me gusta que mi amigo/a sea...

4 🏛 Escribe un pequeño párrafo para describir a tu amigo/a ideal. Usa estas frases para ayudarte. Lee primero los apuntes sobre la gramática.

Para mí el/la amigo/a ideal sería...
Prefiero un chico/una chica que sea...
Lo que no me gusta de un chico/una chica es...
Me gustan los chicos/las chicas...
Me gustan los chicos/las chicas con el pelo... y ojos...

Está **muy** contento.

Está **poco** contenta.

Es **bastante** perezoso.

Es **más** perezosa que...

5 💬 Trabaja con tu pareja. Describe un(a) amigo/a que tu pareja no conozca. Tu pareja tiene que adivinar si te gusta el/la amigo/a o no, y explicarte por qué.

GRAMÁTICA

Using adverbs

You can use adverbs to tell you more about verbs and adjectives.

Match the Spanish words with the English ones:

muy	quite
un poco	less
más	very
bastante	a little bit
poco	more
menos	not very

Make these sentences more interesting by using adverbs from the list above. There could be more than one answer.

1 Pablo es inteligente, guapo y alto.
2 María es simpática, educada, pero tímida.
3 Mi hermana menor es egoísta, aburrida y grosera.
4 Mi profesora preferida es tranquila, cariñosa y simpática.
5 Mi padre es estricto. Me hace trabajar.
6 Mi profesora de dibujo es joven. Tiene paciencia.

GRAMÁTICA

Más...que, menos...que and *tan...como*

*Me gustan los chicos que sean **más** inteligentes **que** yo.*

*Me gustan las chicas que sean **tan** inteligentes **como** yo.*

*Me gustan las chicas que sean **menos** inteligentes **que** yo.*

6a Cada opinión describe una de las cuatro personas famosas. Empareja la opinión con la persona correcta. Utiliza un diccionario, si es necesario.

1 una actriz inglesa
2 una persona carismática
3 una persona deportiva
4 una persona simpática que ha tenido mucho éxito
5 una persona que tiene el pelo largo y rubio
6 un(a) letrista
7 un(a) escritor(a)
8 una persona trabajadora
9 una persona esbelta que tiene ojos verdes
10 una persona muy inteligente

Keira Knightley

Usain Bolt

J. K. Rowling

Bruno Mars

b Escribe una carta de 100 palabras a una de esta personas famosas:

(i) Di que tu ambición es ser cantante, actor/actriz, escritor(a) o deportista.
(ii) Explícale por qué tienes esta ambición.
(iii) Escribe tus ideas sobre lo que implica su profesión.
(iv) Pregúntale su consejo sobre tus posibilidades de éxito.

¡OJO!

Interjections

Interjections are short words or phrases that we utter when we want to express emotion. It is sometimes difficult to pin down the exact meaning of these words, which can stand for different emotions. Here are some examples.

Emotion	Spanish word/ phrase	Approximate meaning
Astonishment, surprise	¡Anda! ¡Vaya!	(My) Goodness!
Anxiety	¡Ay!	Oh (dear)!
Approval, enthusiasm	¡Qué bien!	Great!
Surprise, indignation	¡Caray!	Good heavens!

LENGUA CLAVE

¿A quién admiras?	Admiro a...	¿Cómo es?
		Es muy/bastante/un poco/poco... ...alto(a). ...delgado(a). ...guapo(a). ...británico(a). ...español(a). ...irlandés/esa. ...norteamericano(a).
	Tiene...	...la piel oscura/clara/morena. ...pecas. ...cara redonda/ancha/alargada. ...ojos azules/verdes/castaños. ...barba. ...bigote.
¿Cómo es su personalidad?	Es...	...simpático(a). ...cariñoso(a). ...divertido(a). ...gracioso(a). ...listo(a). ...abierto(a). ...rápido(a). ...majo(a). ...trabajador(a).
	Tiene...	...éxito. ...mérito.
¿Qué hace?	Es...	...cantante. ...escritor(a). ...deportista. ...futbolista. ...actor/actriz.

7 💬 Habla con tu pareja de una persona a quien admiras.

Ejemplo:

A: ¿A quién admiras?
B: Admiro a mi padre.
A: ¿Cómo es?
B: Es alto y fuerte. Tiene el pelo rubio y corto, la cara alargada y la piel clara.
A: ¿Cómo es su personalidad?
B: Es majo y cariñoso y en el campo es rápido y trabajador.
A: ¿Qué hace?
B: Es ingeniero.
A: ¡Qué bien!

¡ojo!

Make your writing more interesting

Conjunctions are 'joining' words that link parts of a sentence. If you are writing about somebody famous, you could write:

La princesa Kate es miembra de la familia real británica (profession). *Es bastante alta, delgada, muy guapa y rica. Tiene los ojos castaños y el pelo largo y moreno* (looks). *Es simpática, sonriente y muy trabajadora* (personality). *Es inglesa* (nationality). *Le encanta el deporte y le parece divertido salir con sus amigos* (likes and dislikes).

This will be the 'bones' of your description. Then make up longer, more complex sentences using conjunctions. The most common conjunctions are:

y	and
o	or
pero	but
ni…ni	neither…nor
aunque	although
cuando	when
para que	so that
porque	because
si	if, whether

Note that:
y becomes *e* before (h)i: *Carlos e Isabel* — Carlos and Isabel
o becomes *u* before (h)o: *setenta u ochenta* — seventy or eighty

Use conjunctions to link words phrases and clauses:
*Es grande **pero** no es gordo.*
He is big but not fat.
*Me gusta **porque** es muy buen cantante.*
I like him/her because he/she is a very good singer.
***Como** es muy fuerte mete muchos goles.*
As he/she is very strong, he/she scores lots of goals.

8a ✏️ Escribe una lista de todos los adjetivos que conoces para describir a una persona y encuentra el contrario. Usa un diccionario si es necesario.

Adjetivo	Contrario
alto	*bajo*
majo	*insoportable*

b ✏️ Escribe cinco frases sobre (a) una persona famosa a quien admiras y (b) una persona famosa que no te guste. Utiliza una conjunción en cada frase.

Ejemplo: Admiro a mi amigo Rubina porque es…
No me gusta X porque es…

9 ✏️ Escribe un artículo sobre gente famosa que te guste.

GRAMÁTICA

More about using adjectives

Adjectives agree in number and gender with the noun they are describing:

masculine singular	***un** chico maj**o*** (a lovely boy)
masculine plural	*oj**os** negr**os*** (black eyes)
feminine singular	***una** piel oscur**a*** (a dark complexion)
feminine plural	***unas** person**as** divertid**as*** (fun people)

In Spanish some adjectives are used with the verb *ser* while others are used with *tener*:

Es guapo.	He is good looking.
Es bastante alto.	He is quite tall.
Tiene el pelo rubio.	He/she has blond hair.
Tiene éxito.	He/She is successful.

Ser is used with nationality:

Soy inglés/esa.	I am English.
Es irlandés/esa.	He/She is Irish.

Completa las frases siguientes con el verbo correcto:
1 Gabriel García Márquez _____ colombiano.
2 Mi novio _____ fuerte y delgado y _____ los ojos morenos.
3 Carlos Slim _____ listo y _____ mucho éxito.
4 Los chicos de Green Day _____ éxito porque _____ simpáticos.
5 Yo _____ alto y un poco gordo.

10 🎧 Escucha lo siguiente. ¿Quién es? ¿María, Suzi, Pili, Juan, Anabel o Pablo?

Ejemplo: 1 — María

1 Le gusta la misma comida.
2 Tiene novia.
3 Está triste.
4 Tiene la misma edad que su amiga.
5 Se lleva muy bien con la persona que vive al lado.
6 Le gusta hacer deporte.
7 Comparte muchas cosas.
8 Cree que su amigo le ayuda.

11 ✏️ Llena los espacios con los verbos entre paréntesis en el perfecto.

1 Tu padre y yo _____ (*hablar*) con tu profesor.
2 En años recientes muchas películas excelentes _____ (*salir*) de Latinoamérica.
3 Y tú, ¿qué le _____ (*decir*)?
4 Su padre _____ (*morir*).
5 ¡Yo no _____ nada! (*hacer*)
6 Aquella canción _____ (*romper*) récords en Argentina.
7 Yo le _____ (*mandar*) muchos correos electrónicos pero él no _____ (*responder*) nunca.

GRAMÁTICA

The perfect tense

The perfect tense is used when you want to talk about a past event and connect it to the present. When you say 'He has arrived', you are calling attention to both the fact that he arrived recently and that he is here now.

The perfect tense in Spanish is formed from the auxiliary verb *haber* and the past participle of the verb. This is the form of the verb ending in -*ado* or -*ido* in regular verbs.

Formation of the perfect tense in regular verbs

	hablar	**comer**	**vivir**
yo	he hablado	he comido	he vivido
tú	has hablado	has comido	has vivido
él/ella/usted	ha hablado	ha comido	ha vivido
nosotros/as	hemos hablado	hemos comido	hemos vivido
vosotros/as	habéis hablado	habéis comido	habéis vivido
ellos/ellas/ustedes	han hablado	han comido	han vivido

He hablado *con ella varias veces, pero no quiere decirme la verdad.*

I've spoken to her several times, but she doesn't want to tell me the truth.

*¡***Hemos comido** *bien!* We've eaten well.

Ha vivido *en esta ciudad por muchos años.*

He's lived in this town for many years.

Irregular past participles

A number of verbs have irregular past participles. The most common ones are:

abrir	to open	abierto	opened		decir	to say	dicho	said
escribir	to write	escrito	written		hacer	to do/make	hecho	done/made
morir	to die	muerto	dead		poner	to put	puesto	put
romper	to break	roto	broken		ver	to see	visto	seen
volver	to return	vuelto	returned					

¿Qué le **han dicho***?*	What have they said to him?
He escrito *dos mensajes.*	I've written two messages.
*¿***Has visto** *Cronos, de Guillermo del Toro?*	¿Have you seen Guillermo del Toro's Cronos?

GRAMÁTICA

The superlative

The superlative is used to compare the most or the least. In English, we add **-est** to the adjective, for example the kind*est*, the rich*est*, the happi*est*, or we add the word 'most', for example the *most* beautiful.

In Spanish, you use the following construction:
el/la/los
+ *más/menos*
+ *noun* + *adjective*.

For example:
- *El chico **más** simpático **de** mi clase.*
  The nicest boy in my class.

- *La persona **menos** inteligente que conozco.*
  The least intelligent person I know.

NB: *mejor* – best; *peor* – worst.

Write two sentences using the superlative for the following set of pictures.

Ana   María   Suzi

12 💬 Trabaja con tu pareja. Habla de tu mejor amigo/a.

Mi mejor amigo/a se llama…
Es el chico/la chica más…
Me encanta su…
Tenemos los mismos gustos en…
Puedo fiarme de él/ella…
Para mí lo más importante es…

13 📖 Lee lo que dice Francisco de su hermano.

Admiro mucho a mi hermano mayor porque es un experto de la informática. Si tengo un problema con mi ordenador o si se estropea, Andrés no tarda nada en recuperar los archivos o vencer a un pirata de informática.

Solo tiene 18 años, pero es superlisto y repara cualquier fallo.

Tiene cuatro ordenadores en total, pero no me deja usarlos porque no tengo éxito con los ordenadores. ¡Con solo mirarlos consigo borrar los archivos! ¡Siempre se me olvida mi contraseña! Lo mejor de Andrés es que es muy tranquilo y explica bien las cosas. ¡También me quema muchos CDs de música popular! ¡Nunca he tenido suerte con los ordenadores!

Uso el ordenador para los estudios y es muy importante entender del 'disco duro', 'lector de disquettes' etc., pero soy un poco tonto porque siempre tengo algún problema. ¡Andrés es mi héroe!

a 🏰 ¿Cuáles de estos adjetivos describen Andrés y Francisco? Rellena la tabla.

> inteligente   divertido   perezoso   generoso
> antipático   antiguo   rápido   agradecido
> trabajador   nervioso   alto   despistado
> aburrido   egoísta   despistado

Andrés	Francisco
inteligente	*agradecido*

b 🏰 Haz una lista de los usos diferentes de *ser* y *tener* en este artículo.

Ejemplo: ser — Es un experto.
tener — Tengo un problema.

14 📖 ¿Qué dice Ángel de la gente a quien admira?

La persona más importante en mi vida es mi madre. Sin ella no sería quien soy. Es cariñosa, simpática y perdona muy fácilmente. Le quiero porque me ha enseñado como ser una persona honrada. También está mi padre. Dicen que me parezco a él, pero prefiero pensar que quieren decir que me parezco con respecto a mi personalidad. Ha sido trabajador y honesto durante toda la vida. Siempre dice algo majo de los demás.

Creo que los amigos son muy importantes. Conozco a mucha gente pero solo tengo una a quien le considero una amiga de verdad. A Ana le conozco de toda la vida y es la única persona con quien puedo hablar porque ella escucha. Es discreta y muy lista, pero modesta. Con Ana puedes ser serio o relajado. Salimos juntos bastante pero no importa si no nos vemos durante un tiempo. Al juntarnos de nuevo todo sigue como antes. No hemos reñido nunca.

🏰 Contesta las preguntas.

1 Según Àngel, ¿cómo es su madre?
2 A Àngel, ¿qué le ha enseñado su madre?
3 ¿Cómo es su padre?
4 ¿Por qué tiene una relación especial con Ana?
5 Cuando Àngel y Ana se juntan de nuevo, ¿qué pasa?

Paper 1: listening

In the following listening task you hear a short advert for a new sports centre. In the first four questions you have to fill in the gaps using what you hear in the recording.

Vas a oír un anuncio sobre un nuevo centro deportivo. Escúchalo con atención y completa la ficha **en español**.

Centro deportivo Quintana

1 Quintana: un .... centro deportivo. **[1]**

2 Tiene una piscina .... **[1]**

3 Hay vistas de un .... natural precioso. **[1]**

4 El restaurante es famoso por sus precios .... **[1]**

[*PAUSA*]

5 En el centro deportivo, además de hacer gimnasia, se puede:

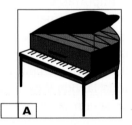
A

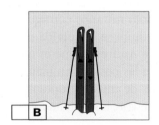
B

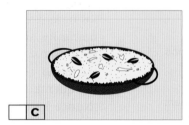
C

[1]

6 Si te haces socio, te dan: *(indica **2** respuestas)*

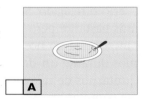
A

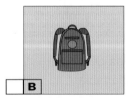
B

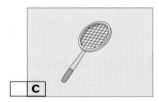
C

D

[2]

[**Total: 7**]

Tips for success

- Use your time for reading the questions productively, to study the questions and the marks allocated.
- Make sure that your answers are short and concise.
- Try to predict the words that fill the gaps from the question. For example, in question 4 think about what a restaurant could be famous for.

Paper 2: reading

This reading task tests your ability to pick out the main points and some details in a short text.

Lee este artículo.

¿Por qué no leen los niños?

Últimamente el hecho de que los niños en edad escolar muestren una tendencia a no leer como pasatiempo preocupa mucho a los expertos. Los resultados de encuestas recientes muestran las siguientes razones que explican esta falta de interés por la lectura:

- Muchos escolares dicen que los libros que leen en el colegio no son interesantes.
- Los resultados de encuestas recientes muestran que los libros que los niños leen en el colegio no son interesantes.
- Parece ser que en su tiempo libre, los niños están demasiado ocupados con otras actividades.
- Los padres de hoy en día leen poco a sus hijos.
- Las actividades informáticas atraen más a los niños.
- Los niños copian las actividades que hacen sus amigos en vez de leer.
- Los libros son muy caros.

Completa cada frase con una palabra española elegida de la lista.

interesa	alto	bajo	duele
anotar	pueden	prefieren	suficiente
nunca	copiar		

1 A los niños no les .... lo que leen en el colegio.   **[1]**

2 Los niños .... hacer otras cosas en su tiempo libre en vez de leer.   **[1]**

3 Los padres no leen lo .... a sus hijos.   **[1]**

4 Los niños prefieren .... lo que hacen sus amigos.   **[1]**

5 El precio de un libro es bastante ....   **[1]**

[Total: 5]

Points to remember

- In this task, for each gap that you have to fill, more than one word in the box makes sense grammatically, but only *one* word fits the context of the text. Read the text carefully so that you are sure of the meaning.

- Try to predict from the questions which words in the box would logically fill the gap, e.g. in question 5 *alto* and *bajo*.

In part 1 of the speaking exam you have to do two role plays, A and B. Below is a sample situation for role play B.

B

Estudiante: tú mismo/a

Profesor(a): amigo/a español(a)

Has quedado con tu amigo/a español(a) para ir al cine, pero no puedes salir esta noche. Llamas a tu amigo/a.

E **(i)** Saluda a tu amigo/a; **y**

  (ii) Explícale por qué llamas.

E Responde a lo que te pregunta.

E **(i)** Discúlpate; **y**

  (ii) Dile cuándo te parece que puedes salir.

E **(i)** Dale las gracias; **e**

  (ii) Invítalo/a a salir.

E **(i)** Sugiere una actividad que quieres hacer; **y**

  (ii) Dile por qué.

Points to remember

- Task 2 in this role play is an unpredictable question. Listen carefully to what you are asked so that you can be sure your answer is appropriate. When planning for this task, try to think of possible questions that you could be asked in this situation.

🎧 Listen to a student carrying out the role play. The dialogue is given below.

P ¡Hola Sonia! Te llamo porque resulta que no puedo salir esta noche.

E ¡Qué pena! ¿Por qué no?

P Es que tengo que hacer demasiados deberes.

E Vale, no te preocupes. Me quedaré en casa viendo la tele yo sola.

P Lo siento mucho, Sonia. Estoy libre el sábado que viene.

E ¡Qué bien! ¡Yo también estoy libre el sábado!

P Gracias, Sonia. ¿Podemos vernos el sábado entonces?

E ¡De acuerdo! Pero, ¿qué hacemos?

P El sábado es la fiesta de cumpleaños de Borja.

Practise this possible dialogue with a partner. Now adapt the highlighted sections to create a different response.

What questions would you ask a new friend about their free time and hobbies? Make up a dialogue of your own and work with a partner to complete it.

Paper 4: writing

In the task below, you have to write a list of eight items in Spanish, all related to the topic of sport.

---

1 Te gusta mucho hacer deporte. Haz una lista de **8** deportes que te interesan **en español.** **[Total: 5]**

Ejemplo: fútbol

Why did you choose these words that you did? Discuss this with your partner.

Points to remember

- When learning vocabulary, sort words into groups or categories. Using spider grams and mind maps can help you. What other strategies could you use to help memorise words? Discuss this with your partner.

Now find at least 8 words to fit the following two categories. Write these words in a list: *los medios de comunicación* and *pasatiempos*.

Read through this next task carefully before you begin.

2 Acabas de pasar un fin de semana inolvidable. Escribe un correo electrónico a tu amigo/a.

Menciona:

(a) adónde fuiste

(b) lo que hiciste

> This suggests it was a weekend to remember. Expressing your opinions is important here.

(c) qué tal lo pasaste y por qué

> This point refers to the future. Beware!

(d) lo que vas a hacer el próximo fin de semana

Debes escribir 80–90 palabras **en español**. **[Total: 15]**

Tips for success

- Remember you need to cover all the points listed in the task when you write your response.
- There are four points, so with a word limit of around 80 words, you need write about 20 words in response to each point in the task.

Read your diary for the week below. Can you use this information to write your e-mail?

viernes	deberes/televisión	aburrido
sábado	ir con amigos al parque y al cine	divertido
domingo	cumpleaños del abuelo — comida en su casa	agradable
semana que viene	fiesta en casa de Jorge — pasar la noche allí	emocionante

Vocabulario

Sports and hobbies

el **ajedrez**   chess
el **alpinismo**   mountain/rock climbing
las **artes marciales**   martial arts
el **atletismo**   athletics
el **bádminton**   badminton
el **baile**   dance
el **baloncesto**   basketball
el **balonmano**   handball
el **béisbol**   baseball
el **billar**   billiards
el **boxeo**   boxing
el **bricolaje**   do-it-yourself (DIY)
el **buceo**   (scuba)diving
la **caza**   hunting
el **ciclismo**   cycling
la **cocina**   cooking
correr   running
la **corrida de toros**   bullfighting
el **críquet**   cricket
los **dardos**   darts
el **deporte**   sport
el **entrenamiento**   exercise, training
la **equitación**   horse riding
la **esgrima**   fencing
el **esquí**   skiing
el **esquí acuático**   water-skiing
el **footing**   jogging
el **fútbol**   football
la **gimnasia**   gymnastics
el **golf**   golf
la **halterofilia**   weightlifting
el **hockey**   hockey
la **informática**   ICT
la **jardinería**   gardening
el **kárate**   karate
la **lectura**   reading
la **lucha**   wrestling
ir en **monopatín**   skateboarding
la **música**   music
la **natación**   swimming
el **patinaje**   skating
la **pesca**   fishing
el **piragüismo**   canoeing
el **rugby**   rugby
la **televisión**   television
el **tenis**   tennis
el **tenis de mesa**   ping pong
el **tiro con arco**   archery
la **vela**   sailing
el **voleibol**   volleyball
el **windsurf**   windsurfing

Verbs

abrir   to open
aburrirse   to get bored

acompañar   to accompany
cerrar   to close
chatear   to chat
coger   to catch; to take
crear   to create
dar   to give
decidir   to decide
encontrar   to find
entrar   to enter
escapar   to escape
escribir   to write
escuchar   to listen (to)
esperar   to wait
estar   to be
hablar   to speak, to talk
hacer   to do/to make
interesarse por/en   to be interested in
invitar   to invite
ir   to go
ir al cine/teatro   to go to the cinema/
theatre
ir de excursión   to go hiking; to go on a
trip
ir de paseo   to go for a walk
jugar (a)   to play (a game)
leer   to read
mandar   to send
navegar por/en Internet   to surf the
internet
poner   to put
practicar   to practise
reír   to laugh
salir   to go out
saltar   to jump
ser   to be
tener   to have
terminar   to finish
tirar   to throw
tocar   to touch; to play an instrument
utilizar   to use
visitar   to visit

Musical instruments

el **arpa**   harp
la **batería**   drumkit
la **corneta**   cornet
la **flauta**   flute
la **guitarra**   guitar
el **piano**   piano
los **platillos**   cymbals
el **saxofón**   saxophone
el **tambor**   drum
el **teclado**   keyboard
el **trombón**   trombone
la **trompeta**   trumpet
el **violín**   violin
la **voz**   voice

Media and communication

los **anuncios**   advertisements
el **artículo**   article
los **correos electrónicos**   e-mails
la **entrevista**   interview
el **informativo**   news programme
(el/la) **Internet**   internet
los **mensajes de texto**   sms
las **noticias**   news
el **ordenador**   computer
el **periódico**   newspaper
la **prensa**   press
el **presentador**   presenter
la **programación**   viewing guide
la **publicidad**   advertising
la **radio**   radio
el **reportaje**   report
la **revista**   magazine
el **tebeo**   comic
el **(teléfono) móvil**   mobile phone
los **titulares**   headlines

Televison, radio and cinema

el **actor**   actor
el **actor secundario**   supporting actor
la **actriz**   actress
la **banda sonora**   soundtrack
la **comedia**   comedy
los **concursos**   game shows
los **créditos**   credits
la **crítica de cine**   film review
el **director**   director
el **documental**   documentary
el **drama**   drama
la **escena**   scene
los **efectos especiales**   special effects
la **estrella de cine**   film star
los **extras**   extras
el **papel (de cine)**   role
las **películas de acción**   action films
las **películas de amor/románticas**
romantic films
las **películas de aventuras**   adventure
films
las **películas de ciencia ficción**   science
fiction films
las **películas de espionaje**   spy films
las **películas de guerra**   war films
las **películas de terror**   horror films
las **películas del Oeste**   Westerns
las **películas históricas**   historical films
las **películas musicales**   musicals
las **películas policíacas**   detective films
el **productor**   producer
el **programa**   programme
los **programas de deportes**   sports shows
el **reparto**   cast

los **subtítulos** subtitles
el **telediario** news
la **telenovela** soap opera
el **tiempo** weather

Opinions
(No) Me gusta(n) I (don't) like
Admiro a I admire
En mi opinión In my opinion
Lo que más me gusta es The thing I like best is
Me da(n) miedo I'm afraid of
Me entusiasma(n) I'm keen on
Me fascina(n) I'm fascinated by
Me hace(n) reír It/They make(s) me laugh
Me impresiona(n) I'm impressed by
Me interesa(n) I'm interested in
Me encanta(n) I love
No aguanto I can't stand
Odio I hate
Prefiero I prefer

Adjectives
abierto/a open
aburrido/a boring
agradable agreeable
anticuado/a old-fashioned
antipático/a unkind
bello/a beautiful
bien educado/a well-brought-up
bueno/a good
cariñoso/a loving
carismático/a charismatic
contento/a content
corto/a short
de buen humor in a good mood
de moda fashionable
deportivo/a sporty
divertido/a fun, amusing
egoísta selfish
elegante smart
exitoso/a successful

famoso/a famous
feliz happy
feo/a ugly
gracioso/a funny
grosero/a rude
hablador/a chatty/talkative
honesto/a honest
inteligente intelligent
interesante interesting
joven young
largo/a long
listo/a clever
loco/a mad
majo/a lovely
malo/a bad
nervioso/a nervous
orgulloso/a proud
pensativo/a thoughtful
perezoso/a lazy
simpático/a kind
tonto/a stupid
tranquilo/a quiet
viejo/a old

Places to go
la **bolera** bowling alley
el **centro** town centre
el **cine** cinema
el **club** club
el **concierto** concert
la **discoteca** club; disco
la **entrada** entrance
el **estadio** stadium
el **gimnasio** gym
la **parada de autobús** bus stop
el **parque** park
el **parque de atracciones** amusement/theme park
la **piscina** swimming pool
la **pista de patinaje** ice rink
la **pista de tenis** tennis court
la **playa** beach

el **polideportivo** sports centre
el **restaurante** restaurant
la **taquilla** ticket office
el **teatro** theatre
las **tiendas** shops

Asking questions
¿A qué hora nos vemos? At what time shall we meet?
¿A qué hora empieza(n)/termina(n)...? At what time does/do... start/finish?
¿A quién admiras? Who do you admire?
¿Cómo es? What is he/she/it like?
¿Cómo pasas tu tiempo libre? How do you spend your free time?
¿Cuál es tu pasatiempo favorito? What is your favourite hobby?
¿Cuánto cuesta(n)? How much does it/do they cost?
¿Dónde está? Where is (it)?
¿Dónde quedamos? Where shall we meet?
¿Practicas algún deporte? Do you do any sports?
¿Por qué? Why?
¿Qué echan en el cine? What's on at the cinema?
¿Qué opinas? What's your opinion?
¿Qué ponen esta noche? What's on this evening?
¿Qué te apetece hacer? What do you feel like doing?
¿Qué quieres hacer? What do you want to do?
¿Te gusta(n)...? Do you like...?

Adverbs
bastante quite
más more
menos less
muy very
tan as
un poco a bit

El mundo del trabajo

1 ¿Qué tal tu cole?

2 Las prácticas de trabajo

3 El futuro

✓ Learn the different school subjects

✓ Talk about daily routine

✓ Talk about school uniform

✓ Use verbs expressing necessity and obligation

✓ Use pronouns

1 ¿Qué tal tu cole?

1a 📖 🏫 ¿Qué estudias? Pon los dibujos en el orden correcto según la lista siguiente.

Ejemplo: **1 — d**

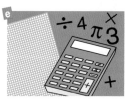

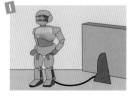

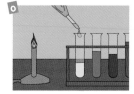

1	el español
2	el diseño
3	las matemáticas
4	la música
5	el inglés
6	el arte dramático
7	la historia
8	la tecnología
9	el alemán
10	las ciencias
11	la religión
12	el dibujo
13	el francés
14	la geografía
15	la informática
16	la educación física

b 💬 Habla con tu pareja. ¿Qué asignaturas te gustan más?

c 📖 ✏️ Cada una de las palabras siguientes es una asignatura. Adivina cuál es cada una.

Ejemplo: **1 — español**

1 pasleoñ
2 narfséc
3 lenaám
4 ticámsameta
5 rosaitih
6 grefogaaí
7 samúci
8 rate tamárdcoi

9 jubdio
10 gtaeíconlo
11 cacdenóiu safíic
12 lerinóig
13 sienacci
14 ficátamrino
15 sediño

2 🎧 ✏️ Rellena los huecos 1–10 con las asignaturas que faltan.

Ejemplo: **1** *— dibujo*

	lunes	martes	miércoles	jueves	viernes
8:00	inglés	geografía	informática	tecnología	español
9:00	ciencias	(2)	(5)	historia	(9)
10:00	(1)	ciencias	(6)	(8)	matemáticas
11:00					
11:30	español	(3)	ciencias	informática	inglés
12:30	matemáticas	deporte	geografía	inglés	dibujo
1:30					
3:00	historia	deporte	(7)	francés	deporte
4:00	geografía	(4)	español	matemáticas	(10)

3 📖 Lee lo que dicen estos jóvenes. Mira el horario. ¿A qué día se refieren?

1 Me encanta estudiar idiomas y hoy ¡tengo la oportunidad de estudiar dos! Es mi día preferido, ¡por supuesto!

2 Me gusta trabajar con ordenadores y como hoy estudiamos esa asignatura dos veces ¡es genial!

3 De veras no me gustan las ciencias así que el único día que no las tenemos es mi preferido.

4 Soy muy deportista y por eso el día que tenemos dos clases de esta asignatura es mi favorito.

5 La verdad es que no me gusta el colegio en absoluto. Pero, como es el día que no hay geografía — ¡la que odio! — tiene que ser mi preferido.

4 💬 Trabaja con tu pareja. Habla de los días escolares que más te gustan y cuáles no. ¿Sabes explicar por qué?

Mi día preferido es…
Hoy tengo…
Una vez a la semana/dos veces a la semana
   tenemos…
Porque se me da(n) bien…
Aunque no me gusta/n…

5a 🎧 📖 Escucha a dos jóvenes hablando de sus colegios y horarios. Lee las frases y decide si son verdaderas (V) o falsas (F).

Ejemplo: **1** *David tiene seis horas de clase al día. — F*

1 David tiene seis horas de clase al día.
2 María va a casa para comer.
3 A David le gusta la informática.
4 David y María están en el mismo año de cole.
5 El recreo de María dura veinte minutos.
6 Las clases de David terminan a las cinco.
7 María no tiene clases el jueves.
8 David no hace ninguna actividad después del colegio.

b 🎧 ✏️ Escucha otra vez. Rellena el cuadro siguiente con la información adecuada.

	María	David
Hora de empezar el colegio	9:00	8:45
Hora de terminar el colegio		
Número de recreos		
Número de clases por día		
Actividades extracurriculares		
Dónde pasa la hora de comer		
Lo que hace durante los recreos y las comidas		
Curso/año del cole		
Opinión del cole		

6a Mira la tabla en la página anterior.
Escribe una pregunta para cada frase
y tu propia respuesta.

Ejemplo: ¿A qué hora empieza el colegio?
Mi colegio empieza a las nueve menos cinco.

b Trabaja con tu pareja. Hazle una
entrevista sobre su colegio.

7a Yésica y Martín están hablando
de su colegio. Encuentra lo que significan
las frases en negrita. Usa un diccionario
para ayudarte.

1 ¿Qué opinas tú de las ciencias, Yésica?

No las aguanto. Son muy difíciles y **el profesor no
hace más que gritar.**

2 ¿Martín, tienes una asignatura preferida — o un profesor
preferido?

Me encantan los idiomas. **Saco buenas notas** porque
**mi profesor explica muy bien las cosas.
Me ayuda mucho.**

3 ¿Qué piensas de la historia y la geografía, Yésica?

No están mal. El Señor Montoya **enseña bien,**
pero **nos pone demasiados deberes.**

4 ¿ Y tú, qué opinas, Martín?

Estoy de acuerdo con Yésica. Considero que estas
asignaturas están bien, pero que el profesor
nos hace escribir demasiado
y es en realidad bastante aburrido.

5 ¿Entonces crees tú, Yésica, que nuestro cole es bueno?

Pues sí. **Nos hacen trabajar mucho** y así
aprobaremos los exámenes, que es lo importante.
Creo que **tienes razón.**

CULTURA

La educación en los países hispánicos

En los países hispánicos, el año escolar dura
entre 9 y 10 meses y se divide, en general,
en trimestres o semestres, según el país: en
España dura de septiembre a junio; en la
mayoría de los países de Hispanoamérica, de
marzo a diciembre. En general, los alumnos
deben aprobar las asignaturas del año antes
de pasar al siguiente.

Los sistemas de educación son diferentes
en los distintos países hispánicos, pero
también hay semejanzas. En España, la
educación es obligatoria para todos los
niños de entre 6 y 16 años. Hay seis años de
educación primaria y cuatro de secundaria.
El certificado de educación secundaria, que
se obtiene a los 16 años, se llama la ESO
(Educación Secundaria Obligatoria). Luego
los alumnos que quieren seguir estudiando
a nivel superior pueden comenzar el
Bachillerato, que dura dos años y prepara al
alumno para la universidad.

b 💬 Trabaja con tu pareja. Haz preguntas sobre lo que estudia en el cole.
Contesta las preguntas de tu pareja.

¿Te gusta(n) ¿Qué te parece(n)	el inglés? la historia? las matemáticas? el dibujo?	(No) me gusta(n)... Odio... Me encanta(n) Detesto... No aguanto... Se me da(n) bien/mal/muy mal
	el(la) profesor(a) de ciencias/español/física?	Grita mucho Me ayuda Enseña/explica muy bien Nos hace trabajar demasiado Nos pone demasiados deberes

8a 🎧 ¿Cuáles son las reglas del cole? Pon los dibujos en
el orden correcto.

Ejemplo: **1 — b**

b 🏫 Escribe una lista de reglas para tu colegio.
¡Usa tu imaginación!

Cambridge IGCSE® Spanish ● International Certificate in Spanish

GRAMÁTICA

Verbs expressing necessity and obligation

To express obligation or necessity
***tener que* + infinitive** can be used. For
example:

Para mantenerme en forma
tengo que comer *las verduras.*
To keep in shape I have to eat
vegetables.

*Amparo **tiene que hacer***
sus deberes.
Amparo has to do her homework.

*Ellos **tienen que** comprar*
un regalo.
They have to buy a present.

María tiene un examen el lunes.
*Ella **tiene que** estudiar.*
María has a test on Monday.
She has to study.

***Hay que* + infinitive** is an alternative.
There is no subject, so the verb form
hay is always used:

Hay que coger *un autobús.*
It's necessary to take a bus.

Hay que *estudiar mucho.*
One must study a lot.

No es fácil aprender español.
Hay que *practicar mucho.*
It isn't easy to learn Spanish.
It's necessary to practise a lot.

Colegio Arturo Soria

Los alumnos tienen la responsabilidad de conocer las reglas del colegio. Tienen que entender su importancia y deben seguirlas todo el tiempo. Se aplican a todas las horas del colegio e incluso durante visitas escolares. Además, deben ser seguidas durante actividades extraescolares.

Para disminuir y quizás eliminar acontecimientos desagradables la seguridad de alumnos y profesores es imprescindible. Por eso se pide todo tipo de cooperación.

Reglas generales

Cada alumno tiene que llevar consigo identificación.

Deben tener un bloc para apuntes, bolígrafos, lápices y libros de texto apropiados para cada clase.

Hay que llevar el uniforme adecuado.

No se permite llevar gorra o zapatillas — ni cascos ni MP3 etcétera.

El colegio no reconoce ninguna responsabilidad por objetos perdidos en el colegio.

No se permiten cerillas o mecheros.

Demostrar respeto.

Hay que ser cortés a toda hora. Los alumnos tienen que tratar a otros alumnos y a adultos con respeto.

Hay que parar e identificarse en cualquier momento si se lo pide un adulto.

Se prohíbe

- Mentir, hacer trampa, copiar y hacer plagio.
- Vender objetos dentro del colegio sin el permiso del director.
- Juegos de azar — con o sin recompensa monetaria.
- Chantaje.
- El uso de MP3, televisores, teléfonos móviles, radios, ipods, juegos electrónicos y todo tipo de cosas semejantes.
- Sacar comida de la cantina — solo se permite comer y beber dentro de la cantina.
- El chicle.
- Tirar misiles sólidos — incluyendo bolas de nieve.
- El uso de patines o monopatines.
- Traer y usar pistolas de agua.
- Actividades ilegales.
- El uso de teléfonos durante el horario escolar sin el permiso explícito de un adulto.

9a 📖 Lee el artículo y contesta las preguntas siguientes.

1 ¿Por qué se pide la cooperación de los alumnos?
2 ¿Para qué sirve el bloc que deben tener los alumnos?
3 ¿Por qué es importante no perder objetos en el colegio?
4 ¿Dónde está permitido comer y beber?
5 ¿Cuándo está prohibido el uso del teléfono?

b 💬 Trabaja con tu pareja para decir lo que, en tu opinión, se debe y lo que no se debe permitir en el cole.

Ejemplo: En mi opinión es importante…
No creo que sea razonable…

10a 📖 Mira los uniformes. Escribe las palabras en el orden correcto.

*Ejemplo: **a** — unas botas*

unas botas   una chaqueta   una camisa
una falda   unos calcetines
una corbata   una camiseta   unas zapatillas
una blusa   un pantalón   unas medias

b 🖉 ¿Puedes describir los uniformes con más detalles?

Ejemplo: *Este chico lleva un pantalón largo y gris.*

c 💬 🖉 ¡Ahora a ti! Describe tu uniforme a tu pareja y escribe unas frases sobre él.

GRAMÁTICA

Agreement of adjectives

Remember that nouns in Spanish are masculine or feminine and adjectives must agree in number and gender with the noun they are describing:

un pantalón blanc**o**
but **una** corbata blanc**a**

unos calcetines blanc**os**
but **unas** zapatillas blanc**as**

Adjectives of colour come after the noun in Spanish. They have to agree with the noun they are describing:

un**a** camiseta negr**a**
a black t-shirt

un**os** pantalon**es** azul**es**
some blue trousers

Make sure you change the adjective endings where necessary!

11 a 📖 🖉 Lee el diálogo siguiente y ponlo en el orden correcto.

A: Muy bien. ¿Qué talla usa?
A: ¿Y qué color prefiere?
A: A ver…un momento…aquí tiene.
B: Talla 38.
B: Gracias.
A: Buenos días. ¿En qué puedo servirle?
B: ¿Cuánto cuestan?
B: Creo que azul marino.
A: En la caja que está allí al fondo.
B: ¿Dónde se paga?
B: Quisiera unos pantalones por favor.
A: Cuestan 38€.

b 🎧 Ahora escucha y corrige.

12 a 🎧 Escucha esta información. Empareja cada artículo con el precio adecuado.

Ejemplo: **1 a — 65€**

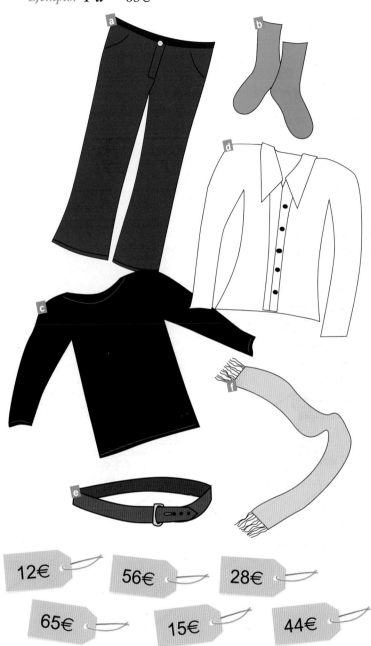

b 💬 Trabaja con tu pareja. Usa el diálogo de arriba. Practica comprando las cosas en los dibujos y los precios siguientes.

La tienda del colegio

13a  Mira el dibujo. ¿Qué compran? ¿Cuánto pagan?

Ejemplo: *1 a — 2€*

b Trabaja con tu pareja. Empareja los nombres de todos los artículos con la imagen adecuada.

Ejemplo: *boli — a*

bolígrafo   lápiz   regla   goma   cuaderno

diccionario   libro   carpeta   agenda   grapadora

paquete de papel   tijeras   sacapuntas   estuche

rotuladores   compás   papel líquido   cola

pluma

c 📖 💬 Lee estas conversaciones y practica con tu pareja para comprar algo de la lista.

A: ¡Hola! ¿Qué desea?
B: Quisiera un bolígrafo azul, por favor.
A: ¡Aquí tiene! ¿Algo más?
B: No, nada más, gracias. ¿Cuánto es?
A: Son 2€, por favor.

A: ¡Hola! ¿Qué quiere, señorita?
B: Quisiera unos rotuladores, por favor.
A: ¡Aquí tiene! ¿Algo más?
B: No, nada más, gracias. ¿Cuánto es?
A: Son 15€, por favor.

A: ¡Buenos días! ¿Qué desea?
B: Quisiera un diccionario, por favor.
A: ¿De qué idioma?
B: Español–inglés, por favor
A: Toma. ¿Algo más?
B: No, gracias ¿Cuánto es?
A: Son 22€, por favor.

GRAMÁTICA

Pronouns

Pronouns are words that replace nouns.

Subject pronouns generally appear before the verb. They explain who is doing the action.

Singular		Plural	
I	yo	we	nosotros/as
you (informal)	tú	you (informal)	vosotros/as
he/it	él	they	ellos
she/it	ella	they	ellas
you (formal)	usted	you (formal)	ustedes

Spanish uses a different word for 'you' according to whether the relationship is:
• informal (talking to a young person or child or an adult you know well), or
• formal (talking to an adult you don't know well or a person who is in authority)

You do not always need to use the subject pronouns, as the ending of the verb tells you who is speaking. Always use them, however, to make things clear. For example:

Él tiene un gato. Yo tengo un perro.
He has a cat. I have a dog.

Direct object pronouns replace nouns that 'receive' the verb. They answer the question 'what?' or 'who(m)?' with regard to what the subject of the sentence is doing. They are often used to avoid repetition. For example:

Pedro compró un helado y se lo regaló a su madre.
Pedro bought an ice cream and gave it to his mother.

Singular		Plural	
me	me	us	nos
you (informal)	te	you (informal)	os
him/it	le/lo	them	les/los
her/it	la	them	las
you (formal)	le/lo/la	you (formal)	les/los/las

Indirect object pronouns also replace nouns that 'receive' the verb, but answer the question 'to what?' or 'to whom?' with regard to what the subject of the sentence is doing. For example:

Voy a traer una taza de café a mi madre.
Le voy a traer una taza de café.

I'm going to bring **my mother** a cup of coffee.
I'm going to bring a cup of coffee **to her**.

Singular		Plural	
to me	me	to us	nos
to you (informal)	te	to you (informal)	os
to him/to her/to it	le	to them	les
to you (formal)	le	to you (formal)	les

Object pronouns generally come before the verb but can also be placed at the end of some forms of the verb, e.g. the infinitive. For example:

Tienes que enviarme una carta.
or *Me tienes que enviar una carta.*
You have to send **me** a letter.

14 🔺 Sustituye las palabras subrayadas con el pronombre adecuado.

Ejemplo: Quiero comprar estos bolígrafos. — Quiero comprarlos.

1 Voy a ver a mi madre esta tarde.
2 Hoy es el día de los exámenes. Voy a llamar a mi profesor.
3 He perdido mis gafas. ¿Has visto mis gafas?
4 Detesto la geografía.
5 Quiero ver el partido de fútbol mañana.
6 Juan prefiere hablar español.

15a 📖 Empareja las frases y los dibujos.

Ejemplo: **1 — d**

1 He perdido mi teléfono móvil. Creo que lo perdí en el patio hace media hora.

2 He perdido mi cartera. La dejé en la cantina ayer. Es roja y contenía cuatro billetes de diez euros.

3 Dejé mis llaves en el laboratorio esta mañana. ¿Las has encontrado?

4 He perdido mi bolsa de deportes. Contiene mi pantalón corto, una camiseta y unas zapatillas. Creo que la dejé en el autobús.

5 ¿Has encontrado un estuche rojo? Contiene dos bolígrafos, un lápiz y una goma. No lo he visto desde esta mañana. Creo que lo dejé en el aula de matemáticas.

6 Busco mi bicicleta. Estaba en el almacén durante el recreo, pero ¡ahora no está! Creo que me la han robado.

a

b

c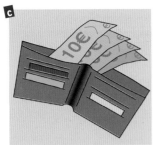

d

e

f

b 🎧 Escucha las conversaciones.
¿Qué han perdido? ¿Cuándo y dónde?
Completa las casillas con la información adecuada.

¿Qué?	¿Cuándo?	¿Dónde?
Ejemplo: mochila	*esta mañana*	*el gimnasio*
1		

c 📖 💬 Trabaja con tu pareja.
Practica estos dos diálogos, a y b.

A: ¿En qué puedo ayudarle?
B: He perdido mi…

a  **b**

A: ¿Dónde la perdió?
B: La perdí…

a 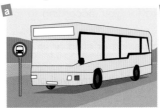 **b**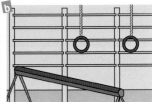

A: ¿Cuándo la perdió?
B: La perdí…

a  **b**
Hoy — Ayer

A: ¿Qué contenía?
B: Contenía…

a  **b**

A: ¿Cómo se llama?
B: Me llamo…..
A: Le informaremos si la encontremos.
B: Gracias.

2 Las prácticas de trabajo

☑ Apply for a job
☑ Learn about workplace activities
☑ Use the imperfect and preterite tenses
☑ Give opinions

1a 🎧 👤 Copia estos títulos en tu cuaderno. Escucha lo que dice la chica. Rellena los detalles que faltan.

Apellido: **Belén**

Nombre:

Fecha de nacimiento:

Edad:

Nacionalidad:

Mejores asignaturas:

Pasatiempos favoritos:

Dónde quiere trabajar:

Por qué:

Cualidades:

Ambiciones:

b 💬 Trabaja con tu pareja. Haz las siguientes preguntas y contéstalas.

1 ¡Hola! ¿Cómo te llamas?
2 ¿Y cuál es tu fecha de nacimiento?
3 ¿Y cuántos años tienes?
4 Muy bien, y ¿de dónde eres?
5 Y ¿cuáles son tus mejores asignaturas en el colegio?
6 ¿Tienes algunos pasatiempos o actividades?
7 ¿Dónde quieres hacer tus prácticas de trabajo?
8 ¿Por qué?
9 Háblame de tus cualidades personales.
10 ¿Me puedes dar otra razón por tu elección?

c 👤 Completa la solicitud de arriba para ti mismo.

2 📖 Quieres hacer prácticas de trabajo. Lee los anuncios.

Anuncios de trabajo

a ¿Te interesa la educación? Hay puestos en colegios de primaria y secundaria por esta región.

b ¿Estás buscando un trabajo en informática? Empresa de informática en centro ciudad busca empleados temporales.

c ¿Te gustan los idiomas y viajar? Considera hacer tus prácticas de trabajo en una agencia de viajes. Hay muchas oportunidades.

d Si te interesa trabajar en el mundo de la hostelería no busques más. Hay puestos en hoteles y pensiones de este barrio.

e Si estás interesado en asuntos sociales te ofrecemos la oportunidad de trabajar en hospitales y residencias de ancianos.

f Si te interesan los medios de comunicación Radio X tiene el puesto que buscas. Escribe inmediatamente.

a 📖 Qué anuncio te interesará si…

1 Eres bueno con los ordenadores.
2 Quieres ser recepcionista.
3 Quieres ser profesor(a).
4 Se te da bien la música.
5 Quieres ser médico.
6 Hablas francés y español.

b 📖 Lee la carta siguiente. ¿A qué anuncio se refiere?

Fecha

Muy señor mío,

Vi su anuncio en la revista de febrero del colegio ofreciendo puestos para las prácticas de trabajo. Me interesa mucho una carrera en medicina y un puesto con ustedes me vendría muy bien. Sería una gran oportunidad.

En el colegio mis mejores asignaturas son las ciencias y la informática. También se me dan bien los idiomas.

Soy un alumno honesto y trabajador. Tengo buen sentido del humor y trabajo bien en equipo.

Creo que tengo las cualidades que busca y le agradecería que me considerara para un puesto.

Le mando adjunto mi currículum y una carta de mi profesor.

Muchas gracias.

Le saluda atentamente,
Angélica Dorado.

c 🏫 Escribe una carta parecida solicitando un puesto de los anunciados en la página 71. Si prefieres, prepárala para otro trabajo de tu elección.

3a 🎧 📖 Escucha y lee. ¿Quién habla? Empareja los nombres con los dibujos.

Ejemplo: Luci — b

Hice mis prácticas de trabajo en un banco. **Luci**

Hice mis prácticas de trabajo en una tienda de animales domésticos. **Pablo**

Trabajé en una fábrica de galletas del barrio. ¡Un rollo! **Juan**

Pasé mis prácticas en una oficina del centro. **Marta**

Trabajé en un colegio. Fue genial. **Suzi**

Trabajé en una agencia de viajes. No fue muy interesante que digamos. **Javier**

b 🎧 🏫 ¿Qué más dicen estos jóvenes? Completa la tabla con los detalles que faltan.

	¿Cuándo?	¿Cuánto tiempo?	Horario	Transporte
Ejemplo: **Luci**	marzo	tres semanas	9–5	coche
Pablo				
Suzi				
Juan				
Marta				
Javier				

c 💬 Trabaja con tu pareja. Usa la información de arriba. Practica preguntas y contéstalas.

Ejemplo: Luci

A: ¿Dónde hiciste tus prácticas de trabajo?
B: Las hice en un banco.
A: ¿Cuándo las hiciste?
B: Las hice en marzo.
A: ¿El trabajo fue difícil?
B: No, lo pude hacer fácilmente.
A: ¿Te gustó la experiencia?
B: No, no me gustó.
A: ¿Por qué?
B: Porque me dieron un trabajo aburrido.

4a 📖 ✏️ Mira el ejemplo. Sigue el código. Usa las imágenes para ayudarte a escribir frases acerca de tus prácticas de trabajo.

Ejemplo:

1 g *Mis prácticas de trabajo duraron quince días.*
   j *Trabajé en una tienda de recuerdos.*
   a *Cada día iba en autobús.*
   o *Empezaba a las diez de la mañana y terminaba a las dos de la tarde.*
   s *En mi opinión el trabajo era aburrido y no me gustaba nada.*

2 e, k, c, m, r
3 h, l, b, p, q
4 f, i, d, n, q

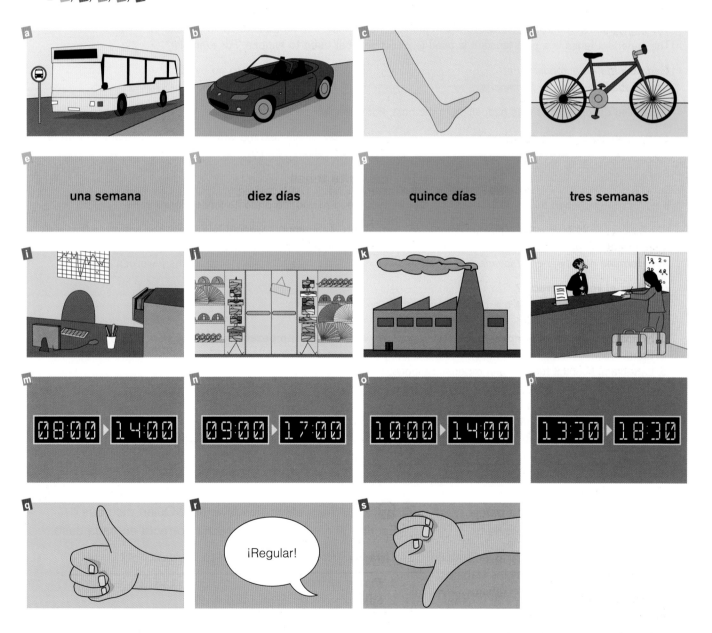

b ✏️ Ahora escribe un pequeño párrafo o una serie de frases sobre tus propias prácticas de trabajo.

The imperfect and preterite tenses

The imperfect tense

*Mis prácticas de trabajo duraron una semana. Trabajé en un supermercado y cada día **iba** a pie. **Empezaba** a las nueve de la mañana y **terminaba** a las cinco de la tarde con un descanso al mediodía. En mi opinión el trabajo **era** poco interesante y no me **gustaba** mucho.*

*Mis prácticas de trabajo duraron dos semanas. Trabajé en una fábrica y cada día **iba** en bicicleta. **Empezaba** a las ocho de la mañana y **terminaba** a las tres de la tarde con dos descansos al día. En mi opinión el trabajo **era** muy fácil y me **gustaba** mucho.*

The highlighted verbs in the text above are in the imperfect tense. You met this tense in Module 1.

The imperfect tense is a past tense. It is used to describe what **used to** happen. For example:

*Cada día **iba** en autobús.*   Every day I **used to** go by bus.

***Empezaba** a las diez de la mañana.*   I **used to** start at 10 a.m.

It can also describe what **was** happening in the past. For example:

*En mi opinión, el trabajo **era** aburrido.*   In my opinion, the work was boring (**while I was there**).

The preterite tense

If the action happened at a particular time in the past, you need to use the preterite tense. For example:

*El mes pasado **trabajé** en una tienda.*   Last month I worked in a shop. (the activity is **finished**)

*En junio del año pasado **empecé** a trabajar en el restaurante.*   In June last year I began to work in the restaurant.

*Ayer **terminé** el trabajo en el joyería.*   Yesterday I finished work in the jeweller's.

¿Cuál es el verbo correcto?

1 El mes pasado **hice/hacía** mis prácticas de trabajo en un restaurante.

2 Cada día **fui/iba** en metro.

3 Normalmente **empecé/empezaba** a las seis pero el lunes **empecé/empezaba** a las siete.

4 En mi opinión, trabajar en un hospital **fue/era** poco interesante.

5 La visita al hospital **fue/era** una experiencia inolvidable.

6 El trabajo **fue/era** repetitivo y no muy variado.

7 **Trabajé/trabajaba** en la cantina de un hospital.

8 El primer día **olvidé/olvidaba** traer dinero para comprar comida.

9 Lo peor **fue/era** hacer el café.

10 El trabajo **fue/era** variado y no **estuvo/estaba** mal.

5 💬 Haz un diálogo con tu pareja. Usa las preguntas para ayudarte.

- ¿Dónde hiciste tus prácticas de trabajo?
- ¿Cuánto tiempo duraron los trabajos?
- ¿Cuándo empezabas los trabajos por la mañana?
- ¿Cuándo terminabas por la tarde?
- ¿Cómo ibas al trabajo?
- ¿Cómo era el trabajo?

6 🎧 Escucha a estos dos jóvenes. ¿Quién dice qué? Escribe el nombre de la persona correcta en cada caso.

Ejemplo: 1 Iba en bicicleta. Mari Carmen.

1 *Iba en bicicleta.*

2 Sus trabajos duraron quince días.

3 El trabajo era muy aburrido.

4 Trabajó en una tienda.

5 El día era demasiado largo.

6 Le gustó el trabajo.

7a 📖 🖊 Lee en el recuadro de al lado
lo que dice alguna genta sobre sus
experiencias de trabajo. Decide cuáles
son negativas, cuáles son positivas y cuáles
no estaban mal.

era aburrido	había mucha variedad
era interesante	mi jefe era antipático
era fácil	me llevaba bien con todos los demás
era útil	el día era demasiado largo
era insoportable	el trabajo era un poco repetitivo

b Busca más comentarios que puedas
dar sobre tus prácticas de trabajo.
Usa un diccionario para ayudarte.
Escríbelos en la tabla también.

Me gustaba	No estaba mal	No me gustaba
Ejemplo: era interesante		

8 📖 🖊 Lee los siguientes párrafos. Mira la lista de abajo
y escribe las palabras que faltan en cada hueco.

1
Pasé dos semanas
trabajando en una
peluquería en el
centro de la cuidad.
Era muy interesante
pero el trabajo era
un poco repetitivo.
Cada día tenía que

para los clientes,

y también

.

2
Trabajar en una oficina estaba
bastante bien. Tenía que

 , y ,

lo que no me gustaba mucho.
Pero la oportunidad de

 y

era, en mi opinión, una
experiencia muy útil.

3
Hice mis prácticas de trabajo
en una agencia de viajes.
Tenía muchas oportunidades.
Por ejemplo:

 ,  ,

y mucho más. Lo único que
no me gustaba era mi jefe:
era un poco frío y yo tenía que

cada día.

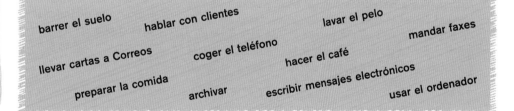

barrer el suelo　　hablar con clientes　　lavar el pelo　　mandar faxes

llevar cartas a Correos　　coger el teléfono　　hacer el café

preparar la comida　　archivar　　escribir mensajes electrónicos　　usar el ordenador

9 💬 Haz una encuesta entre tus compañeros
de clase. Averigua dónde hicieron sus
prácticas de trabajo, qué horario tenían que
hacer, y qué opinan de sus experiencias.
Usa las siguientes preguntas.

- ¿Dónde hiciste tus prácticas de trabajo?
- ¿Qué tenías que hacer?
- ¿Te gustó? ¿Por qué (no)?

10 🖊 Escribe una carta a tu corresponsal acerca
de tus prácticas de trabajo. ¡No te olvides de
dar tus opiniones! Menciona lo siguiente.

- dónde trabajaste
- durante cuánto tiempo
- cómo llegabas al trabajo
- las horas que trabajabas
- lo que tenías que hacer

Al teléfono

11a 📖 Empareja las frases en negrita con sus equivalentes en inglés de la lista de abajo. Utiliza un diccionario para ayudarte.

- phases
- don't be distracted
- file
- successful
- abroad
- note
- fears
- don't worry
- company
- arise
- call
- scares

Llamando por teléfono

A pesar de que muchísima gente hoy en día tiene teléfono móvil, una gran cantidad de personas tienen problemas con usar el teléfono convencional en su lugar de trabajo. A mucha gente le causa ansiedad ¡e incluso trauma! Cada empleado tiene que vencer sus **temores** y encontrar una manera de superar esas preocupaciones. Si tienes problema con usar el teléfono, a lo mejor te ayudan los consejos siguientes.

Haciendo la llamada

Hacer una llamada se puede dividir en tres **fases** principales:

- la preparación
- la **llamada**
- la evaluación

La preparación

Asegúrate de a quién estás llamando. Apunta la razón de la llamada y de lo que te quieres enterar y ten eso delante de ti antes de llamar. Antes de hacer una llamada superimportante practica con un colega. Eso te ayudará a relajarte y a saber cuáles pueden ser los problemas que **surgen**. Si tienes una lista de llamadas ponlas en orden de dificultad con la que te parece la más fácil primero. Así ganarás confianza antes de hacer la que más te **asusta**. No dejes para luego llamadas difíciles — eso solo servirá para hacerlo más estresante todavía.

La llamada

A menudo lo más difícil es conseguir comunicar con la persona a quien llamas. Si contesta una operadora, por ejemplo, ten a mano el número de extensión de la persona y su nombre. Si hace falta, explícale brevemente por qué llamas. Sé flexible con lo que dices y ante todo muéstrate tranquilo y bien educado y habla despacio — sobre todo si estás llamando **al extranjero**.

La evaluación

Apunta lo que pasa durante la llamada para tener un **archivo** de los hechos. Si una llamada no ha sido demasiado **exitosa**, intenta decidir por qué para evitarlo en el futuro. Mantén una actitud positiva y acuérdate de que con la práctica las llamadas se hacen más fáciles.

Recibiendo llamadas

Solo contesta las llamadas cuando estás preparado. Aprende frases apropiadas que puedas usar al contestar. Saluda a la persona que llama; da el nombre de tu **empresa** y tu nombre y pregunta en qué puedes ayudarle. Si recibes la llamada en un sitio donde hay mucha gente o ruido **no te distraigas** — concéntrate en la llamada. **No te preocupes** por los silencios — es bastante común. La persona que te llama a lo mejor puede estar nerviosa también.

b 👥 Contesta las preguntas siguientes

1 ¿A qué se refieren las tres fases principales?
2 ¿Por qué es importante practicar con un colega antes de hacer la llamada?
3 ¿Por qué no debes posponer llamadas difíciles?
4 Menciona tres adjetivos que describan la actitud que debes adoptar por teléfono.
5 Según el artículo, ¿qué debes hacer si estás llamando al extranjero?
6 ¿Por qué es importante analizar las llamadas no exitosas?
7 ¿Cómo es posible mejorar la habilidad de hacer una llamada?
8 ¿Qué información debes dar al contestar una llamada?
9 ¿Por qué no debes preocuparte por los silencios?

12a 🎧 📖 Escucha y lee lo que dicen estas personas.

① Buenos días. Hotel Bella Vista, ¡Dígame!

Quisiera hablar con el señor Fidel, por favor.

¿De parte de quién?

Señora Delibe.

Ya le pongo.

② Buenas tardes. Oficina de turismo. ¡Dígame!

Quisiera hablar con el señor Fidel, por favor.

Lo siento. No está en este momento. ¿Quiere dejar un recado?

③ Buenos días. Restaurante Tía Miranda. ¡Dígame!

Quisiera hablar con la señora Orenes.

Está al teléfono. ¿Quiere esperar?

Sí, gracias.

b 📖 Empareja el inglés con el español.

¡Diga! ¡Dígame!	Thank you very much.
¿Puedo hablar con …..?	Hello!
Quisiera…	Can I take a message?
De parte de…	He/She isn't here.
Lo siento…	Don't mention it/You're welcome.
Está ocupado/a…	Would you like to wait/hold on?
No está.	I would like to…
¿Puedo coger un recado?	Goodbye.
¿Puedo dejar un recado?	Can I leave a message?
Muchas gracias.	On behalf of…
De nada.	He/She is on the phone.
Está al teléfono.	I'm sorry…
¿Quiere esperar?	Can I speak to…?
Adiós.	He/She is busy.

13 💬 Trabaja con tu pareja. Practica esta conversación. Úsala como ejemplo para practicar tus propias conversaciones.

Ejemplo:

A: Dígame. Arquitectos López. ¿En qué puedo servirle?

B: Oiga. Quisiera hablar con el señor Albani, por favor.

A: ¿De parte de quién?

B: Soy Conchita González.

A: Desafortunadamente no está aquí.

B: ¿Cuándo volverá?

A: No estoy seguro. ¿Quiere dejar un mensaje?

B: Sí. Pídele al señor Albani que me llame a las cuatro.

A: Por supuesto.

B: Muchas gracias. Hasta luego.

14 📖 Lee el texto.

Las prácticas de trabajo

Las prácticas de trabajo ofrecen amplias oportunidades.

Hoy en día no es suficiente con el título para conseguir el trabajo de tus sueños. Hace falta tener experiencia y habilidades más allá de lo académico.

Habrás estudiado mucho y habrás aguantado mucho estrés y cantidad de preocupación para lograr tu plaza en la universidad. Querrás descansar un poco, disfrutar de la vida con tus nuevos amigos además de estudiar para la carrera. ¿Pero qué pasa después de terminarla?

Ser licenciado no es todo. Cada vez más los empresarios quieren más. Quieren a individuos con experiencia, y que sepan tratar con la gente. Quieren a personas que estén dispuestas a seguir mejorando su nivel profesional. **Tendrás que convencerles** que tú eres la persona a quien buscan y que tienes las cualidades adecuadas. Así que **nunca es demasiado temprano** para conseguir experiencia en el mundo del trabajo. ¡Nunca es temprano para empezar tu currículum! Hoy no es extraño empezar un pequeño trabajo durante los fines de semana o las vacaciones a la edad de catorce años.

¿Qué piensa la gente?
Preguntamos a unos jóvenes acerca de su experiencia de trabajo. Lee lo que dijeron:

Silvia, 14 años
'Trabajé en el departamento de pediatría de un hospital cerca de donde vivo. Fue una experiencia verdaderamente positiva para mí. Aprendí mucho. Cada día fue diferente. Ayudaba a preparar las comidas y jugaba con los niños. Los empleados eran majos y nos llevábamos muy bien. **Creo que me gustaría ser** enfermera cuando deje el colegio y esta experiencia me ha ayudado a entender de lo que trata este trabajo.'

Enrique, 15 años.
'**Siempre he querido ser** mecánico así que tuve mucha suerte conseguir hacer mis prácticas en un garaje del barrio. **Sin embargo** la verdad es que me desilusioné un poco porque no me dejaron trabajar en los vehículos. **La mayoría del tiempo** tenía que preparar el café o lavar los coches. A veces acompañaba a un mecánico si había una avería, lo cual me gustaba mucho. El horario estaba bien. Empezaba a las nueve y terminaba a las cuatro. Creo que haré otra cosa cuando deje el colegio. Ser mecánico es bastante duro.'

Pablo, 16 años
'Pasé tres semanas trabajando en una peluquería. Fue una experiencia valiosa y es lo que de verdad quiero hacer cuando termine el colegio. **Antes de hacer mis prácticas** pensaba que era un trabajo fácil, pero no lo es. Hay que estar de pie todo el día, lo que cansa mucho. Algunos de los clientes son desagradables y hay que estar sonriente todo el rato – cosa que no encuentro fácil. De todos modos ahora sé mucho más y tengo una buena idea de lo que tengo que hacer **para tener éxito** en esta profesión.'

¿Has hecho ya las prácticas de trabajo? Dónde las hiciste? ¿Qué hiciste? ¿Cómo fue? Escríbenos para contar tus experiencias y opiniones.

a 📖 👤 Empareja las expresiones en negrita con sus equivalentes en inglés. Luego escoge **tres** de las expresiones e inventa una frase que muestre su uso en español.

Ejemplo: hoy en día — nowadays

- nevertheless
- it's never too early
- I think I'd like to be
- I've always wanted to be
- most of the time
- before doing my work experience
- to be successful
- you'll have to convince them

b 📖 Según lo que dice el artículo, indica si las frases siguientes son verdaderas (V) o falsas (F). Si son falsas, escribe una frase en español para corregirlas.

1 Todos los chicos quieren trabajar en lo que hicieron en sus prácticas.
2 Todos piensan que la experiencia fue útil.
3 A Enrique lo que más le gustaba fue lavar los coches.
4 Sus experiencias les han ayudado a tomar decisiones con respecto a su futuro.
5 Les dejaban hacer todo tipo de tareas.
6 A Pablo le costaba ser agradable con los clientes.

c 👤 Escribe una contestación a la revista dando tus ideas y opiniones sobre tus propias prácticas de trabajo. Menciona:

- dónde trabajaste
- durante cuánto tiempo
- qué hiciste exactamente cada día
- si era una experiencia positiva o negativa y por qué
- tu opinión sobre las prácticas de trabajo en…

3 El futuro

1  Escucha para saber lo que piensa hacer esta gente y pon las letras en el orden en que se mencionan.

Ejemplo: **1 — b**

Agencia de trabajo

Instituto

Banco

Trabajos
Se buscan aprendices

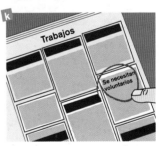
Colegio
Trabajos
Se necesitan voluntarios

GRAMÁTICA

The immediate future

To form the immediate future tense use *ir + a*.

The verb *ir* (to go) is formed as follows:

voy

vas

va

vamos

vais

van

2 ¿Qué quieren hacer? Empareja las personas con las frases correctas. Piensa en qué persona del verbo es apropiada en cada caso.

1 Ana	¿qué vas a hacer el año que viene?
2 Pablo y Marta	voy a trabajar en el banco.
3 Iñigo,	va a seguir estudiando.
4 Conchi y yo	van a ir a Inglaterrra.
5 Yo	¿vais a hacer algo?
6 Juan y Susana,	vamos a buscar un empleo.

3 Pregunta a tus compañeros de clase lo que van a hacer el año que viene.

Ejemplo: ¿Qué vas a hacer el año que viene?
El año que viene voy a…

4 🎧 📖 Escucha a estos jóvenes hablando de su futuro. Rellena los huecos en las frases siguientes con los verbes correctos.

Ejemplo: **1** — *Buscaré un trabajo.*

1 _____ un trabajo.
2 _____ más. Quiero estudiar ciencias y diseño.
3 _____ un año y luego _____ a estudiar.
4 _____ un poco antes de empezar a trabajar.
5 _____ como voluntaria en el extranjero.
6 _____ un aprendizaje. Quiero ser mecánico.

trabajaré   haré   buscaré
viajaré   descansaré
estudiaré   volveré

¡OJO!

Todas estas palabras son verbos.
¿Qué tienen en común?

GRAMÁTICA

The future tense

This verb tense is used when talking about future actions: 'I will' and 'I shall'. For example:

Buscaré un trabajo
I will look for a job

Esta tarde haré mis deberes. This afternoon **I will do** my homework

The future tense is formed by adding the following endings to the infinitive (the part found in the dictionary):
-é
-ás
-á
-emos
-éis
-án

For example: *estudiar* **(to study)**

estudiaré	I **will** study
estudiarás	you **will** study
estudiará	he/she **will** study
estudiaremos	we **will** study
estudiaréis	you **will** study
estudiarán	they **will** study

Remember where accents are and are not necessary.

---

5 🎧 📖 Ahora escucha otra vez. Empareja cada persona con la frase adecuada abajo.

Quiere un puesto pagado. *Ejemplo:* **1**
Quiere aprender mientras trabaje.
Quiere conocer el mundo.
Seguirá con sus estudios.
Quiere unas vacaciones antes de estudiar.
No le importa el dinero.

6a 🎧 📖 Escucha y lee lo que dicen estos jóvenes sobre sus planes futuros. Haz una lista de todos los verbos en el futuro que encuentras.

> Tengo planes y sueños. Hay una diferencia entre los dos, pero el futuro no siempre es seguro. Primero, lo que sí es seguro, es que me iré del colegio. Me gusta estar aquí, pero creo que la gama de asignaturas es aburrida. Seguiré estudiando y quiero ser ingeniero. Después de mis estudios cogeré un año de descanso y me iré de viaje. Haré algún trabajo voluntario — construyendo carreteras y pozos en África o algo así. Más tarde buscaré un trabajo mejor pagado. En mis sueños, el futuro ideal para mí es así: compraré una casa grande y me casaré. Pero el tiempo decidirá. Ya veremos.

Toni, 17 años

> El año que viene me quedaré en el cole para terminar mis estudios. Luego me iré a la universidad y estudiaré idiomas. Si es posible, trabajaré en el extranjero, en Estados Unidos o en China. No estoy segura. Dentro de diez años, en el mundo de mis sueños, tendré mi propia empresa. Seré rica y famosa. ¿Casarme? Sé que no me casaré — por lo menos dentro de los próximos diez años.

Ana, 16 años

b Decide cuáles de estas frases son verdaderas (V) y cuáles son falsas (V). Si son falsas, escribe una frase en español para corregirlas.

Ejemplo: *Toni va a seguir estudiando en el cole.* F
— *Toni se irá del colegio.*

1 Toni quiere estudiar asignaturas más interesantes que las del cole.
2 Toni quiere visitar otras partes del mundo.
3 A Toni no le importa ayudar a los demás.
4 Ana se va inmediatamente del cole.
5 Ana quiere viajar.
6 Para Ana un matrimonio es más importante que su carrera.

GRAMÁTICA

Verbs with irregular stems in the future

Note that some verbs have *irregular* stems. For example:

hacer: haré, harás, hará, haremos, haréis, harán

Can you find the future stem for the following verbs?

decir	querer	tener
poder	saber	valer
poner	salir	venir

7a 📖 ✏️ Lee lo que dice Alberto de sus planes para el futuro. Apunta todos los verbos en el futuro.

Alberto

¿Qué pienso hacer en el futuro? Pues, seguiré estudiando hasta terminar la universidad y buscaré un trabajo. Por supuesto, cuando tenga éxito mi grupo, viajaré con ellos por todo el mundo. Me haré famoso y ¡tendré mucho dinero! Entonces ayudaré a la gente pobre en, por ejemplo, África. Veré todos los sitios que me han interesado durante muchos años, como África o Cuba. Más adelante me imagino que conoceré a mi media naranja. Me casaré porque creo en ello, y a lo mejor tendré algunos hijos. Si tengo suerte, disfrutaré de buena salud y ¡seré feliz! ¡Y esto es todo!

b ✏️ Ahora usa lo que dice Alberto para escribir sobre lo que harás en el futuro.

8a La mayoría de la gente no consigue cumplir sus sueños. Lee con lo que soñaban estas personas y lo que les pasó.

¡ojo!

All the verbs in bold are in the conditional tense. What do they mean?

1

Inés, 6 años
Me gustaría ser conductor de trenes. **Viviría** en una casa pequeña cerca de la estación y **sería** muy feliz.

Inés, 40 años
Soy dentista. Vivo en un pequeño piso en el centro de la ciudad con mi marido y mis dos hijos.

2

Marisol, 16 años
Me gustaría ser azafata. **Viajaría** por todo el mundo y **hablaría** muchos idiomas diferentes.

Marisol, 22 años
Trabajo en una agencia de viajes. Sueño con vacaciones exóticos pero no gano suficiente dinero de momento.

3

Adalia, 12 años
En mi mundo ideal **tendría** dos hijos — un chico y una chica. No **trabajaría**. **Viviría** en una casa del campo.

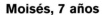

Adalia, 35 años
Tengo dos hijos. Trabajo en una oficina en la ciudad. Estoy muy contenta pero no es lo que pensaba.

4

Ico, 15 años
Me encanta cantar y bailar. **Me encantaría** ser famoso. **Actuaría** en el teatro y bailaría en todos los mejores espectáculos.

Ico, 50 años
Soy profesor de música en un colegio secundario. Me encanta mi trabajo, pero ¡no es exactamente lo que tenía planeado! ¡Quizás un día uno de mis estudiantes será famoso!

5

Moisés, 7 años
Me encantaría ser piloto o quizás piloto de un coche de carreras. **Sería** famoso y muy rico.

Moisés, 26 años
Soy mecánico. Trabajo para mi padre en un garaje y ¡es genial! No es el futuro con que soñaba, pero la verdad es que es el mejor trabajo del mundo para mí y ¡eso me gusta!

b Empareja el español con el inglés.

Ejemplo: 1 — b

1 Me gustaría ser…	**a** I would be
2 Viviría	**b** I would like to be…
3 Estaría	**c** I would be
4 Viajaría	**d** I would live
5 Hablaría	**e** I would act
6 Tendría	**f** I would love to
7 No trabajaría	**g** I would have
8 Actuaría	**h** I would speak
9 Me encantaría	**i** I would not work
10 Sería	**j** I would travel

9a 🎧 Escucha los sueños de estos jóvenes. Pon las actividades en el orden en que se mencionan.

Ejemplo: **1 — f**

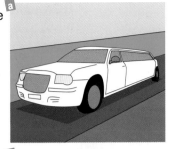

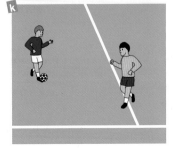

GRAMÁTICA

The conditional tense

The conditional is used when talking about events that ***would*** happen. For example:

Buscaría *un trabajo.*	**I would look** for a job.
Compraríamos *una casa en las montañas.*	**We would buy** a house in the mountains.

The conditional tense of regular verbs is formed by adding the following endings to the infinitive (the part found in the dictionary):

-ía	-íamos
-ías	-íais
-ía	-ían

For example: ***estudiar*** **(to study)**

estudiaría	I **would** study
estudiarías	you **would** study
estudiaría	he/she **would** study
estudiaríamos	we **would** study
estudiaríais	you **would** study
estudiarían	they **would** study

b 💬 Mira la lista de actividades de ensueño. Trabaja en pareja. Decide lo que te gustaría o lo que no te gustaría hacer.

Ejemplo: *comprar un coche de lujo*
Compraría un coche de lujo./
No compraría un coche de lujo.

comprar un coche de lujo
visitar América del Sur
tocar un instrumento
bailar en un escenario
cantar en público
escribir una obra maestra
hablar un idioma nuevo
aprender a cocinar
montar a caballo
conocer a alguien famoso

c ✏️ Escribe tu lista. Empieza con lo más importante para ti.

10 🎧 📖 Escucha y lee lo que dice Manolo sobre un mundo perfecto.

Mi vida ideal

Durante mi vida ideal tendría muchas experiencias emocionantes para contar a mis nietos. Querría seguir estudiando, así por fin sabría mucho más que ahora acerca de mis asignaturas favoritas – la historia y la literatura. Como tendría un trabajo interesante, bien remunerado y que valdría la pena, podría permitirme el lujo de viajar mucho y conocer otras culturas. Saldría con mis amigos todos los fines de semana o les invitaría a mi casa, que sería grande y bonita – muy lejos de los vecinos. ¡Pondría mi música favorita a todo volumen sin que nadie se quejara! Habría un cine y una piscina en el jardín. Vendría mi familia a visitarme también. Me gustaría tener suficiente dinero para ayudarles. ¡Mucho más tarde diría la gente que yo había sido una persona inteligente, generosa, simpática y divertida! No pido mucho, ¿¡verdad!?

Manolo Montoso-Sánchez, 16 años

✏️ Escribe una lista de todos los verbos condicionales en el texto y lo que significan en inglés. Lee otra vez la gramática que explica cómo formar el condicional e identifica cuáles de los verbos en tu lista son regulares y cuáles no. Practica deletrearlos.

GRAMÁTICA

Irregular verbs in the future and conditional tense

The following verbs are all **irregular**. They form the conditional using the **future stem** and **not** the **infinitive**.

Infinitive	Future	Conditional
decir	diré	diría
hacer	haré	haría
poder	podré	podría
poner	pondré	pondría
querer	querré	querría
saber	sabré	sabría
salir	saldré	saldría
tener	tendré	tendría
venir	vendré	vendría

¿Qué significan estos verbos?
Usa un diccionario para ayudarte si hace falta.

¡OJO!

Remember there are many cognates. These are words which sound, mean or are spelt similarly to English words. For example:

fotógrafo — photographer
veterinario — vet
ingeniero — engineer
parque — park
garaje — garage
león — lion
cebra — zebra

How many other examples do you know?

11 ✏️ ¿Cómo sería tu vida ideal? Escribe tu propio párrafo.

12 ✏️ ¿Cuántos trabajos, profesiones y lugares de trabajo conoces en español? Haz una lista así:

Profesión/ trabajo	Inglés	Lugar de trabajo	Inglés
profesor	teacher	colegio	school

13 📖 Lee este artículo sobre las cualidades necesarias para realizar las ambiciones.

¿Qué es lo que hace falta para lograr tus sueños? Preguntamos a unos alumnos que se están preparando para sus exámenes qué es lo que les parece esencial para realizar sus ambiciones. Aquí están los resultados:

Usar lógica
Repasar
Hablar con soltura
Leer las instrucciones

- Un 35% dice que lo importante es estudiar y repasar **cuidadosamente** para aprobar los exámenes.
- Un 15% habla de cómo hay que leer **exactamente** las instrucciones para contestar **bien** las preguntas en los exámenes.
- La mayoría de los alumnos creen que al escribir es imprescindible expresarse **claramente**.
- Con respecto a los exámenes orales, un 37% dice que lo más importante es hablar con **soltura**.
- Un 13% da importancia a tratar los problemas de matemáticas **lógicamente**.

✏️ ¿Cómo los estudiantes logran mejor sus objetivos en los exámenes? ¿Qué destrezas hacen falta? Contesta las preguntas.

1 ¿Cómo deberían repasar los temas?
2 ¿Cómo deberían leer las instrucciones?
3 ¿Cómo deberían escribir?
4 ¿Cómo deberían hablar?
5 ¿Cómo deberían tratar los problemas de matemáticas?

14 📖✏️ ¿Qué adverbios conoces en español? Haz una lista.

*Ejemplo: cuidadosamente, con cuidado;
hábilmente, con habilidad*

15a 📖✏️ Cambia estos adjetivos a adverbios añadiendo '–mente'. ¿Qué significan en inglés? ¡Se permite usar un diccionario!

Ejemplo: afortunado, afortunadamente — fortunately

- afortunado
- agradable
- alegre
- claro
- correcto
- cortés
- falso
- feliz
- furioso
- igual
- lento
- normal
- nuevo
- perfecto
- primero
- reciente
- útil
- verdadero

GRAMÁTICA

Adverbs

The words highlighted in the article are all adverbs. Adverbs tell you how something is done. They often end in –ly in English. For example: carefully, exactly, well, clearly, fluently, logically.

To form most adverbs in Spanish, first choose the adjective, make it feminine and then add –*mente*.

Adjective	Feminine form	Adverb	English
ciudadoso	*cuidadosa*	*ciudadosamente*	carefully
tranquilo	*tranquila*	*tranquilamente*	quietly
fácil	*fácil*	*fácilmente*	easily

Remember that some adjectives do not change in the feminine form.

When two adverbs appear together, the first one you use does **not** have –*mente*. For example:

*Para aprobar mis exámenes estudié **cuidadosa y tranquilamente.***
To pass my exams I worked **carefully** and **calmly.**

The following adverbs do not end in –*mente*:

bien *Mi profesora de inglés es muy buena, enseña muy **bien.***
My English teacher is very good, she teaches very well.

mal *El trabajo está muy **mal** escrito.*
The work is very badly written.

despacio *No entiendo. ¡Habla más **despacio**, por favor!*
I don't understand. Speak more slowly, please!

The adverb 'quickly' has two forms: **rápido** and **rápidamente.**

b 💬 Trabaja con una pareja. Usando adverbios, busca maneras de hacer estas acciones.

*Ejemplo: ¿Cómo se puede hablar bien español?
Se puede hablar claramente.*

- hablar bien español
- trabajar
- aprobar exámenes
- jugar al fútbol

Paper 1: listening

Vas a oír la opinión de cuatro jóvenes sobre sus colegios. Escucha lo que dicen con atención y escribe una X en la casilla si la afirmación es **Verdad.**

Hay que marcar **solo 6** casillas (XXXXXX).

Vas a oír lo que dicen dos veces, pero antes tienes unos segundos para leer las afirmaciones.

Verdad

Ana

(a) Hay que llevar uniforme en todos los colegios e institutos españoles. ☐

(b) Si llegas tarde al colegio, te castigará el director. ☐

(c) La educación es obligatoria hasta los dieciséis años. ☐

Martín

(d) En su colegio no hay descansos. ☐

(e) Prefiere las asignaturas prácticas. ☐

(f) Participa en actividades fuera de las horas de clase. ☐

Carla

(g) Su colegio tiene muchas instalaciones deportivas. ☐

(h) Su colegio tiene piscina cubierta. ☐

(i) Tienen una pequeña granja. ☐

Roque

(j) Tiene buena relación con todos sus profesores. ☐

(k) En su colegio hay bastante disciplina. ☐

(l) Los profesores tienen expectativas altas. ☐

[Total: 6]

Points to remember

- This listening task requires good concentration to understand precisely what the speakers say.
- There are 12 statements made by four speakers, six of which are true.
- At least *one* of the speakers must make more than one true statement.
- Use the pause time wisely. Read all the statements before you begin.

Paper 2 : reading

This question type requires you to answer the questions in Spanish. Only single words or short phrases are required.

Mi vida escolar en Colombia

The heading is important because it gives you a first clue about the content. This text is about schools in Colombia.

Lee este correo electrónico de tu amigo/a por correspondencia colombiano/a sobre su colegio y contesta a las preguntas **en español.**

Make sure you do this before you look at the questions. Remember that you are not expected to understand every word. Try picking out key points. What strategies can you use to work out the meanings of less familiar words and phrases?

¡Hola Kirstie!

Gracias por tu correo. Me resultó muy interesante saber cómo es tu colegio. Hay aspectos parecidos a la vida escolar aquí en Colombia, pero también hay diferencias.

Tu horario es mejor – nosotros empezamos el cole a las ocho y terminamos a las cinco.

Me dices que en tu país se pueden elegir las asignaturas que quieres estudiar. Aquí es obligatorio estudiar matemáticas, español, inglés, ciencias, geografía e historia. Los idiomas me parecen difíciles porque no se me dan bien, así que no los soporto.

¡Me parece que tenéis suerte de poder trabajar durante las vacaciones! Aquí no es posible porque vivimos en el campo. Yo tengo que cuidar a mis hermanos cuando no tengo cole y mi amigo tiene que ayudar a sus padres en su granja. ¡Por supuesto que no nos pagan, lo que me parece bastante injusto!

Me preguntas por las instalaciones y los clubs de mi cole. Tenemos unos edificios bonitos. Hay espacio para todos y tenemos buenos laboratorios y una biblioteca muy grande.

Soy miembro del club de atletismo. Entreno tres veces a la semana y he ganado varias medallas.

Tengo que estudiar mucho este año para aprobar mis exámenes. Después pienso hacer las *pruebas de Estado* para poder ir a la universidad. Quiero ser contable.

¿Y tú? ¿Qué piensas hacer?

Un abrazo,

Lucas

Tips for success

- The skimming and scanning techniques you have just used are an effective way to help you to find key information you need to answer the questions.
- Read through all the questions before you begin. Remember that they follow a logical sequence, so the answer to the first question is at the start of the text.

1 ¿Sobre qué tema había escrito Kirstie en su último correo? **[1]**

2 ¿Qué opina Lucas del día escolar de Kirstie? **[1]**

3 Respecto a lo que estudian, ¿qué es diferente en Colombia, según Lucas? **[1]**

4 ¿Qué asignaturas no le gustan? **[1]**

5 ¿Por qué? **[1]**

6 ¿Qué hace Lucas durante las vacaciones? **[1]**

7 ¿Por qué se queja? **[1]**

8 ¿Qué piensa de las instalaciones de su colegio? **[1]**

9 ¿Qué tal se le da el deporte? **[1]**

10 ¿Qué quiere hacer en el futuro? **[1]**

[Total: 10]

Paper 3: speaking

Presentation and discussion

In the speaking exam you have to give a presentation. Remember that you have to speak for about 2 minutes on a subject of your choice, which you prepare in advance. Then you answer questions about your presentation.

Here is an example of a topic you could choose. The questions and short texts will help you develop your technique for making the presentation, working with a partner.

Tips for success

- Choose a topic that interests you, like the one we have suggested below.
- You may use a photo to help make your presentation more interesting.
- To time your presentation it is a good idea to read it to a partner.
- Make sure you are well acquainted with the vocabulary related to the topic you have chosen, so that you can answer the follow-up questions.

School life

Aquí hay un imagen de un colegio. ¿Cómo contestarías estas preguntas?

- ¿Cómo se llama tu colegio?
- ¿Qué tipo de colegio es?
- ¿Cuántos alumnos hay?
- ¿Qué asignaturas estudias?
- ¿Cómo es un día típico?

🎧 Escucha la información sobre la vida escolar. Empareja cada comentario con el título adecuado (A–D).

A las instalaciones	**B** el horario	**C** los profesores	**D** sus planes futuros

Sample student answer

1 Empiezo el colegio a las ocho de la mañana. Hay seis horas de clase al día y cada clase dura cincuenta minutos. Tengo un recreo de media hora a las diez y entonces juego al fútbol en el patio o charlo con mis compañeros en el aula. Terminamos a las cinco de la tarde. **B**

2 Tengo profesores buenos y malos. El profesor de matemáticas es muy severo, pero puede ser simpático también. En mi opinión, la profesora de geografía enseña muy mal, grita todo el tiempo y nos pone demasiados deberes. ☐

3 Nuestro colegio es mixto. Tiene mil alumnos y unos ochenta profesores más o menos. Está en el centro de la ciudad y es bastante moderno aunque ahora el edificio resulta demasiado pequeño para tantos alumnos. Lo mejor es que hay buenas instalaciones, como aulas con ordenadores y pizarras interactivas. ☐

4 ¿Qué estudiaré el año próximo? No sé qué pasará en el futuro, pero pienso quedarme en el colegio para terminar mis estudios. Quiero ser profesora de inglés, así que necesitaré estudiar idiomas. ☐

Now use the texts above to prepare a presentation of your own on the same topic. Read it out loud and discuss it with your partner. Take care to:

- Put the different parts of the presentation in a logical order (e.g. it might be better to start with a description of the school rather than with your daily timetable).
- Link the different parts of your presentation by using connectives such as: *también* (also), *luego* (then), *por lo tanto* (so), *porque* (because), *para que* [+ subjunctive] (so that), *cuando* (when), *mientras* (while), *en mi opinión* (in my opinion).

hacer las prácticas de trabajo to do work experience
ir a reuniones to go to meetings
lavar el pelo to wash hair
repartir el correo to deliver the post
trabajar en un/una… to work in/on a…
usar el ordenador to work on the computer
la **agencia de viajes** travel agency
el **banco** bank
la **empresa** company
la **fábrica** factory
el **garaje** garage
el **hotel** hotel
la **oficina** office
la **peluquería** hairdresser's
el **restaurante** restaurant
la **tienda** shop

Jobs and professions
el/la **abogado/a** lawyer
el/la **agricultor/a** farmer
el **albañil (*no feminine form*)** builder
el/la **arquitecto/a** architect
el/la **asesor/a** consultant
el/la **auxiliar de vuelo** flight attendant
el/la **azafato/a** flight attendant
el/la **bombero/a** firefighter
el/la **cajero/a** cashier
el/la **camarero/a** waiter/waitress
el/la **cantante** singer

el/la **cartero/a** postman/woman
el/la **científico/a** scientist
el/la **cirujano/a** surgeon
el/la **cocinero/a** cook, chef
el/la **conductor/a** driver
el/la **dentista** dentist
el/la **dependiente/a** shop assistant
el/la **electricista** electrician
el/la **empleado/a** employee
el/la **enfermero/a** nurse
el/la **farmacéutico/a** pharmacist, chemist
el/la **fontanero/a** plumber
el/la **ingeniero/a** engineer
el/la **marinero/a** sailor
el/la **mecánico/a** mechanic
el/la **médico/a** doctor
el/la **modelo** model
el/la **obrero/a** labourer
el/la **oficinista** office worker
el/la **peluquero/a** hairdresser
el/la **periodista** journalist
el/la **piloto** pilot
el/la **policía** policeman/woman
el/la **político/a** politician
el/la **recepcionista** receptionist
el/la **reportero/a** reporter
el/la **técnico/a** technician
el/la **torero/a** bullfighter
el/la **veterinario/a** vet

Future plans
Espero I hope to
Intento I try to
Me apetecería I'd like to
Me gustaría I'd like to
Quiero I want to
Quisiera I'd like to
Voy a I'm going to
buscar un trabajo to look for a job
cogerse un año sabático to take a year out
estudiar to study
hacer un aprendizaje to do an apprenticeship
ir a la universidad to go to university
ir de viaje to go travelling
seguir estudiando to carry on studying
ser famoso/a to be famous
trabajar como voluntario/a to work as a volunteer

Question words
¿Qué? What?
¿Quién/Quiénes? Who?
¿Cuál/Cuáles? Which?
¿Cómo? How?
¿Cuándo? When?
¿Cuánto/a/os/as? How much/many?
¿Por qué? Why?

El mundo es un pañuelo

1 El transporte

2 De vacaciones

3 El tiempo y el medio ambiente

☑ Talk about travelling around

☑ Compare types of transport

☑ Use interrogatives

☑ Use prepositions

1 El transporte

¿Cómo viajar?

1a 📖 Empareja las palabras con la imagen adecuada.

Ejemplo: a — el coche

a

b *Renfe*

c *Metro*

d ✈

e

f ZONA PEATONAL

g

h

i

j Estación de autobuses

k

el autobús   la bicicleta   el avión   a pie
el autocar   el coche   el metro
el taxi   la moto   el tren   el barco

b 💬 Trabaja con tu pareja. Habla de los transportes que usas.

Ejemplo: ¿Cómo viajas al colegio?
Para ir al colegio siempre voy a pie.
¿Cómo viajas cuando tienes prisa?
Cuando tengo prisa prefiero ir en taxi.

- para ir al colegio
- para ir de vacaciones
- para ir de compras
- cuando tienes dinero
- para estar seguro
- cuando tienes prisa
- para visitar la región
- para salir con amigos
- para salir con la familia
- cuando hace mal tiempo

c 🎧 Escucha lo que dicen estos jóvenes de los modos de transporte que usan. ¿Qué modos de transporte menciona cada persona?

1 Raquel
2 Sabrina
3 Miguel Ángel
4 Rafa
5 Mario
6 Enrique

2a 🎧 📖 Escucha y lee lo que dicen estos jóvenes acerca de cada método de transporte. ¿Qué piensan?

Ejemplo: metro = más rapido — underground is quicker

a Creo que es más rápido viajar al centro en metro.

b En mi opinión los autobuses son demasiado lentos.

c Es muy peligroso ir a pie

d Ir en autocar es muy interesante pero es caro.

e Ir en bicicleta es más sano y también es práctico.

f No me gusta viajar en avión, prefiero viajar en barco.

g Los trenes son incómodos y sucios.

h Ir en taxi es fácil pero cuesta demasiado dinero.

i Viajar en coche daña el ambiente.

b 📝 Usando la tabla para ayudarte, escribe tus opiniones de los diferentes métodos de transporte.

Creo que En mi opinión Prefiero (No) me gusta	ir viajar	en coche a pie	es	muy demasiado bastante	barato caro rápido lento cómodo incómodo práctico sano seguro peligroso

c 💬 ¿Estás de acuerdo? Compara tus opiniones con las de tu pareja.

Ejemplo: A: En mi opinión ir en avión es peligroso. También es demasiado caro. Prefiero viajar en coche.
B: No estoy de acuerdo. Me gusta viajar en avión. Aunque es caro, es muy rápido y práctico.

3 🎧 ¿Quién viaja? ¿Adónde van? ¿Cómo? ¿Por qué? Completa la tabla con los detalles que faltan.

	¿Quién?	¿Adónde?	¿Cómo?	¿Por qué?
Ejemplo:	*padre*	*Londres*	*avión*	*rápido*
1				

4a 📖 ✏️ Lee lo que dicen los jóvenes. Rellena la tabla.

Persona	✈️	🚶	🚗	🚲	🚈	🚌	🚂	Ⓜ️	Otro
Ejemplo: Raquel		✓						✓	
Sabrina									
Miguel Ángel									
Rafa									
Mario									
Enrique									

El modo de transporte que a diario uso para ir al colegio es el metro. Vivo en el centro de la ciudad y mi colegio, San Vincente de la Vega, está a unos 15 minutos en metro. A veces voy andando con mis amigos. ¡En primavera, por ejemplo!

Raquel

A mí me gusta estar en forma y me preocupo por el ambiente, así que voy todos los días a la facultad en mi bicicleta de montaña. Tardo unos 30 minutos. Sin embargo, los fines de semana me encanta ir de compras a uno de los grandes centros comerciales y para llegar allí necesito ir en coche. Me lleva mi hermana mayor, Patricia, que tiene coche.

Sabrina

Después del cole, ¡que por cierto está al lado de mi casa!, voy a visitar a mis amigos. Como es un pueblo bastante pequeño y no hay tanto tráfico, voy patinando sobre ruedas. También voy a veces en mi pequeña moto.

Miguel Angel

Vivo en las afueras de la ciudad y tengo que coger un tren de cercanías para ir al colegio o quedar con mis amigos. Después voy unos 15 minutos a pie. ¡Es un viaje bastante largo!

Rafa

GRAMÁTICA

Interrogatives

These are the words used to ask a question. Look at the following table.

Singular	Plural	Meaning
¿Qué?	*¿Qué?*	What?
¿Cuál?	*¿Cuáles?*	Which (one(s))?
¿Quién?	*¿Quiénes?*	Who?
¿Cuánto/a?	*¿Cuántos/as?*	How much/many?

Remember, when asking the question 'Which?' in front of a noun, use *¿Qué?* rather than *¿Cuál?*:

*¿**Cuál** prefieres, el tren o el coche?*
Which do you prefer, train or car?

*¿**Qué** método de transporte prefieres, el tren o el coche?*
Which method of transport do you prefer, train or car?

Write out the following sentences in Spanish:

1 How much does it cost to travel to work by taxi?
2 Who travels by bus?
3 How do you get to your friend's house?
4 How many people go to school on foot?
5 What form of transport do you prefer?

Durante la semana voy al colegio en un autobús que pasa al lado de mi casa. Los fines de semana trabajo en una granja y para ir allí tengo que coger un autocar hasta el pueblo.

Mario

Como ahora soy famoso no puedo ir andando, ¡sin que me reconozcan! Por eso, me llevan a todos los sitios en coche... ¡en una limusina! Para ir a los conciertos o en los viajes de promoción, voy mucho en avión.

Enrique

b ✏️ Contesta las preguntas.

Ejemplo: **1** *¿Cómo va Raquel al colegio?*
Raquel va al colegio andando y en metro.

2 ¿Cómo va Sabrina a la facultad?
3 ¿Qué módo de transporte usa Sabrina para ir de compras?
4 ¿Cómo va Miguel Angel a casa de sus amigos?
5 ¿Qué módo de transporte usa Rafa?
6 ¿Cómo va Mario al trabajo?

c 💬 Trabaja con tu pareja. Contesta las preguntas.

1 ¿Cómo vas al colegio/al trabajo/a casa de tus amigos?
2 ¿Qué módo de transporte usas cuando estás con amigos/con tus padres?
3 ¿Cómo viajas de una ciudad a otra?
4 ¿Cómo viajas al extranjero?

d 🗺 Haz una encuesta. Pregunta a tus compañeros cómo van a los sitios. Usa esta información para escribir frases como en el ejemplo.

Ejemplo: *Katie siempre va al colegio en autobús. Para ir de compras va en el coche de su madre. Va andando a la pista de tenis.*

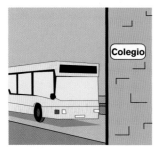  

e 📖 Empareja las frases con la imagen adecuada.

a Prefiero ir en bicicleta.
b Ir en tren es muy cómodo.
c Me encanta viajar en barco.
d El jueves voy a ir a Lima en autocar.
e Siempre vamos andando.
f Salen de su casa a las ocho y cogen el autobús.

GRAMÁTICA

Prepositions

Most forms of transport take the preposition *en*, for example *en tren*. There is one exception: *a pie*. When using *andando*, there is no preposition: *voy andando*.

To talk about going and travelling, use the prepositions: *a* (to) or *de* (from). For example:

*Voy **a** Madrid.*
*Voy **de** mi casa.*
I am going to Madrid.
I am going from my house.

When *a* or *de* appear before the word *el*, they are shortened to *al* or *del*. This is because it is easier to pronounce. For example:

*Voy **al** colegio…(a + el)* I go to school…

*Vuelvo **del** trabajo…* (de + el)
I come home from work…

Read the following sentences. Where there are errors, write out a corrected version.

1 Me gusta ir a el cine.
2 ¿Vas a menudo a la playa?
3 ¿Cuántas veces viajas a pie?
4 ¿Te gusta ir en coche?
5 Voy todos los días a el colegio andando.
6 Marta vuelve de el colegio a las cinco.
7 ¿A qué hora vuelves del trabajo?
8 ¿A qué hora vuelves a el trabajo?

¿Cómo vamos?

5a 🎧 🖊 Marta y Alex deciden qué transporte usar para el viaje fin de curso. Escucha lo que dicen. Copia la tabla abajo y escribe los aspectos positivos y negativos de cada modo de transporte. ¿Qué deciden al final?

Modo de transporte	Ventajas	Desventajas
Ejemplo: avión	*rápido*	*caro*
barco		
autocar		
tren		

b 💬 Pregunta a tu pareja qué opina de cada modo de transporte.

Ejemplo: A: *¿Qué opinas de viajar en barco?*
B: *En mi opinión ir en barco es muy cómodo y barato, pero se tarda más.*

6 🖊 Lee el mensaje electrónico de Luisa. Escribe tu respuesta.

> ¡Hola!
>
> Las vacaciones se acercan y, como sabes, voy a ir a Salamanca con mi familia. Vivimos bastante cerca y por eso vamos a ir en coche. Es más práctico y barato. En Salamanca hay muchos autobuses, pero prefiero ir andando porque es más sano…¡y barato! Dime, ¿adónde vas a ir de vacaciones? ¿Cómo vas a ir? ¿Y por qué?

7 💬 Haz diálogos con tu pareja.

- Quisiera un billete de ida/de ida y vuelta para…, por favor.
- ¿Cuánto cuesta (un billete sencillo)?
- Necesito un bonometro.
- ¿A qué hora sale el próximo/último tren/ autobús/metro para…?

Ejemplo:
A: *Buenos días. En que puedo servirle?*
B: *Quisiera un billete de ida para Pinto.*
A: *Aquí tiene. 3 euros.*
B: *Gracias. ¿A qué hora sale el último tren?*
A: *A las once y media.*

El Metro en dos capitales hispánicas

El Metro es un sistema de trenes subterráneos o al aire libre. Actualmente puedes viajar en metro en la capital de España, Madrid, pagando una tarifa plana, a cualquier destino. Para viajar más barato, puedes comprar un bonometro, un billete de 10 viajes, a un precio reducido. Los billetes se compran de la taquilla o de una máquina automática. También hay abonos mensuales y anuales. Hay 12 líneas y un 'metro ligero' bastante nuevo, de 3 líneas, que se desarrolla en superficie y que sirve ciertos distritos de la capital.

En la capital de Argentina, Buenos Aires, también existe un metro, que se llama el Subte (= *subterráneo*). El sistema es extensivo — hay 5 líneas — pero menos grande que el de Madrid. Es el modo más rápido y barato para viajar por la ciudad. Aquí también se paga una tarifa plana a cualquier destino y se puede comprar un billete más barato de 10 viajes.

Después de leer el texto contesta las preguntas:

1 ¿En qué se parecen los sistemas de metro de Madrid y Buenos Aires?

2 ¿En qué se diferencian?

3 En Madrid, ¿cómo se diferencia el Metro del Metro Ligero?

4 ¿Cómo se puede viajar más barato en Buenos Aires?

De viaje

8 📖 ¿Dónde están estas personas? Empareja las señales con cada declaración.

Ejemplo: **1 — b**

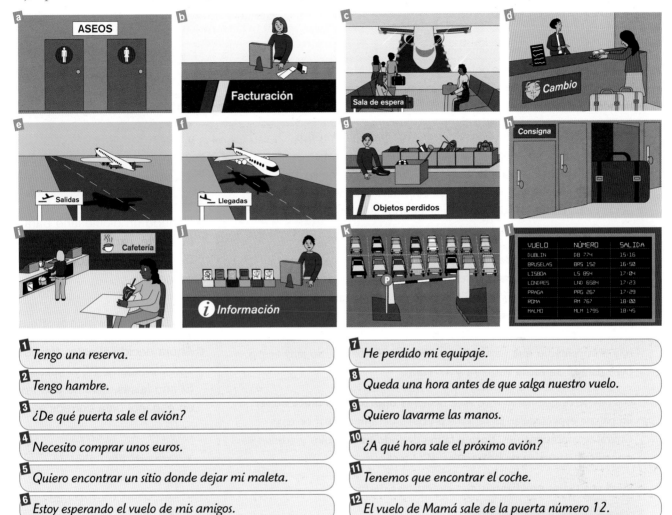

1 Tengo una reserva.

2 Tengo hambre.

3 ¿De qué puerta sale el avión?

4 Necesito comprar unos euros.

5 Quiero encontrar un sitio donde dejar mi maleta.

6 Estoy esperando el vuelo de mis amigos.

7 He perdido mi equipaje.

8 Queda una hora antes de que salga nuestro vuelo.

9 Quiero lavarme las manos.

10 ¿A qué hora sale el próximo avión?

11 Tenemos que encontrar el coche.

12 El vuelo de Mamá sale de la puerta número 12.

9 🎧 🏠 En la agencia de viajes. Escucha a la gente hablando con el empleado. Completa la tabla de abajo.

- ¿Adónde quieren ir?
- ¿Cómo quieren viajar?
- ¿Cuándo quieren ir?
- ¿Qué más quieren saber?

	Ejemplo:	1	2	3
Destino	Madrid			
Transporte	avión			
Día/Fecha	lunes 14 de julio			
Hora de salir	08:00			
Hora de llegar	12:30			
Otros detalles	sin equipaje			

10a 🎧 📖 Escucha y lee el texto.

Un viaje en tren asombroso

Cada año en México muchísima gente hace el largo viaje de 673 kilómetros en tren entre Chihuahua y Los Mochis, **que se sitúa** en la costa pacífica. Una de las **rutas** más **pintorescas** del mundo, es un viaje a través de un paisaje impresionante.

Noventa años en construcción, el ferrocarril Chihuahua Pacífico, **conocido como** El Chepe, viaja a través de la sierra mejicana, **también llamada** El Cañón de Cobre. **Se completó** por fin en 1961 después de un esfuerzo increíble y **se considera una** de las grandes obras de ingeniería del siglo XX. Tiene en total 86 túneles y 36 puentes.

Hay **compartimentos de primera y segunda clase** y sale **a diario** en cada dirección. Cada año este ferrocarril transporta a más de medio millón de pasajeros. Para los turistas a quienes les encanta la comodidad, primera clase es **la única opción**. Los compartimentos tienen aire acondicionado y **asientos cómodos**. Hay un restaurante buenísimo. A veces, **no hay más remedio que** viajar en segunda clase. Es básico, no muy limpio, pero barato. **Se tarda** entre 14 y 17 horas.

Los pasajeros que hacen este viaje tienen **la oportunidad única** de ver un paisaje espectacular. Es un viaje precioso durante el cual se ven cataratas impresionantes, **flora y fauna** de todo tipo y color y árboles magníficos que salen de las paredes de la roca.

¡Será una de las experiencias más inolvidables de tu vida!

b Usando un diccionario para ayudarte, explica lo que significa en cada caso el texto en negrita.

Ejemplo:
que se sitúa — which is situated

c Ahora decide si estas frases son verdaderas (V) o falsas (F). Si son falsas, escribe una frase en español para corregirlas.

Ejemplo: 1 — (V)

1 *Este artículo habla de un viaje en tren.*
2 Las vistas no son nada buenas.
3 Es un viaje corto.
4 Se tardó mucho en construir.
5 Los trenes salen con frecuencia durante el día.
6 Se come muy bien en el tren.
7 Viajar en segunda clase cuesta poco.

d 🏕 Tus padres te han comprado dos billetes para hacer este viaje con un(a) compañero/a. Escribe 150 palabras, narrando lo que os pasó en el viaje y dando tus impresiones de lo que viste de México.

2 De vacaciones

Talk about holiday plans

Use of *ir a* + infinitive

Talk about hotels and accommodation

Using a dictionary

1 🎧 Escucha lo que dicen estos jóvenes de sus próximas vacaciones. Une los dibujos y los números.

GRAMÁTICA

The immediate future

When talking about things that are about to happen, we use the immediate future tense (see also Module 3 p. 79). This is expressed in exactly the same way in both Spanish and English. We use the verb *ir* (to go) followed by *a* and the infinitive form of the main verb. For example:

Voy a ir de vacaciones.
I'm going to go on holiday.

¿Dónde vas a alojarte en vacaciones?
Where are you going to stay on your holiday?

María va a visitar las montañas.
Maria is going to visit the mountains.

Ivan y Ana van a montar a caballo.
Ivan and Ana are going to go riding.

2a 🎧 📖 Identifica todas las veces que se usa '*voy a*' o '*vamos a*'. Traduce las frases al inglés.

Ejemplo: <u>*Voy a*</u> *ir a Estados Unidos.*
I'm going to go to the USA.

1
Este año voy a ir a Estados Unidos con mis amigos del colegio. Vamos a pasar 15 días en Nueva York y vamos a visitar todos los sitios de interés. ¡Va a ser genial!

2
En verano creo que voy a ir a Francia con mis padres. Voy a ir a la playa todos los días y al cine o a la discoteca por la tarde.

3
Voy a ir de vacaciones a Italia. Voy a pasar tres semanas con unos primos que tengo allí. ¡Me encanta! Voy a estudiar italiano y a aprender cómo preparar pasta.

4
En septiembre voy a ir a África de safari. Voy a pasar dos semanas buscando animales salvajes. Además voy a descansar y a leer.

5
En Semana Santa voy a ir con mi familia a Gran Canaria, una de las islas Canarias. Vamos a tomar el sol, visitar las islas, descansar e ir al parque acuático. ¡Guay!

b 📝 Escribe un pequeño párrafo sobre lo que vas a hacer de vacaciones este año.

3 📖 🖋 Lee el texto. Para cada destino, da razones en español para escogerlo para sus vacaciones.

Ejemplo: Voy a ir a Salamanca porque me interesa la cultura y quiero estudiar.

Destinos de vacaciones

1 Salamanca

Ésta es la ciudad de universidad por excelencia: la Universidad de Salamanca fue la primera en ser fundada en España y es también una de las más antiguas de Europa. Los edificios hermosos con su gran valor cultural han sido hogar para algunos de los mayores pensadores, artistas y escritores españoles.

2 Granada

Esta ciudad tiene un sabor árabe inequívoco. Sus platos típicos, sus artes y edificios son una consecuencia de la historia gloriosa de la ciudad. Este lugar tiene un encanto inolvidable. Forma parte del patrimonio universal, junto con la Alhambra y el Generalife, y ha sido un centro cultural importante a lo largo de siglos, tanto durante el período musulmán como el cristiano.

3 Madrid

La capital de España es una ciudad cosmopolita y vibrante. Como un centro de economía, finanzas, administración y servicios, esta ciudad combina la infraestructura más moderna con una herencia cultural y artística importante.

4 Mallorca

Famosa por sus playas hermosas y mar de aguas transparentes, esta isla tiene todo lo que hace falta para unas vacaciones relajantes, sobre todo para aquellos que disfrutan con los deportes acuáticos. El paisaje costero es resplandeciente con calas, playas y acantilados preciosos. Una isla hermosa y diversa con una vida cultural muy rica.

5 Barcelona

De origen romano, Barcelona tiene una larga e interesante historia. Para visitantes que disfrutan de museos, exposiciones y esculturas al aire libre esta ciudad tiene en programa durante todo el año música, teatro y baile.

6 México

Se puede hacer una visita diferente a Chichén Itzá, un enclave arqueológico maya en la Península de Yucatán. Éste era el centro político y económico de la civilización maya entre 750 y 1200 A.C. Sus extraordinarios edificios ilustran el interés de los mayas por el espacio arquitectónico y la composición, así como sus conocimientos astronómicos amplios.

7 Cuba

La isla de Cuba es la más grande de las Antillas Mayores. Localizada muy cerca de la costa del sur de Florida entre el Océano Atlántico y el Mar Caribe, la isla tiene un clima subtropical que es ideal durante todo el año.

8 Argentina

Cosmopolita y vibrante, Buenos Aires es una ciudad moderna con un aire claramente europeo. La arquitectura es espectacular; tiene excelentes museos y parques en abundancia. Las calles se llenan de vida los domingos con el

mercado de antigüedades semanal. Hace falta descubrir esta ciudad, lugar de sepultura de Eva Perón. Al anochecer se puede cenar en uno de los muchos restaurantes excelentes, asistir a una obra de teatro en el famoso Teatro de Colón, o simplemente disfrutar aprendiendo un tango argentino tradicional.

4 📖 ¿Adónde van y qué piensan hacer? Lee lo que piensan hacer estos chicos para sus vacaciones. Empareja las personas 1–8 con la letra de la imagen que corresponda.

Ejemplo: 1 — g

1 Voy a ir a Mallorca para pasar mis vacaciones descansando en la playa.

2 Las próximas vacaciones voy a ir al bosque porque me gusta mucho pasear con el perro y estar al aire libre.

3 Me gusta dormir al aire libre, así que tengo preparadas la mochila y la tienda. ¡Me voy!

4 Yo busco vacaciones con aventura y emoción y por eso voy a ir a los parques de atracciones de Florida.

5 Voy a ir de vacaciones a los ríos de Canadá porque me gustan los deportes acuáticos.

6 Como creo en la terapia que proporcionan las compras, me voy de vacaciones a la ciudad de París, donde hay cantidad de tiendas y centros comerciales.

7 En Semana Santa voy a ir con mis padres a esquiar.

8 Vamos a ir al campo para las próximas vacaciones. Preferimos estar muy lejos del ruido del tráfico y de las ciudades grandes.

CULTURA

¿Sabías que el español es la tercera lengua más hablada del mundo? Haz una investigación para descubrir cuáles de los países abajo tiene el español como primera lengua.

Argentina
Austria
Bélgica
Bolivia
Chile
China
Cuba
República Dominicana
Dinamarca
Ecuador
El Salvador
Nueva Zelanda
Nicaragua
Panamá
Paraguay
Perú
Polonia
Eslovenia

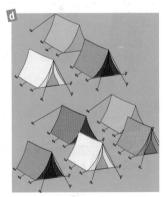

El alojamiento

5 🎧 📖 ¿Dónde se van a alojar? Empareja las imágenes con la palabra adecuada.

Ejemplo: 1 b — un camping

 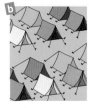   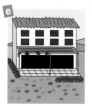

un hotel
un albergue juvenil
un camping
un chalet
un apartamento
una casa

6a 💬 Trabaja con tu pareja. Pregunta y contesta sobre tus planes de vacaciones, como en el ejemplo.

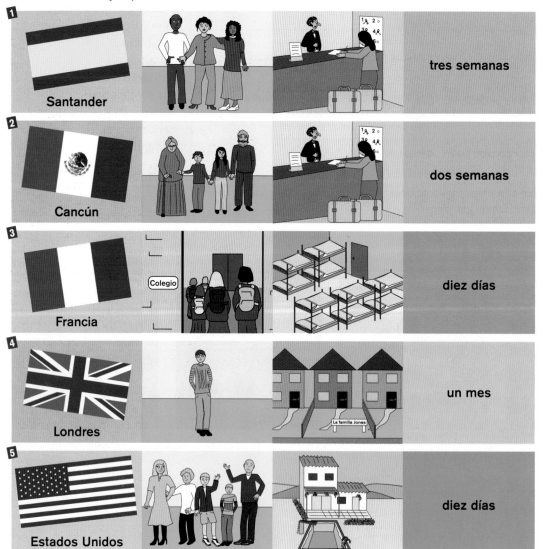

1. Santander — tres semanas
2. Cancún — dos semanas
3. Francia / Colegio — diez días
4. Londres / La familia Jones — un mes
5. Estados Unidos — diez días

Ejemplo: 1

A: ¿Adónde vas a ir de vacaciones este verano?
B: Voy a ir a Santander este verano.
A: ¿Con quién vas a ir de vacaciones?
B: Voy a ir con mis padres.
A: ¿Cuánto tiempo vas a pasar?
B: Voy a pasar tres semanas.
A: ¿Dónde vas a quedarte?
B: Voy a quedarme en un hotel.

b ✏️ Elige unas vacaciones de la lista arriba. Escribe un correo electrónico a un amigo hablándole de tus vacaciones.

Ejemplo: Este verano voy a…

7a 📖 Empareja las imágenes con la palabra adecuada.

Ejemplo: 1 — f

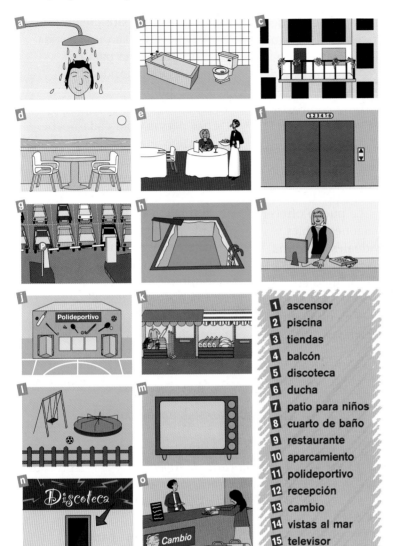

b 🎧 Escucha lo que dice esta gente. Empareja las imágenes del ejercicio 7a con lo que escuchas.

Ejemplo: 1 — e

c 💬 Trabaja con tu pareja. ¿Cuántas preguntas puedes hacer acerca de lo que tiene el hotel?

Ejemplo: ¿Hay una piscina?
¿A qué hora es el desayuno?
¿Dónde se puede comprar postales?
Por favor, ¿me puede cambiar dinero?

1	ascensor
2	piscina
3	tiendas
4	balcón
5	discoteca
6	ducha
7	patio para niños
8	cuarto de baño
9	restaurante
10	aparcamiento
11	polideportivo
12	recepción
13	cambio
14	vistas al mar
15	televisor

CULTURA

Turismo consciente

Cada vez más gente descubre las preciosas islas Galápagos. Son un conjunto de 14 islas y una serie de islotes ubicados a 972 kilómetros de la costa continental ecuatoriana. Son de alto interés ecológico por su parque nacional y la reserva biológica marina.

De origen volcánico, disfrutan de especies únicas como iguanas, tortugas Galápagos, albatros, piqueros y leones marinos, entre muchas otras.

8 🎧 Escucha estas conversaciones y contesta las preguntas en español. Pon una ✗ en la casilla del alojamiento que mejor corresponda con las frases indicadas.

	Hotel Bella Vista	Albergue Las Olas	Camping Río Grande
Ejemplo: Es un camping.			✗
Está en la costa.			
Se puede comer allí.			
Hay que compartir con más de una persona.			
Se puede llevar mascota allí.			
Quieren pasar dos semanas allí.			
Se puede dejar el coche allí.			
Es un grupo escolar.			

9 📖 💬 Practica los tres diálogos con tu pareja.

1

A: Buenos días, hotel Bella Vista. En qué puedo servirle?

B: Nos gustaría reservar dos habitaciones con cuarto de baño para quince días a partir del quince de agosto, si es posible.

A: ¿Pensión completa o media pensión?

B: Pensión completa, por favor, y a ser posible con vistas al mar o a la piscina.

A: Todas nuestras habitaciones tienen vistas al mar. ¿Algo más?

B: Sí, una cosa más. ¿Hay aparcamiento?

A: Sí, señor.

2

A: ¿El albergue juvenil Las Olas?

B: Sí, ¿en qué puedo servirle?

A: ¿Tiene habitaciones libres para un grupo de estudiantes desde el 27 de julio hasta el 16 de agosto?

B: ¿Cuántos estudiantes son?

A: Seis chicos, seis chicas y dos profesores.

B: ¿Les importaría compartir habitación?

A: Los estudiantes pueden compartir sin problema, pero para los profesores individuales, por favor.

B: Muy bien. Le puedo ofrecer seis habitaciones dobles y dos individuales cada una con ducha. ¿Eso le vale?

A: Vale. ¿Está incluido el desayuno?

B: Sí, pero la cena es aparte.

A: Muchas gracias.

3

A: Hola, aquí el camping Río Grande.

B: Hola. Llamo para preguntar si tiene sitio para una tienda y una caravana para tres noches empezando el 12 de julio.

A: Sí, tenemos. El precio es por persona por cada noche. La caravana y la tienda cuestan más.

B: Muy bien. ¿Aceptan perros?

A: Sí, pero hay que llevarlos con la correa puesta.

B: ¿Me puede decir si hay cafetería y restaurante?

A: No hay restaurante en el camping, pero cerca hay muchos sitios donde se puede cenar.

B: Muchas gracias.

10 📖 Lee la carta abajo.

lunes el 4 de agosto

Querida Angelina,

¡Escribo para contarte mi plan de vacaciones para el verano y, por supuesto, ¡para averiguar lo que vas a hacer! Sabes que mis padres acaban de comprar un chalet en el sur de España y naturalmente allí es adonde vamos este verano. Viajamos en coche y como es un camino muy largo vamos a pasar una noche en un hotel por el camino. ¡A mi familia no nos gusta nada pasar todo el día en el coche! No voy a estudiar en absoluto para mis exámenes durante las vacaciones, solo voy a descansar y a pasar el tiempo en la piscina o en la playa. Tendré tiempo para estudiar cuando volvamos.

¿Y tú? ¿Vas a Florida otra vez este verano? Si la respuesta es sí, ¿a qué parques vas esta vez? ¿Qué tiempo hará? Mi amigo Javier, que estuvo allí el año pasado, dice que hace muchísimo calor. ¿Vas a comprar mucho? Mi padre dice que todo es muy barato en los EE.UU. ¿Va tu hermana contigo este año o va a buscar un trabajo? Salúdala de mi parte, ¿vale?

Contéstame y cuéntamelo por favor.

Un saludo de tu amigo

Alberto

a 📖 Busca las seis frases correctas.

Ejemplo: 1

1 *Es una carta de Alberto.*
2 Pasa sus vacaciones en un hotel.
3 Su familia viaja a España.
4 El viaje durará mucho.
5 Alberto tiene que estudiar para sus exámenes.
6 Va a quedarse en la costa.
7 Va a estar muy ocupado durante las vacaciones.
8 Alberto busca información.
9 En Florida hay pocos parques temáticos.
10 Estados Unidos no es caro.
11 La hermana de Angelina trabaja en los EE. UU.

b ✏️ Imagínate que eres Angelina. Escribe una respuesta a la carta de Alberto. Asegúrate de que contestas a todas sus preguntas y luego pregúntale algo tú. Por ejemplo, pregúntale cuándo se va de vacaciones; cuánto tiempo se queda allí; dónde está su casa.

11a 📖 Lee esta carta.

Av Cleto González 11
Distrito de la Catedral
42011 San José
Costa Rica
E-mail: famjuan@yahoo.cr

10 de mayo

Estimado señor,

Me gustaría reservar dos cuartos individuales en su hotel, cada uno con cuarto de baño y balcón, por una semana desde el 6 hasta el 12 de julio. Nos gustaría pensión completa.

Le ruego decirme cuánto cuesta esta reserva.

En espera de su respuesta,
Atentamente,
Juan García-Mendez

Pienso... Quisiera... Me gustaría...	...pasar quince días ...una semana	...desde el 2 de agosto. ...hasta el 20 de agosto.
Me gustaría reservar una habitación...		...con una cama para dos personas ...con dos camas ...con una ducha ...con cuarto de baño
¿Tiene sitio libre...		...para una caravana? ...para una tienda?
Quisiera...		...pensión completa ...media pensión
Me gustaría saber... ¿Puedes decirme...		
En espera de su respuesta...		

1
Hotel María Cristina, Puerto Banus

4 estrellas ★★★★

Muy cerca del casco viejo

Rodeado de paseos y jardines

A cuatro manzanas de la playa principal

Piscina grande y restaurante

2
Delfin el-Verde

4 estrellas ★★★★

Es imposible no volver a casa bronceado dado su playa, sol interminable, arena y deportes. Querrás volver aquí año tras año.

Abierto desde el 31 de marzo hasta el 14 de septiembre.

b 📖 💬 Practica una conversación en la oficina de turismo con tu pareja.

¿Dónde está Correos? ¿Dónde hay un banco/ una oficina de Correos/un cine por aquí?

Quisiera un mapa de la ciudad/ información sobre.../un horario.

¿Qué se puede hacer por aquí?

Buenos días. ¿En qué puedo servirle/ ayudarle?

Aquí tiene un mapa/un folleto/ un horario.

Aquí se puede visitar los monumentos y museos, hacer compras, hacer deportes acuáticos y se celebra(n) la(s) fiesta(s) de...

12 ¿Qué tal tu geografía? Encuentra estos países en un atlas y busca los nombres en español. Después, añade las nacionalidades apropiadas en la tabla siguiente.

Europa	
País	**Nacionalidad**
España	español/la
Inglaterra	inglés/esa
Francia	francés/esa

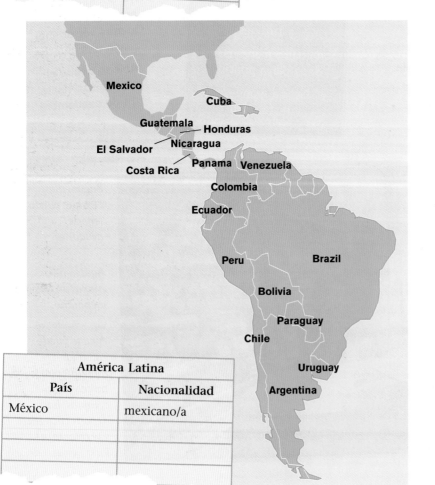

América Latina	
País	**Nacionalidad**
México	mexicano/a

LENGUA CLAVE

When you look up a word in a bilingual dictionary, it is followed by a number of related words. The part of speech of each word is indicated as follows:

- (v.) — verb
- (n.m.) — masculine noun
- (n.f.) — feminine noun
- (adj.) — adjective

For example:
viajar (v.) — to travel
viaje (n.m.) — journey
viajero (n.m.) — traveller/passenger

Look up the following verbs related to travel and transport. Can you find the Spanish for the English nouns listed?

- *parar* (to stop) — bus stop
- *sentarse* (to sit) — seat
- *entrar* (to enter) — entrance
- *salir* (to go out) — exit
- *volar* (to fly) — flight
- *conducir* (to drive) — driver
- *visitar* (to visit) — visitor
- *llegar* (to arrive) — arrival

Can you find any more related words?

3 El tiempo

☑ **Talk about the weather**
☑ **Compare climates**
☑ **Use different tenses and verbs to describe the weather**
☑ **Learn about fiestas**

1 📖 Une los dibujos y las frases.

Ejemplo: 1 — d

1	hace calor
2	hace mal tiempo
3	llueve
4	hace frío
5	hay hielo
6	hace viento
7	hace sol
8	hace buen tiempo
9	está nublado
10	hay niebla
11	hay tormenta
12	nieva

2a 🎧 Escucha el pronóstico del tiempo y empareja el tiempo con la ciudad correcta.

b 🗣 Trabaja con tu pareja. Usa la información en 2a para hablar del tiempo en diferentes ciudades de España.

Ejemplo: ¿Qué tiempo hace en Madrid?
En Madrid hace calor y hace sol.

3a Mira el mapa de Chile. Usa la información para decidir cuáles de las frases siguientes son verdaderas (V) y cuáles son falsas (F).

PERU

BOLIVIA

Iquique •

22°
Antofagasta •

CHILE

Pacific
Ocean

ARGENTINA

SANTIAGO • 30°

Concepción •
22°

Temuco •

Atlantic
Ocean

Punta Arenas
10°

1 Hoy hace sol en Antofagasta.
2 Hoy hace calor en Santiago.
3 Hoy está nublado en Temuco
4 Hoy hay nieve en Punta Arenas.
5 Hoy llueve en Concepción.

b Mira el mapa otra vez. Con tu pareja, contesta las preguntas utilizando las expresiones en la página 109 (Grámatica).

Ejemplo:

A: ¿Qué tiempo hace hoy en Concepción?
B: Hoy en Concepción hace calor, pero está lloviendo.

1 ¿Qué tiempo hace hoy en Santiago?
2 ¿Qué tiempo hace hoy en Antofagasta?
3 ¿Qué tiempo hace hoy en Temuco?
4 ¿Qué tiempo hace hoy aquí?

4 Empareja la estación del año con la imagen adecuada.

1 verano
2 invierno
3 primavera
4 otoño

5 Trabaja con tu pareja. Rellena la tabla siguiente con palabras y frases que asocies con diferentes estaciones.

Verano		Invierno	
Tiempo	Actividades	Tiempo	Actividades
hace sol	*ir a la playa*	*llueve*	*ir al cine*

6 Escucha la descripción del clima de Chile. Copia los puntos cardinales de la brújula abajo y haz apuntes sobre el tiempo.

CHILE —

norte
noroeste / noreste
oeste / este
suroeste / sureste
sur

7 Completa las frases siguientes con el nombre correcto de las estaciones según el hemisferio.

*Ejemplo: En junio, julio y agosto en Chile es **invierno** y en España es **verano**.*

1 En diciembre, enero y febrero en Chile es _____ y en España es _____ .
2 En septiembre, octubre y noviembre en Chile es _____ y en España es _____ .
3 En marzo, abril y mayo en Chile es _____ Y en España es _____ .

8 🎧 📖 💬 Escucha otra vez la información sobre el clima de Chile, pero esta vez léela también y hazle preguntas a tu pareja sobre el clima.

Ejemplo: *A: ¿Qué tiempo hace en el norte de Chile en verano?*
B: En el norte de Chile en verano hace calor.

La República de Chile es uno de los muchos países hispanohablantes. Como se ve en el mapa, se encuentra en América del Sur, a lo largo de la costa, entre las montañas de los Andes y el océano Pacífico. Comparte su frontera con Argentina al este, Bolivia al noreste y Perú hacia el norte.

Dado que el país tiene cuatro mil kilómetros de largo, no es ninguna sorpresa que el clima de Chile sea tan variado como sus tierras.

El verano en Chile es de diciembre a marzo. En el centro del país durante esta estación el clima es cálido y seco, con pocas lluvias, y la temperatura llega a unos 30 grados centígrados. En invierno, sin embargo, la región central recibe muchas precipitaciones, mientras que sus zonas más expuestas experimentan vientos violentos.

En las zonas del sur, donde hay muchos lagos, en verano las temperaturas no llegan a más de 14 grados. Aquí el clima es más lluvioso y más fresco. En invierno llueve más que en el centro. En el extremo sur incluso se registran vendavales. Las lluvias son abundantes excepto en Patagonia, donde tienen un clima muy seco.

En el este del país está la cordillera de los Andes, que sirve de frontera entre Chile y Argentina. Aquí el clima es típico de las regiones montañosas. En las elevaciones altas hay un clima de hielo.

La zona del norte de Chile se caracteriza por veranos cálidos e inviernos suaves. En esta región está el desierto más seco del mundo, el Atacama: aquí las lluvias son escasas y las temperaturas muy altas.

vendaval = gale

GRAMÁTICA

Different tenses and verbs to describe the weather

To talk about the weather in Spanish, we usually use the third person of *hacer*, *estar* or *haber*.

¿Qué tiempo hace en Inglaterra?	What's the weather like in England?
Hace frío.	It's cold.
Hace calor.	It's hot.
Hace sol.	It's sunny.

To say it's very hot, cold or sunny, just add *mucho*:

Hace mucho calor.	It's very hot.
Hace mucho frío.	It's very cold.
Hace mucho sol.	It's very sunny.

However, when talking about any form of precipitation (rain, snow etc.), use *estar*:

Está lloviendo.	It's raining.
Esta nevando.	It's snowing.
Está nublado.	It's cloudy.

Mucho can be used after the verb, except with *está nublado*, which requires *muy* (*está muy nublado*)

It is also possible to use *hay* plus a noun:

Hay sol.	It's sunny.
Hay niebla.	It's foggy.
Hay lluvia.	It's raining.

If you want to talk about the weather in the past, simply use the past tense of *hacer*, *estar* or *haber*:

Hizo sol.	It was sunny.
Estuvo lloviendo.	It was raining.
Hubo tormenta.	There was a storm.

An easy way to talk about the weather in the future is to use the third person of the present tense of *ir* with the infinitive of the relevant verb:

Va a hacer sol.	It's going to be sunny.
Va a hacer calor.	It's going to be hot.
Va a haber tormenta.	There will be a storm.

Finally, there are two verbs relating to the weather, namely *llover* and *nevar*, that can be used on their own in the relevant tense:

Llovió.	It rained.
Llueve.	It's raining.
Va a llover.	It's going to rain.
Nevó.	It snowed.
Nieva.	It's snowing.
Va a nevar.	It's going to snow.

Care must be taken with these verbs as they are radical changing.

9 🏔 Haz investigaciones por Internet para descubrir el clima de otro país hispanohablante, y después úsalo como modelo para escribir y dar tu propia presentación sobre ese país. ¡Podrías hacer un PowerPoint para acompañarlo!

10 📖 Empareja el español con la frase adecuada en inglés.

1 En mi pueblo hace mucho frío en invierno.	**a** Tomorrow it's going to be very windy.
2 Ayer hizo mucho calor en la playa.	**b** In my town it's very cold in winter.
3 Mañana va a hacer mucho viento.	**c** At Christmas it snowed every day.
4 En vacaciones hizo mucho sol.	**d** Yesterday it was very hot on the beach.
5 En otoño llovió todos los días.	**e** On holiday it was very hot.
6 Hoy está nublado.	**f** In autumn it rained every day.
7 En el centro del país normalmente hace mucho calor.	**g** It's cloudy today.
8 En Navidades nevó todos los días.	**h** In the centre of the country it's usually very hot.

11a 🎧 📖 Escucha y lee la información de cómo afecta al Polo Norte el cambio de clima. Toma apuntes y decide cuál de las frases siguientes es la más apropiada.

1 El clima mundial es más o menos consistente y constante y no debemos estar preocupados.
2 No tienen importancia para la raza humana los cambios que están ocurriendo en el clima global.
3 Ha habido unos cambios en el clima mundial que ya tienen consecuencias significativas.

Estamos destruyendo nuestro mundo

Parece ser que durante los últimos **cien años** la temperatura **del mundo ha aumentado** medio grado. No parece mucho, pero incluso medio grado puede tener un efecto profundo en nuestro planeta.

La principal causa de este calentamiento global es la actividad humana, que genera gases contaminantes, sobre todo en los países industrializados. Estos gases retienen el calor del sol en la atmósfera, lo que produce el llamado "efecto invernadero".

Según muchos estudios, el nivel del mar ha subido entre seis y ocho pulgadas (quince a veinte centímetros).

Se piensa que estas temperaturas **elevadas** están causando la descongelación de las capas polares, y que son una **consecuencia** del calentamiento global.

Esa subida de temperaturas aumenta **el volumen** de agua en el océano, lo cual hace que algunas partes del mundo hoy en día **sufran** inundaciones catastróficas — como en partes de Gran Bretaña, India y Bangladesh. También **quiere decir** que aumenta la cantidad de icebergs.

Otras consecuencias graves del calentamiento global son los huracanes y las tormentas, que son cada vez más frecuentes en ciertas regiones. También aumentará el número de muertes por enfermedades como la malaria y el cólera, que afectarán a más población porque las zonas tropicales van a extenderse.

Lo que **está claro** es que está cambiando el clima global y tendremos que prepararnos para las consecuencias.

b 📖 🏛️ Ahora, con la ayuda de un diccionario, busca las palabras del texto en negrita que correspondan con las palabras o frases siguientes.

Ejemplo: **1** *un siglo — cien años*

1 un siglo
2 se ha hecho más grande
3 altas
4 de la Tierra
5 la cantidad
6 resultado
7 es obvio
8 significa
9 padezcan de
10 creen que

12 📖 Mira las imágenes. ¿Puedes emparejar cada una con estas actividades? Usa un diccionario para ayudarte.

Ejemplo: *a — una corrida de toros*

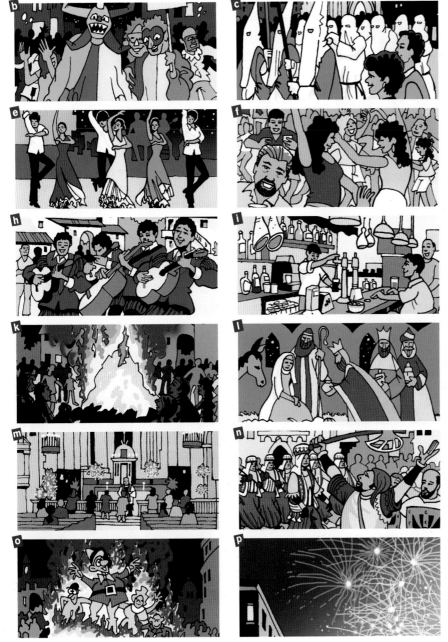

cantar
una procesión
una hoguera
beber
una fiesta
un belén
el baile flamenco
una corrida de toros
una verbena
la misa
una batalla
una imagen
un disfraz
montar a caballo
fuegos artificiales
comer

España, ¡el hogar de las fiestas!

En cada uno de sus múltiples pueblos y ciudades se puede ver algún tipo de fiesta casi todas las semanas del año. Estas fiestas hacen que la gente salga a la calle para compartir las celebraciones. Puede ser esto el motivo de las buenas relaciones y camaradería entre los vecinos en la península.

Las fiestas más famosas en el extranjero son los encierros de Pamplona, las Fallas de Valencia con sus impresionantes fuegos artificiales, las batallas de moros y cristianos representadas en Alcoi, o quizás las fiestas de Semana Santa por toda Andalucía, sin olvidarse de la enorme Feria de Abril de Sevilla.

En Andalucía hay corridas de toros, flamenco, conciertos, música y fiestas de vino, mientras que en otros sitios se puede encontrar todo tipo de celebraciones extrañas, como la fiesta del caracol en Lleida, la del marisco en Logroño y la de la paella de Chueca.

Cara, la revista del momento, les ofrece aquí toda la información imprescindible sobre dos de las fiestas inolvidables de España. ¡No te las pierdas!

San Isidro – Madrid

San Isidro es el patrón de la capital de España, Madrid. El 15 de mayo los madrileños van andando hacia el Prado de San Isidro donde es costumbre tomar agua bendita que sale de una fuente que hay en el patio. Es tradicional vestirse de chulapo o chulapa (el traje típico de la ciudad de Madrid).

A pesar de su significado religioso, San Isidro es una buena excusa para celebrarlo con comida, copas, música y baile hasta la madrugada. Es típico, por ejemplo, comer barquillos y rosquillas. Esta fiesta dura varios días repletos de actividades culturales — concursos de chotis, conciertos de música y ferias de artesanía.

Las Navidades españolas

Las tradiciones más comunes de Navidad incluyen la construcción de enormes belenes — representando el Nacimiento, árboles de navidad, mercadillos por todo el país, donde se venden frutas, flores, dulces de navidad (mazapanes, turrones y polvorones), velas, decoraciones y artesanías — y por supuesto hoy en día regalos para todos. A menudo, con la aparición de la estrella navideña en el cielo, se encienden lámparas de aceite. Con el avance de la noche disminuyen

las muchedumbres y se puede ver a la gente que se retira hacia sus hogares. La alegría familiar se interrumpe con el canto de las campanas que llaman a todos a la iglesia para celebrar la Misa del Gallo. La más bella de estas celebraciones se ve en el monasterio de Montserrat, que se sitúa en lo alto de una montaña cerca de Barcelona. Se distingue por el coro de niños que cantan con una voz dulce y única.

No se come la cena hasta después de medianoche. Es una celebración familiar y uno de los platos típicos

es el pavo trufado. Después de la cena se cantan los villancicos y a continuación los jóvenes salen de juerga. Las celebraciones siguen hasta la madrugada que como dice en la canción: 'Esta noche es Nochebuena, Y no es noche de dormir'.

El Día de Navidad se va otra vez a la iglesia antes de los aperitivos y la comida.

En España Santa Claus y los regalos en Navidad no es una costumbre tradicional. Los regalos los traen el día 6 de enero los Reyes Magos. La víspera del día 6 los niños dejan sus zapatos limpios fuera para que los encuentren los Reyes. Si el niño ha sido bueno durante el año, le dejan regalos. Si ha sido malo solo recibe carbón de reyes (un dulce hecho de azúcar de color negro que parece carbón). El día 6 es fiesta nacional, y lo tradicional es comer el roscón de reyes (un bollo dulce en forma de anillo grande que contiene frutos secos y a menudo relleno de nata). Quien encuentre al comer su trozo la sorpresa escondida en la masa, se supone que tendrá suerte durante el resto del año.

GRAMÁTICA

Se puede + infinitive

This means 'one/you can do something'. For example:

En mi pueblo se puede pasear a orillas del mar.
In my village you can walk by the sea.

14 💬 Trabaja con tu pareja. Contesta las preguntas siguientes usando las pistas en la casilla.

Ejemplo:
¿Qué se puede hacer en la fiesta de San Isidro? En la fiesta de San Isidro se puede bailar hasta la madrugada.

> San Valentín
> El día de los Inocentes
> Semana Santa
> La Víspera de Todos los Santos
> Navidad

1 ¿Qué se puede hacer en _____?
2 ¿Qué fiestas celebras?
3 ¿Qué se puede hacer?
4 ¿Qué se puede ver?

15 🏰 Escribe una carta a un(a) amigo/a español(a) de 130 palabras comparando tus experiencias de Navidad con las Navidades españolas (según el artículo). Comenta sobre todo:
(i) lo que pasa, durante la Nochebuena
(ii) la tradición de dar regalos
(iii) la importancia de celebrar la fiesta en familia

📖 Según lo que dice el artículo sobre la tradiciones navideñas en España, indica si las frases siguientes son verdaderas (V) o falsas (F). Si son falsas, escribe una frase en español para corregirlas.

1 Mientras avanza la noche la mayoría de la gente vuelve a casa.
2 Se come la cena de Navidad a las 12 de la noche en punto.
3 Después de la cena los jóvenes salen para divertirse.
4 El Día de la Navidad se bebe algo antes de ir a la misa.
5 El día 6 de enero los niños malos no reciben nada.
6 El roscón de reyes tiene una sorpresa para algunos.

Paper 1: listening

This question is divided in two parts. Each of the first set of five statements contains an incorrect word. You have to listen for the correct word from the context and supply it. The second set of four questions requires you to provide short answers in Spanish.

Vas a oír una entrevista con Margarita, una chica que cuenta lo que pasó durante sus vacaciones del año pasado. Escucha la entrevista con atención y contesta a las preguntas. Habrá una pausa durante la entrevista.

Primera parte: Preguntas 1 a 5. En cada frase hay algo que no corresponde con lo que dicen en la entrevista. Escucha la entrevista y escribe la palabra correcta en español.

Vas a oír la primera parte dos veces, pero antes tienes unos segundos para leer las preguntas 1 a 5.

1 Margarita fue de vacaciones con su ~~familia~~ por primera vez.

.... **[1]**

2 Se alojaron en un ~~hotel~~ en la costa.

.... **[1]**

3 Les gustó mucho ~~la playa~~.

.... **[1]**

4 Por la tarde iban a ~~beber~~ al pueblo.

.... **[1]**

5 Hizo ~~bastante~~ calor.

.... **[1]**

[PAUSA]

Segunda parte: Preguntas números 6 a 9. Vas a oír la segunda parte de la entrevista dos veces. Escúchala y contesta a las preguntas en español. Tienes unos segundos para leer las preguntas.

6 ¿Qué fue lo mejor de las vacaciones para Margarita?

.... **[1]**

7 ¿Qué fue lo que más le sorprendió?

.... **[1]**

8 ¿Qué piensa hacer Margarita el verano que viene?

.... **[1]**

9 ¿Por qué piensa hacer eso?

.... **[1]**

[Total: 9]

Points to remember

- Before you listen to the extract, take time to read carefully the five statements and the four questions.
- Concentrate on grasping the meaning of the extract. Understanding the context is the key to success.
- The answers to questions 1–5 are each a word taken from the audio.

Paper 2: reading

Lee este artículo e indica si las afirmaciones que siguen son verdaderas o falsas. **Si son FALSAS, escribe una frase en español para corregirlas.**

ATENCIÓN: hay 2 afirmaciones que son **VERDADERAS** y 3 afirmaciones que son **FALSAS.**

México: una tierra llena de cultura e historia

Soy Ramón Casales y acabo de pasar el verano viajando por México para descubrir un nuevo mundo y para conocer la vida y la cultura de la familia de mi madre, Carmen. Para ello, me instalé en casa de mis abuelos, que viven en Mérida, no lejos de Cancún, un lugar de veraneo.

Mérida es un centro de negocios lleno de vida que mezcla con éxito y gracia su pasado y la modernidad de los edificios nuevos.

Pasé muchas tardes estupendas explorando la ciudad y visitando los monumentos históricos y sobre todo las iglesias, que me encantan. También me fui a visitar lugares de interés maya para saber más sobre esta sociedad que siempre me fascinaba en las clases de historia del colegio. Era bastante fácil moverse a pie por la ciudad, o también podías coger uno de los muchos taxis, que eran muy baratos. Además, había autobuses bastante cómodos y frecuentes para ir a las afueras.

Durante mi estancia aproveché la oportunidad para viajar un poco más lejos. Cogí un tren y un ferry para ir a Cuba, donde pasé unos días alucinantes. Me pareció un lugar limpio y optimista y la gente era muy acogedora. Me encantaron, sobre todo, los coches antiguos, que son muy populares allí.

Si no has estado nunca en México, es muy difícil imaginar el clima que tienen. Es lo que se llama clima cálido y subhúmedo — lo que quiere decir que hace mucho calor — con temperaturas que oscilan de 22°C a 26°C, a pesar de una humedad constante, y llueve mucho. Así que, siempre tienes un calor impresionante y resulta bastante incómodo hasta que te acostumbras.

Fue una experiencia maravillosa que no olvidaré nunca.

Ejemplo: **VERDADERO**   **FALSO**

Ramón habla de su visita a Cancún. [ ] [X]
Ramón habla de su visita a Mérida.

1 La cultura maya fue algo completamente nuevo paro él. [ ] [ ]

2 El transporte en Mérida es bueno. [ ] [ ]

3 Descubrió que los cubanos eran muy antipáticos. [ ] [ ]

4 El clima de esa parte de México es templado. [ ] [ ]

5 Le impresionó la fiesta que vio. [ ] [ ]

[Total: 8]

Tips for success

- In true/false questions it is essential to read the text with great care, since your answers depend on your precise understanding of the gist and detail of the passage.
- The false statements often contradict a statement made or implied in the text. When explaining why a statement is false, you may have to manipulate the language rather than reproduce the text verbatim.

Paper 3: speaking

The text below is an example of a good presentation about a holiday. It is based around a picture prompt.

Follow the text as you listen to the recording. Notice how and when the interviewer steps in to ask extra relevant questions. The transcript is annotated to show errors that you should try to avoid.

Accurate use of complex structure.

Careful with the preterite tense of *ser.* What should it be?

Check verbs. This should be *sentarse.* Do you know what *sentirse* means?

Clear demonstration of ability to move from one verb tense to another with ease (from present *está* to past *pasó*).

Effective use of past tense.   This should be *estupendas.*

El año pasado **pasé** unas vacaciones **estupendos** en el Caribe. Pero **antes de poder llegar allí**, tuvimos que pasar veinticuatro horas en el aeropuerto porque **hubo** huelga de pilotos. **Fui** incomodísimo porque no había ningún sitio donde **sentirse** y tuve que dormir en el suelo. Mi madre **está muy mal de la espalda**, así que pasó la noche con mi padre en un hotel cerca del aeropuerto y mis hermanos y yo nos quedamos allí en el suelo. Nos trataron bien porque nos dieron comida, y bebida, y más tarde **pagaron una compensación mis padres**. Pero fue un gran desilusión y una mal comienzo para unas vacaciones de ensueño. Fui a Jamaica con mi familia y con amigos nuestros. Después de ese problema, todo fue bien. Una vez allí, nos alojamos en un hotel de lujo en la playa con media pensión.

Effective use of past tense.

Don't forget the personal a. This should read: *pagaron una compensación a mis padres.*

¿Y qué tiempo hace en Jamaica?

¡Pues siempre hace sol! **A pesar de** ser octubre, no hacía demasiado calor, lo que **quería decir** que **podía** bañarme en el mar todos los días.

Good use of connectives.

Good use of imperfect tense.

¿Y qué más pueden hacer los turistas allí?

Se pueden hacer, por ejemplo, muchos deportes. Cada tarde jugábamos todos al voleibol en la playa. Me puse morena y muy en forma.

¿Y dónde comiste cuando no lo hiciste en el hotel?

Había muchos sitios diferentes donde cenar, pero el que más me gustó fue un restaurante en el puerto donde se come pescado fresco que se compra a los barcos pesqueros. Se llama Sami's.

This student missed the opportunity to show off a future tense. The teacher sets this up with the question about the future.

¿Crees que volverás?

Sí. **Nos reímos mucho y fueron mis mejores vacaciones. Tengo muchas ganas de volver** allí otra vez algún día.

Practise with a partner. How would *you* answer each of the interviewer's questions? What would you include in a presentation about your holidays?

Now look at this photo. What could you say about it? Prepare a short presentation. Work with a partner to prepare then present this topic.

Paper 4: writing

Here you have to write a response of 130–140 words in Spanish. You should prepare for different purposes and contexts, real or imaginary subjects and be able to express and justify ideas and points of view.

Vas a ir a una fiesta. Escribe una carta a tu amigo/a. Menciona:

(a) cuándo y dónde es la fiesta

(c) el tipo de fiesta que prefieres

(b) con quién vas a ir y por qué

(d) lo que hiciste la última vez que fuiste a una fiesta.

Debes escribir 130–140 palabras **en español.**

Read the following answer, taking note of the good points of language and the places highlighted where you can develop ideas so as to fulfil the required number of words.

Sample student answer

You could give details about the timing.	¡Hola Marta! ¿Vas a ir a la fiesta de Loli la semana que viene?
	Voy a ir con mi hermano, porque tiene coche y es más seguro.
You could mention who is invited.	Va a ser el martes doce de enero y va a celebrarlo en el restaurante Rumba que está en el centro. ¿Lo conoces?
	Voy a decirles a todos los invitados que vayan vestidos de gala y ya he comprado mi traje en las rebajas. Es un vestido largo,
You could give more detail on how you expect people to dress.	de seda verde, y es precioso.
Accurate use of the subjunctive.	Espero que sea tan divertida como el año pasado, que terminamos en casa de Jorge. ¡Nos lo pasamos fenomenal!
Accurate use of imperative.	Llámame y hablamos a ver qué te parece.
	Besos,
	Cristina

Good use of future tense here.

Good use of the present with reference to the future.

Accurate use of the subjunctive.

Good use of description.

Accurate use of preterite tense.

Note the accurate use of a variety of tenses in this sample answer, which ensures higher marks for this type of question.

Ahora escribe tu carta. Intenta cambiar los detalles lo máximo posible.

Vocabulario

Transport
el **autobús** bus
el **autocar** coach
el **avión** plane
el **barco** boat
la **bicicleta** bicycle
el **coche** car
el **metro** underground/tube
la **moto** motorbike
a **pie** on foot
el **taxi** taxi
el **tren** train

Adjectives
barato/a cheap
caro/a expensive
cómodo/a comfortable
fácil easy
incómodo/a uncomfortable
lento/a slow
limpio/a clean
peligroso/a dangerous
práctico/a practical
próximo/a next
rápido/a fast
sucio/a dirty
último/a last

Travelling
el **andén** platform
los **aseos** toilets
el **billete** ticket
la **cafetería** café
el **cambio** bureau de change
(el billete) de ida y vuelta return (ticket)
el **equipaje** luggage
la **maleta** suitcase
objetos perdidos lost property
la **puerta de embarque** departure gate
el **puerto** port, harbour
la **reserva** reservation
la **sala de espera** waiting room
la **salida** exit
(el billete) sencillo single (ticket)
el **viaje** journey, trip
el **vuelo** flight

Countries
Alemania Germany
Argentina Argentina
Austria Austria
Bélgica Belgium
Brasil Brazil
Canadá Canada
Chile Chile

Chipre Cyprus
Colombia Colombia
Dinamarca Denmark
España Spain
los **Estados Unidos** United States
Francia France
Gales Wales
Grecia Greece
Hungría Hungary
Inglaterra England
Irlanda Ireland
Islandia Iceland
Italia Italy
Luxemburgo Luxembourg
Marruecos Morocco
Méjico, México Mexico
Nueva Zelanda New Zealand
(los) Países Bajos the Netherlands
Perú Peru
Polonia Poland
(el) Reino Unido United Kingdom
Sudáfrica South Africa
Suecia Sweden
Suiza Switzerland
Venezuela Venezuela

Places to stay
el **albergue juvenil** youth hostel
el **apartamento** apartment
el **camping** campsite
el **campo** countryside
la **casa** house
el **chalet** bungalow, house, cottage
la **costa** coast
el **hotel** hotel
las **montañas** mountains
el **parador** (Sp) state-run hotel
el **piso** flat

Accommodation
el **aparcamiento** car park
el **ascensor** lift
el **balcón** balcony
la **cama** bed
la **caravana** caravan
la **discoteca** disco
la **ducha** shower
(la) media pensión half board
(la) pensión completa full board
la **piscina** swimming pool
la **recepción** reception
el **sitio** place; pitch; space
la **terraza** terrace; balcony
la **tienda** shop
vistas al mar sea views

Weather
el **clima** climate
Está lloviendo. It's raining.
Está nevando. It's snowing.
Está nublado. It's cloudy.
Hace buen tiempo. The weather is good.
Hace calor. It's hot.
Hace frío. It's cold.
Hace mal tiempo. The weather is bad.
Hace sol. It's sunny.
Hace viento. It's windy.
Hay hielo. It's icy.
Hay niebla. It's foggy.
Hay relámpagos. There's lightning.
Hay tormenta. There's a storm.
Llueve. It is raining.
Nieva. It is snowing.
el **pronóstico** weather forecast
el **tiempo** weather

Seasons and months
las **estaciones** seasons
la **primavera** spring
el **verano** summer
el **otoño** autumn
el **invierno** winter
el **mes** month
enero January
febrero February
marzo March
abril April
mayo May
junio June
julio July
agosto August
septiembre September
octubre October
noviembre November
diciembre December

Festivals and celebrations
el **Año Nuevo** New Year
bailar to dance
la **batalla** battle
beber to drink
el **belén** crib
la **boda** wedding
brindar to drink a toast
cantar to sing
celebrar to celebrate
el **champán** champagne
comer to eat
la **corrida de toros** bullfight
el **cumpleaños** birthday
el **Día de la Madre** Mother's Day

el **disfraz**   disguise, costume
los **dulces**   sweets
la **feria**   festival, fair
la **fiesta**   party, (public) holiday
el **flamenco**   type of dance
los **fuegos artificiales**   fireworks
la **hoguera**   bonfire
la **iglesia**   church
la **imagen**   image; picture; photo
la **misa**   mass
montar a caballo   to ride a horse
la **Navidad**   Christmas
la **Nochebuena**   Christmas Eve
la **Pascua**   Easter
el **pavo**   turkey
la **procesión**   procession
el **regalo**   present
religioso/a   religious
los **Reyes Magos**   Three Kings, Magi
San Valentín   Valentine's day

la **Semana Santa**   Holy Week
la **tarjeta**   card
la **tradición**   tradition
el **turrón**   nougat (Sp)
la **verbena**   festival
el **villancico**   carol

Holiday activities

bañarse en el mar   to swim in the sea
comprar recuerdos   to buy souvenirs
descansar   to relax
hacer surf   to go surfing
ir de compras   to go shopping
dar un paseo   to go for a walk
montar en bici   to go for a bike ride
practicar deporte   to do sports
sacar fotos   to take photos
salir a cenar   to go out to eat
tomar el sol   to sunbathe
visitar lugares de interés   to visit places of interest

Places of interest

la **agencia de viajes**   travel agency
el **banco**   bank
el **bar**   bar
la **bodega**   wine cellar; winery
el **castillo**   castle
la **catedral**   cathedral
Correos   post office
el **jardín**   garden
el **mercado**   market
el **museo**   museum
el **museo de arte**   art gallery
la **oficina de turismo**   tourist office
el **palacio**   palace
el **parque de atracciones**   amusement park
la **playa**   beach
la **plaza**   square
el **río**   river
el **teatro**   theatre
el **zoo**   zoo

Así es mi vida

1 Una vida sana

2 De compras

3 ¡A comer fuera!

4 ¡Vivir a tope!

☑ Learn the parts of the body

☑ Discuss health, healthy eating and exercise

☑ Use informal and formal imperatives

☑ Use impersonal verbs

☑ Use the pluperfect tense

1 Una vida sana

1a 📖 ✏️ ¿Qué sabes ya? Descifra las palabras y emparéjalas con la imagen adecuada.

Ejemplo: **a** — *la cabeza*

al bazeca
sol ídsoo
al zíran
al cabo
le razob
al ripnea
le ipe
al noam
le locule
le bromho
al drollia
al palesad
le joo
le masetógo

b 🎧 En el gimnasio. Apunta las partes del cuerpo en el orden en que las oyes. Usa el vocabulario del ejercicio arriba.

c 🏃 💬 Inventa tu propia rutina de ejercicio. Pruébalo con tu pareja.

GRAMÁTICA

The imperative

To give someone an instruction or to tell him or her what to do we use the imperative. There are two forms for the informal imperative, singular (*tú*) and plural (*vosotros*).

Look at the box below

	-ar	-er	-ir
tú	*habla*	*come*	*escribe*
vosotros	*hablad*	*comed*	*escribid*

A few imperatives are irregular in the *tú* form:

decir	*di* (say)
salir	*sal* (go out)
hacer	*haz* (do/make)
ser	*sé* (be)
ir	*ve* (go)
tener	*ten* (have)
poner	*pon* (put)
venir	*ven* (come)

Fill the gaps with the correct form of the verb in brackets.

1 _____ hondo. (*respirar, tú*)

2 _____ las manos. (*levantar, vosotros*)

3 _____ las piernas. (*estirar, tú*)

4 _____ unos ejercicios de calentamiento. (*hacer, tú*)

5 _____ las piernas. (*doblar, vosotros*)

6 _____ los ojos. (*abrir, tú*)

7 _____ cuidado cuando haces ejercicios. (*tener, tú*)

8 _____ conmigo al gimnasio. (*venir, tú*)

9 _____ las manos. (*levantar, tú*)

10 _____ hacia el suelo. (*agacharse, tú*)

2 Lee este artículo y apunta verdadera (V) o falsa (F) para cada una de las frases abajo. Si son falsas, escribe una frase en español para corregirlas.

¿Qué tipo de ejercicio debería ser parte de mi rutina diaria?

Mantenerse sano requiere una rutina adecuada de actividad física. El ejercicio aeróbico es un buen ejemplo. Aumenta el pulso, trabaja los músculos, y altera la respiración. Para la mayoría de la gente es mejor intentar hacer 30 minutos diarios por lo menos 4 veces a la semana. Si llevas bastante tiempo sin hacer ejercicio, puedes empezar con 5 o 10 minutos al día y aumentarlo poco a poco. Por ejemplo, se puede comenzar con un paseo de 10 minutos después de cada comida. Otro beneficio del ejercicio es que ayuda a controlar el peso. Unos ejemplos de ejercicio aeróbico son:

- dar un paseo rápido cada día dentro, en una máquina de correr, o al aire libre
- bailar
- hacer una clase de aerobic
- nadar
- patinar o hacer patinaje sobre ruedas
- jugar al tenis
- montar en bicicleta

Además, hay muchas posibilidades cada día para ser más activo. Si te mueves mucho gastarás muchas calorías! Cuanto más te mueves, más calorías gastas. Lo siguiente puede ayudarte a aumentar tu actividad:

- Cuando tengas la oportunidad, anda en vez de coger el autobús o pedir que te lleven tus padres en coche.
- Sube por las escaleras en vez de usar el ascensor.
- Trabaja en el jardín o haz algo de limpieza en casa cada día.
- Baja del autobús una parada antes del colegio y anda desde allí.

1 Hace falta hacer ejercicio para mantenerse en forma.
2 El ejercicio aeróbico es bueno para el corazón.
3 Hay que hacer 30 minutos de ejercicio cada día.
4 Hay que descansar después de comer.
5 Para los paseos rápidos las máquinas de correr son mejores.
6 El ejercicio aumenta la energía.
7 Cuando vas al colegio, siempre es preferible tomar el autobús.
8 Hacer tareas de casa es buen ejercicio.

3 ¿Cómo puedes llevar una vida sana? Escucha la grabación y contesta las preguntas.

1 ¿Qué quiere decir el mágico número 5?
2 ¿Cuántas horas de sueño recomienda la Señora Fernández?
3 ¿Qué hay que evitar por la noche? Menciona dos cosas.
4 ¿Qué más hay que evitar? Menciona 3 cosas.
5 Según la Señora Fernández, ¿qué se debe hacer para llevar una vida sana basada en el sentido común? Menciona 3 cosas.

4a 🗣️ Haz una entrevista con tu pareja. Utiliza el cuadro de abajo para ayudarte.

Ejemplo: **A:** *¿Qué haces para estar en forma?*
B: *Duermo ocho horas cada noche y bebo mucha agua.*
A: *¿Qué actividades me aconsejarías para estar en forma?*
B: *Haz deportes y evita el estrés.*
A: *¿Qué hay que hacer para llevar una vida sana?*
B: *Hace falta relajarse durante el día y no se debe fumar o tomar alcohol.*

¿Qué haces para estar en forma?	Duermo/Como/Bebo/Evito/Hago...
¿Qué actividades me aconsejarías para estar en forma?	Duerme/Come/Bebe/Evita/Haz...
¿Qué hay que hacer para llevar una vida sana? ¿Qué actividades sanas hiciste la semana pasada?	Hay que descansar/dormir... Hace falta comer/acostarse... No se debe fumar/tomar drogas/estresarse. Jugué al fútbol y fui de paseo con mi familia.

b ✏️ Escribe un párrafo contestando a las preguntas.

5 📖 ¿Qué te pasa? Empareja las imágenes con las frases.

Ejemplo: **1 — d**

1. Me duele la garganta.
2. Me duele el oído.
3. Tengo el brazo roto.
4. Tengo una insolación.
5. Tengo un resfriado.
6. Me duele la espalda.
7. Tengo tos.
8. Tengo una picadura.
9. Estoy mareado.
10. Me duele el estómago.
11. Tengo una quemadura.
12. Tengo dolor de cabeza.
13. Tengo fiebre.
14. Tengo el tobillo torcido.
15. Tengo dolor de muelas.

Paper 4: writing

Here is an example of a longer writing task, which requires you to know some set phrases for writing a formal letter. See if you can tackle it. You need to write between 130 and 140 words.

Buscas empleo en un hotel para este verano. Escribe una carta al director para solicitar trabajo.

Menciona:

(a) el trabajo que buscas y por qué

(b) tu experiencia laboral en este tipo de trabajo

(c) lo que quieres saber sobre el trabajo: por ejemplo horario, responsabilidades.

Debes escribir 130–140 palabras en español.

Points to remember

- Remember to cover each of the three points more or less equally. This will give you the best chance of covering all of the points raised.
- As this task is a letter, make sure it is set out appropriately, as in the example below. Beware of making the kind of errors that are explained in some of the marginal comments.

Sample student answer

Sevilla, **6 de junio de 2013** — Always include the date, in the appropriate format.

Muy señor mío: — Decide whether your letter is formal or informal. Informal letters and some formal ones start with *Querido…*

Me dirijo a usted **por** pedirle información sobre las posibilidades de hacer mi prácticas de trabajo en su tienda. — *Por* and *para* are easy to confuse. This should be *para*. Check you understand when to use which one.

Entiendo que ha ayudado antes a otros **alumnos** de mi colegio, San Agustín de la Vega. — Take care to check and correct spelling (*alumnos*).

Estoy muy interesada en trabajar en su empresa y le mando adjunta información sobre mi experiencia laboral. — Agreement needed here, so 'my' needs to be plural: *mis*.

Le saluda atentamente, — This is an appropriate ending for a formal letter. How might you finish a letter to a friend? Discuss.

Sofía Marcos

Sofía Marcos — Good use of reference to accompanying paperwork/information.

Now write your answer to the question as asked.

Points to remember

Follow this recipe for success.

- Start with a general greeting. You can begin a formal letter with *Muy señor/a mío/a:…* or *Estimado/a señor/a:…*
- Set the context – for example, *acabo de terminar mis exámenes.*
- For part (a) you must refer to the type of job you would like to do: *Me gustaría…* Make sure you remember to say why.
- Link parts (a) and (b) together. Your work experience must be linked to the job you would like to do.
- Use part (c) as your conclusion. Remember to ask questions as well. For example, ask about dates, salary and working conditions.
- End the letter with the appropriate formal ending as given in the example text.

Vocabulario

School subjects

las actividades extra-escolares	extra-curricular activities
el alemán	German
la biología	biology
las ciencias	science
las ciencias naturales	natural sciences
la danza	dance
los deportes	sports
el dibujo	art
el diseño	design
la educación cívica	PHSE
la educación física	PE
el español	Spanish
la física	physics
el francés	French
la geografía	geography
la historia	history
la informática	ICT
el inglés	English
el italiano	Italian
el latín	Latin
la literatura	literature
las matemáticas	maths
la química	chemistry
la religión	RE
el teatro	drama
la tecnología	technology

School timetables

las asignaturas	subjects
el castigo	detention
la clase	class; lesson
los deberes	homework
los días	days
la hora	time; hour
la hora de comer	lunch time
el horario	timetable
el recreo	break
el trimestre	term
las vacaciones	holidays
el lunes	Monday
el martes	Tuesday
el miércoles	Wednesday
el jueves	Thursday
el viernes	Friday
el sábado	Saturday
el domingo	Sunday

School uniform

el abrigo	coat
la blusa	blouse
las botas	boots
la bufanda	scarf
los calcetines	socks
la camisa	shirt
la camiseta	T-shirt
el chándal	tracksuit
la chaqueta	jacket
el cinturón	belt
la corbata	tie
la falda	skirt
la gorra	cap
los guantes	gloves
las medias	tights
los pantalones	trousers
los pantalones cortos	shorts
la sudadera	sweatshirt
el suéter	jumper
el traje de entrenamiento	tracksuit
los vaqueros	jeans
el vestido	dress
las zapatillas de deporte	trainers
los zapatos	shoes
amarillo/a	yellow
azul	blue
blanco/a	white
gris	grey
marrón	brown
morado/a	purple
naranja	orange
negro/a	black
rojo/a	red
rosa	pink
verde	green

School equipment

la agenda	diary
el bolígrafo	biro, ballpoint pen
la calculadora	calculator
la carpeta	folder
el compás	compass
la computadora (LA)	computer
el cuaderno	exercise book
el diccionario	dictionary
el estuche	pencil case
la goma	rubber
la grapadora	stapler
el lapicero	pencil
el lápiz	pencil
el lápiz de color	coloured pencil
el libro	book
el maletín (Sp)	briefcase
la mesa	table
la mochila	backpack
el ordenador (Sp)	computer
el papel	paper
el pegamento	glue
la pluma	fountain pen
el portafolio (LA)	briefcase
la regla	ruler
el rotulador	felt-tip pen; marker pen

Schools and buildings

la silla	chair
las tijeras	scissors
el/la alumno/a	pupil
el aula (f)	classroom
la biblioteca	library
el campo de deportes	sports field
el comedor	dining room; canteen
el/la director/a	headteacher
el edificio	building
la entrada	entrance
la escalera	staircase, stairs
el/la estudiante	student
el gimnasio	gymnasium
el guardarropa	cloakroom
el laboratorio	laboratory
los lavabos	toilets
la oficina	office
el pasillo	corridor
el patio	playground
el portero	caretaker
el/la profesor/a, el/la profe	teacher
la sala de profesores	staff room
la secretaría	secretary
el taller	workshop
el teatro	theatre
el vestíbulo	hall

School types and qualifications

aprender	to learn
aprobar un examen	to pass an exam
el colegio, el cole (coll.)	school
el colegio de primaria	primary school
el colegio de secundaria	secondary school
el curso	course; school year
la escuela	primary school
estudiar	to study
el instituto	high school
la licenciatura	degree
el rendimiento escolar	school performance
repasar	to revise
suspender un examen	to fail an exam
la universidad	university

Workplaces and activities

archivar	to file
barrer el suelo	to sweep the floor
coger recados	to take messages
contestar el teléfono	to answer the phone
escribir	to write
escribir correos electrónicos	to send e-mails
hablar con clientes	to talk to clients
hacer el café	to make the coffee

6a 🎧 📝 En la farmacia. Escucha el diálogo. Luego completa la tabla con los detalles que faltan.

	Problema	Remedio	Precio
Ejemplo:	*dolor de cabeza*	*aspirinas*	*6 euros*
1			

b 💬 Trabaja con tu pareja. Adapta el diálogo de abajo para practicar comprando medicamentos en una farmacia.

Ejemplo: **A:** *Buenos días.*
　　　　B: *Buenos días. ¿Qué le pasa?*
　　　　A: *No me siento bien. Me duelen la garganta y la cabeza.*
　　　　B: *Le recomiendo estos comprimidos y estas pastillas. ¿Qué tamaño quiere?*
　　　　A: *Grande por favor. ¿Cuánto le debo?*
　　　　B: *Son … euros.*
　　　　A: *Aquí tiene. Gracias. Adiós.*

7 📖 Lee el artículo siguiente. Pon títulos para los contenidos como en el ejemplo.

GRAMÁTICA

Impersonal verbs

To talk about ailments and symptoms in Spanish, the verb *doler* is very important.

Me duele(n) + body part
Te duele(n)
Le duele(n)
Nos duele(n)
Os duele(n)
Les duele(n)

Look at the examples below:

Me duele la cabeza.	My head hurts.
Me duelen los dedos.	My fingers hurt.
Me duele la garganta.	My throat hurts.
Me duelen las piernas.	My legs hurt.

Doler as an impersonal verb is similar to the verb *gustar*. See page 34.

Alternatively, *tengo dolor de* + body part can be used:
Tengo dolor de cabeza.
Tengo dolor de dedos.
Tengo dolor de garganta.
Tengo dolor de piernas.

Note that the article is not necessary here.

Guía para exploradores

Botiquines

Un botiquín bien provisto de cosas para primeros auxilios es imprescindible. Elige una caja resistente y suficientemente grande para tener el contenido visible y accesible sin tener que sacar todo a la hora de usarlo. Guarda una lista del contenido y manténlo en un sitio apropiado.

Sugerencias para el contenido del botiquín:

- jabón
- vendas
- tiritas
- termómetro
- tijeras
- pinzas
- crema de sol
- linterna
- algodón hidrófilo
- agua esterilizada
- imperdibles
- crema antiséptica

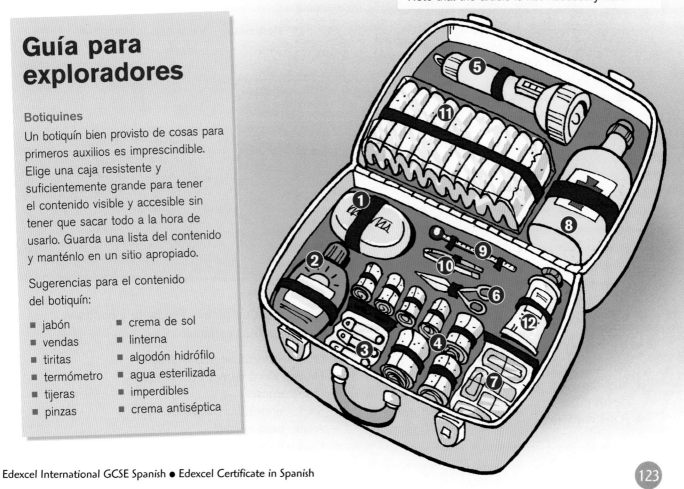

8 🎧 📖 Escucha la grabación, lee este artículo y contesta las preguntas.

La comida sana

¿Sabías que la mayoría de las personas deberíamos comer más?

Una dieta bien equilibrada puede ayudar a mantener un peso corporal sano, mejorar el bienestar general y reducir el riesgo de enfermedades serias. Sigue estas simples reglas para asegurarte de la mejor rutina alimenticia posible.

Primero y lo más importante es elegir una variedad de estos cuatro grupos de alimentos cada día:

1 pan, otros cereales y patatas
2 fruta y verduras
3 leche y productos lácteos
4 carne y pescado
5 aceite, mantequilla, azúcar

Las comidas del quinto grupo que contienen grasa y azúcar pueden formar parte de tu régimen, pero solo si no sustituyen alimentos de los otros grupos. Tampoco es bueno comerlas en cantidades grandes o muy a menudo. Aprovechar de una amplia variedad de alimentos en tu dieta es importante para la salud. Por último, sigue los siguientes consejos adicionales:

- Disfruta de lo que comes.
- Come una dieta variada.
- Bebe mucha agua.
- Come lo suficiente para mantener un peso sano.
- Come muchos alimentos ricos en carbohidratos y fibra.
- Come mucha fruta y verdura.
- No comas demasiados alimentos con mucha grasa.
- No comas demasiados alimentos abundantes en azúcar.

1 ¿Cuáles son las ventajas de mantener una dieta sana? Menciona dos cosas.
2 ¿Qué comida no es bueno comer en cantidades grandes?
3 Menciona **un** tipo de comida de cada uno de los cinco grupos.
4 ¿Qué consejo se da acerca del agua?

9 📖 ✏️ Completa esta tabla añadiendo las palabras adecuadas del recuadro. ¿Cuántas palabras puedes añadir a la lista? Usa un diccionario para ayudarte.

Pan y cereales	Vitaminas y fibras	Productos lácteos	Carne y pescado	Azúcar y grasas
pan	naranjas	leche	pollo	mantequilla

zanahorias queso pasta aceite yogur
mermelada atún huevos nata arroz
manzanas jamón patatas zumo de frutas

10 💬 Trabaja con tu pareja. Habla de las comidas que tomaste ayer. Decide si eran sanas o no.

Ejemplo: **A:** *Ayer comí pizza con patatas y bebí agua.*
B: *Eso no es sano. Debes tomar ensalada.*

11a 🎧 📖 Escucha a Ana y Carlos. ¿Qué comen y beben? Copia la tabla y complétala con la información correcta, utilizando las palabras del recuadro.

	Desayuno	Almuerzo	Merienda	Cena
Ana	cereales	ensalada		
Carlos	leche		yogur	carne

zumo de frutas mantequilla chocolate pan galletas
ensalada cereales café tostada
mermelada arroz fruta
helado atún carne tortilla leche
sopa pizza yogur pollo
carne tarta manzana pescado agua mineral

b 💬 Trabaja en pareja. Pregunta y contesta las siguientes preguntas.

- ¿Qué desayunaste esta mañana?
- ¿Dónde vas a comer esta noche?
- ¿Qué comes?
- ¿Sueles merendar durante el día?
- ¿A qué hora cenas?
- ¿Qué sueles comer y beber para la cena?

12a 🎧 Escucha lo que dicen estas personas. Luego completa la tabla.

	Desayuno	Mediodía	Tarde	Otra información
Elena				
Ramón				
Conchi				

b 🖊 Escribe un párrafo sobre lo que comes y bebes y lo que haces para mantener la salud.

Ejemplo: *Suelo desayunar cereales con leche cada mañana. Intento no beber café o té porque no son buenos para la salud…*

13a 📖 Lee este correo electrónico de Laura. Busca los cuatro ejemplos del pluscuamperfecto del verbo.

> Hace dos años tenía un gran problema de sobrepeso. No podía hacer nada para adelgazar: mi familia había intentado ayudarme; yo había pedido consejos de mis amigos y del médico. Finalmente me había dado por vencido. Estaba convencido de que no iba nunca a recuperarme.
>
> Entonces me puse en contacto con una consejera por Internet, quien me explicó que mi problema podría resolverse con una dieta más sana y con hacer más ejercicio físico. Así comencé a comer más verduras y fruta, y a dar un paseo por lo menos una vez al día. Tampoco suelo sentarme muchas horas frente a la tele, como había hecho antes. Ahora he bajado de peso a un nivel saludable y llevo una vida mucho más sana. ¡Aun he comenzado a practicar yoga!
>
> Laura

GRAMÁTICA

The pluperfect tense

This tense is used to describe actions which took place before another action in the past, e.g. 'I had eaten my breakfast before they arrived'. The pluperfect is formed from the imperfect tense of *haber* plus the past participle.

Formation of the pluperfect tense in regular verbs:

hablar	comer	vivir
había hablado	había comido	había vivido
habías hablado	habías comido	habías vivido
había hablado	había comido	había vivido
habíamos hablado	habíamos comido	habíamos vivido
habíais hablado	habíais comido	habíais vivido
habían hablado	habían comido	habían vivido

*Mi madre estaba contenta conmigo, porque **había hecho** mis deberes.*
My mother was pleased with me because I had done my homework

*Cuando llegamos, ya **habían preparado** la cena.*
When we arrived, they had already prepared the meal.

b Contesta las preguntas siguientes.
  1 ¿Por qué Laura se había dado por vencido?
  2 Qué consejo se le ofreció por Internet?
  3 ¿Qué había hecho ella para bajar de peso? Menciona 4 cosas.

14 📖 Descifra estas palabras y emparéjalas con la imagen adecuada. Usa un diccionario para ayudarte.

Ejemplo: **a** — *mantel*

talpolil   cochulil   naltem
llivtersea   zaat   lapot
osva
rachacu   raraj   netoder
y las neitimpa
topal donoh

15 📖 Lee este artículo. Pon una X en las casillas con las cuatro frases correctas en la tabla abajo.

Querido Doctor David,

¿Me pregunto si es grosero comer con los codos en la mesa? Tengo dos hijos, de 9 y 10 años, que me miran con cara de alucine cuando les digo que eso no se hace. Le agradecería cualquier consejo sobre las buenas maneras en la mesa que pudiera ofrecerme. Quiero que mis hijos crezcan bien educados.

¡Espero que pueda ayudarme!
Una madre preocupada
Málaga

Querida preocupada,

En comidas informales es aceptable tener los codos encima de la mesa. Pero solo si no estás comiendo. Mientras comes, hay que evitarlo.

Sería aconsejable decirles a tus hijos que las normas de la mesa no solo tratan de comer educadamente, sino que también son consideración hacia los demás. Diles que aunque tú sabes que son majos y bien educados, los demás también les juzgarán.

Ser bien educado en la mesa da una buena impresión a los demás. Tus hijos no querrán ser maleducados. ¿Verdad?

No importa si estás en casa o en un restaurante, aquí hay diez normas básicas para tus hijos:

1 Come con cuchillo y tenedor a no ser que sea comida en plan estilo *buffet*. ¡Solo los bebés comen con sus dedos!

2 No te llenes la boca demasiado – queda horrible y no es sano.

3 Mastica siempre con la boca cerrada. Nadie quiere verte la comida. Eso quiere decir que no se debe hablar con comida en la boca.

4 No digas cosas despectivas sobre la comida que te sirvan. Eso ofende mucho.

5 Siempre di 'gracias' cuando alguien te sirve. Es cortesía básica y demuestra que aprecias al chef o al anfitrión.

6 No empieces hasta que todos tengan la comida servida en sus platos.

7 Come despacio. Alguien habrá pasado bastante tiempo preparando la comida, así que es apropiado disfrutarlo como es debido. Eso quiere decir que debes esperar por lo menos 5 segundos después de tragar antes de meter más comida en la boca.

8 No te asomes para coger algo por delante de otra persona – pide que te lo pasen.

9 Siempre usa una servilleta para limpiarte la boca o las manos. Mantén la servilleta en tus rodillas cuando no la estás usando.

10 Siempre recuerda dar las gracias al cocinero y decirle lo delicioso que es la comida – ¡incluso si no te gustó!

Ejemplo:	*Normalmente hay que usar cuchillo y tenedor.*	**X**
1	No se debe mantener la boca cerrada.	
2	¡Habla y canta con la boca llena!	
3	Solo di cosas positivas sobre la comida servida.	
4	A veces hay que dar las gracias.	
5	Es de buena educación esperar a los demás.	
6	No hay que darse prisa comiendo.	
7	Las servilletas no sirven para nada.	
8	Hay que echar piropos al cocinero.	
9	Hay que pelear para conseguir la comida.	

2 De compras

☑ **Talk about shops and places of business**
☑ **Learn quantities, sizes and shapes**
☑ **Discuss eating out**
☑ **Use ordinal numbers**

1a 🎧 ¿Cómo es donde vives? Pon las imágenes en el orden en que oyes los lugares.

Ejemplo: **1** — *c*

b 📖 Empareja las palabras con las imágenes.

Ejemplo: **a** — *la carnicería*

el quiosco de periódicos
la farmacia
Correos
la carnicería
el estanco
los grandes almacenes
la panadería
el supermercado
el mercado
la frutería
la librería
la pescadería
la tienda de ropa
el banco
la floristería

2a 🎧 Escucha la grabación. Escribe el nombre de la persona que corresponda con las frases abajo.

Ejemplo: *Vive en una ciudad turística.* — *Alina*

1 Dice que las compras son más baratas en su barrio.
2 No compra comida en su barrio.
3 Le entusiasma el ambiente de donde compra.
4 De vez en cuando va de compras a la ciudad — pero no sola.
5 Compra por Internet.
6 Le gusta leer.

b 💬 Trabaja con tu pareja. Pregunta y contesta las preguntas siguientes.

• ¿Te gusta ir de compras?
• ¿Qué tiendas hay en tu barrio?
• ¿Adónde vas normalmente para comprar?
• ¿Por qué?

c Escribe un correo electrónico a tu amigo/a para decirle lo que hiciste la última vez que fuiste de compras a la ciudad (120–130 palabras).

- ¿A qué tiendas fuiste?
- ¿Qué compraste?
- ¿Te gustó el día? ¿Por qué (no)?

3a Lee este correo electrónico y haz una lista de las tiendas del barrio de Sergio. Luego, escribe una frase para describir cada tienda.

Ejemplo: La panadería abre temprano.

¡Hola!

Me has pedido información sobre las tiendas de mi barrio. Sé que es muy diferente en Inglaterra y que no tenéis muchas tiendas pequeñas. Pero aquí en España todavía hay muchos locales pequeños – sobre todo en los barrios de las afueras y en los pueblos.

La gente no suele ir lejos para comprar, a pesar del sistema de transporte público maravilloso. Por ejemplo, tenemos una panadería donde compramos pan. Nos conviene porque abre temprano cada mañana, así que tenemos pan recién hecho cada día para desayunar.

La mayoría de la gente hace la compra en los supermercados porque es práctico y ahorra mucho tiempo, lo que supongo es una verdadera ventaja. Tenemos mercadillo los miércoles y sábados donde compramos fruta y verduras frescas. También hay hipermercados que normalmente se ubican en las afueras de las ciudades.

En todos los barrios suele haber una farmacia y a veces también una librería. Por todas partes hay quioscos donde se compran bonos de lotería o quinielas.

Para tiendas buenas especializadas – como las de ropa o música – hay que ir a las ciudades. En pueblos turísticos normalmente hay también tiendas de recuerdos. Las tiendas suelen estar abiertas más horas que en tu país, aunque las tiendas pequeñas cierran a la hora de comer y de echar la siesta.

Si compras en el barrio normalmente resulta barato. Sin embargo, en las ciudades las cosas suelen ser más caras.

Bueno, espero que esto te ayude con tus estudios – y que estés bien.

Por favor, escríbeme pronto con noticias tuyas.

Un abrazo,
Sergio

b Escribe una respuesta a Sergio. Háblale de las tiendas que hay donde vives y de tus hábitos a la hora de hacer la compra. Dile qué has comprado recientemente.

En mi barrio hay…

Las tiendas españolas

¿Has visto que la mayoría de las tiendas terminan en *-ía*? Haz una lista de estas y otra lista de las que no terminan en *-ía*.

Aun hoy día, los comercios en España cierran, en general, entre las 2 y 5 de la tarde. Así, los tenderos en los pueblos y barrios pueden tomar la comida principal del día y, en muchos casos, echar la siesta. Los grandes almacenes, los hipermercados y los centros comerciales no cierran durante estas horas; muchos están abiertos de las 9 de la mañana a las 9 de la noche. Sin embargo, ¡en los días de fiesta, que son frecuentes en España, todos cierran!

¡OJO!

Intenta acordarte de estas frases útiles que tienen que ver con las compras.

echar un vistazo	to have a look
buscar una ganga	to look for a bargain
tres por el precio de uno	three for the price of one
de oferta	on offer
las rebajas	the sales
la caja	the checkout/pay point
los probadores	the changing rooms

¿Dónde se compra?

4a  ¿Dónde se encuentra cada cosa en la lista de compras?

Ejemplo: **1 — e**

Lista de compras

1 manzanas
2 leche
3 gambas
4 pasta de dientes
5 aceite
6 patatas fritas
7 mermelada
8 periódico
9 panecillos
10 limonada

Sección de congelados

Panadería

Pescadería

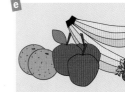
Quiosco

Frutería

Bebidas

Lácteos y huevos

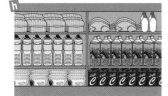
Sección de alimentación

Droguería

Ultramarinos

b ¿En qué tienda/puesto están? ¿Qué quieren comprar? ¿Cuánto gastan? Completa la tabla.

	Puesto	Artículo	Precio
Ejemplo:	*frutería*	*naranjas*	5,60€
1			

5 Completa la lista siguiente añadiendo una cantidad apropiada.

Ejemplo: una lata de sardinas

Lista de compras

sardinas   pasteles
tomates   azúcar
jamón   aceitunas
queso   zanahorias
vino   café
leche   pan

6 Trabaja con tu pareja. Practica comprando comida y bebida.

¿Qué desea?   ¿Algo más?   ¿Tiene…?   ¿Cuánto es?

Quisiera…   Déme…   Eso es todo.

LENGUA CLAVE

un kilo	a kilo
medio kilo	half a kilo
un cuarto kilo	quarter of a kilo
cien gramos	100 grams
quinientos gramos	500 grams
un litro	a litre
medio litro	half a litre
un vaso	a glass
una botella	a bottle
una lata	a tin
un paquete	a packet
un pedazo	a slice
un trozo	a piece
una bolsa	a bag
una caja	a box
una docena	a dozen
un cartón	a carton
un tubo	a tube
una barra	a loaf

7 📖 En los grandes almacenes. Mira el directorio de abajo. ¿En qué planta se compra cada artículo?

Ejemplo: **a — 1a**

Directorio

6ª	Cafetería, Agencia de viajes
5ª	Electrónica, sonido, informática
4ª	Deportes
3ª	Moda Él y Ella
2ª	Regalos de boda y juguetes
1ª	Papelería
PB	Complementos moda: cinturones, bolsos, zapatos
Sot	Supermercado

6a	Sexta planta
5a	Quinta planta
4a	Cuarta planta
3a	Tercera planta
2a	Segunda planta
1a	Primera planta
PB	Planta baja
Sot	Sótano

8 💬 Trabaja con tu pareja. Usa el directorio de arriba. ¿Adónde hay que ir para ver las cosas en las imágenes?

Necesito unos zapatos — *Hay que ir a la planta baja.*

una camiseta   un cinturón   un refresco   un CD

un bolígrafo   un balón de fútbol   unos tomates   una muñeca

130

GRAMÁTICA

Ordinal numbers

An ordinal number is an adjective that describes the numerical position of an object, for example first, second, third etc.

Below are the ordinal numbers, first to tenth:

primero	first	*sexto*	sixth
segundo	second	*séptimo*	seventh
tercero	third	*octavo*	eighth
cuarto	fourth	*noveno*	ninth
quinto	fifth	*décimo*	tenth

Like many other adjectives, the ordinal numbers have both a masculine and a feminine form, singular and plural. In other words, ordinal numbers have four forms, just like other adjectives that end in -o.

For example:
primero(s), primera(s)
segundo(s), segunda(s)
tercero(s), tercera(s)

When used before a noun, *primero* and *tercero* drop the -o in the masculine singular form:
el primer día, el tercer año.

Ordinal numbers usually precede the noun. However, if the noun they refer to is royalty, a pope or a street, they come after the noun:

Isabel II (segunda)	'segunda' comes after 'Isabel' (royalty)
Alejandro VI (sexto)	'sexto' comes after 'Alejandro' (pope)
la calle octava	'octava' comes after 'calle' (street)

Ordinal numbers are not normally used after 10:
el siglo veintiuno   the twenty-first century

1st, 2nd, 3rd, 4th and so on are normally indicated in Spanish as *1°, 2°, 3°, 4°*.

Escoge la forma correcta del número en cada frase.

1 Vivo en el tercer/tercero piso.
2 Hay que ir al primer/a la primera planta.
3 Julio es el quinto/la quinta hijo de mi vecina.
4 Hoy es el primer/el primero/la primer de julio.

9 Lee el artículo y contesta las preguntas.

De compras en Madrid y en Buenos Aires

A pesar de la gran cantidad de supermercados e hipermercados que hay ahora tanto, en Madrid como en Buenos Aires y otras partes del mundo hispanohablante, todavía existen algunas tiendas que pertenecen a empresas familiares. Como en otros países, los centros comerciales, que ahora son tan populares, tienden a estar en los alrededores de las ciudades.

La mayor diferencia entre ir de compras en estas dos ciudades es que Buenos Aires tiene muchas 'calles por rubros'. Básicamente son zonas de muchas tiendas individuales que venden cosas especializadas, como por ejemplo instrumentos de música o utensilios de cocina. Si te encuentras en una de esas calles, pasarás mucho tiempo encontrando el mismo tipo de cosas. Incluso hay centros comerciales donde muchas de las tiendas venden productos parecidos.

Horarios

En las dos capitales las tiendas suelen seguir horarios tradicionales y abren entre 08.30 y 09.30 (o más temprano si son tiendas de comida) y cierran de las 14.00 hasta las 17.00, y abren por la tarde hasta las 21.00. Este horario se debe a las temperaturas altas que hay durante los meses de verano y justifican la popular siesta. Antes, en un país católico las tiendas no abrían los domingos. Ahora, sin embargo, se puede hacer compras todo el fin de semana sin problema. ¡Los tiempos han cambiado mucho!

Muchos grandes almacenes y centros comerciales tienen horarios alargados — de 09.30 o 10.00 hasta las 20.00 o las 22.00 de lunes a sábado.

¿Qué comprar?

En Madrid y en Buenos Aires los productos hechos de cuero son muy populares entre los turistas — zapatos, bolsos, chaquetas y calzado. Los famosos zapatos castellanos son típicos de Madrid, mientras las alpargatas son muy populares en Buenos Aires. Se compra mucha música tradicional en los dos lugares, pero por supuesto lo típico en Madrid es el flamenco mientras en Buenos Aires es el tango. Otra compra popular es ropa y las dos capitales atraen mucho interés en las tiendas de sus diseñadores famosos — como Ágata Ruiz de la Prada y Adolfo Domínguez en España y Pablo Ramírez y Martín Churba en Argentina.

Mercados

El mercado sigue siendo una institución. Todavía hay un mercado cubierto en cada barrio, donde se encuentran puestos de todo tipo de comida y bebida. Suelen seguir el mismo horario que las demás tiendas de los barrios.

En ciertos lugares hay mercados tradicionales cada semana o varias veces al mes donde se pueden ver calles enteras de puestos variados. Un buen ejemplo de esto es el Rastro de Madrid o el Rastro de Pulgas en Buenos Aires, famosos también por la cantidad de puestos dedicados a artículos de segunda mano. Siempre se puede encontrar una ganga, pero como en todos los sitios ¡hay que tener cuidado con los posibles engaños y la seguridad personal! Como se suele decir, ¡no es oro todo lo que reluce!

1 ¿Dónde están ubicados los centros comerciales en estas dos ciudades?

2 ¿Qué tipo de mercancías venden en las 'calles por rubros'?

3 ¿Por qué cierran las tiendas entre las 14.00 y las 17.00?

4 Qué tipo de mercancía se vende típicamente en los Rastros?

10 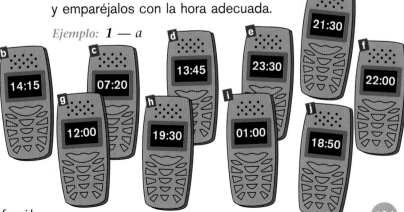 ¿A qué hora? Escucha los mensajes y emparéjalos con la hora adecuada.

Ejemplo: **1** — *a*

3 ¡A comer fuera!

1a 📖 Empareja las imágenes con las palabras adecuadas del menú. Usa un diccionario si hace falta.

Ejemplo: **b** — *fruta del tiempo*

Restaurante Casa Guanche
Menú del día

Primer plato
Sopa de fideos
Ensalada mixta con jamón
Cóctel de gambas

Segundo plato

Carne y aves
Chuletas de cordero
Pollo asado
Bistec en salsa de fruta

Pescados
Langostinos y almejas
Merluza

Arroces y pastas
Paella valenciana
Espaguetis a la boloñesa

Postres
Fruta del tiempo
Flan
Helados

Pan, vino, agua y café incluidos
No se admiten propinas

b 🎧 ¿Qué pide cada persona? Copia y completa la tabla con los detalles que faltan.

	Primer plato	Segundo plato	Postre
Ejemplo:	*sopa*	*chuletas*	*helado*
1			

2 🎧 Pon las imágenes en el orden correcto según el diálogo.

a

b

c

Menú

d

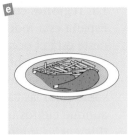
e

3a 🎧 📖 Escucha el diálogo.
Pon las frases en el orden correcto.

1 *Para empezar, para mí, paté, y para mi amigo melón.*

2 *De acuerdo.*

3 *¿Y qué quieren para beber?*

4 *Un helado de piña para mí y para mi amigo un helado de vainilla.*

5 *Gracias. Tráiganos el menú, por favor.*

6 *Muy bien. ¿Y de segundo plato?*

7 *Entonces, dos helados de vainilla.*

8 *Pollo con patatas para dos, por favor.*

9 *Una botella de vino tinto y una botella de agua mineral con gas.*

10 *¿Y de postre?*

11 *Buenas tardes. ¿Tiene una mesa para dos personas?*

12 *Aquí tiene. ¿Qué van a tomar?*

13 *Sí. Hay esta mesa aquí, en la terraza.*

14 *Lo siento, señor, pero de piña no hay.*

b 💬 Trabaja con tu pareja. Practica el diálogo.
Inventa tus propias conversaciones.

4 📖 Busca la palabra intrusa. Usa un diccionario para ayudarte.

Ejemplo: *desayuno almuerzo cena* **comedor** *merienda*

1 zumo	naranja	pomelo	melocotón
2 sopa	consomé	tortilla	gazpacho
3 merluza	gambas	bacalao	cerdo
4 carne	pescado	aves	legumbres
5 arroz	postre	pasta	patatas
6 queso	mantequilla	huevos	leche

GRAMÁTICA

Disjunctive pronouns

Look at the following example phrase
from the dialogue in Exercise 3a:

Para *mí* paté.   Pâté for *me*.

Here, *mí* is a disjunctive pronoun. It is
used because the word *mí* (me) follows
the preposition *para* (for). Disjunctive pronouns
are used after prepositions
and are listed in the table below.

	Singular	Plural
First person	*mí* (me)	*nosotros/as* (us)
Second person	*ti* (you) *usted*	*vosotros/as* (you)
Third person	*él* (him) *ella* (her)	*ellos* (them) *ellas*

Escribe estas frases en español.

1 A coffee for me and a tea for her.
2 I'd like chicken for them, Pablo and Juan.
3 Water for him and wine for us.
4 An ice cream for her and fruit for him.
5 Ana and María? A glass of water for them.

5 📖 Lee el artículo y contesta las preguntas.

Las regiones culinarias de España

España está rodeada de mar; tiene tres lados de costas. En el norte tiene el mar Cantábrico; al oeste está el océano Atlántico y hacia el este hay el mar Mediterráneo. Justo al otro lado del estrecho de Gibraltar están Marruecos y Argelia. Con tantas millas de costa se puede entender por qué los españoles comen tanto marisco y pescado. En el pasado, las barreras naturales — sobre todo las cadenas montañosas — hicieron difícil la comunicación entre las regiones. Así, aunque ciertos ingredientes, como el aceite de oliva y el ajo, son comunes, se desarrollaron diferencias importantes entre las regiones. Los alimentos de cada región son, en general, sencillos y típicos de la zona. Los españoles tienen una dieta muy variada y sana.

España se caracteriza por la diversidad culinaria de sus regiones.

¡Hola! Me llamo Arturo y soy de Bilbao en el norte de España. Mi región es famosa por el pescado, sobre todo el bacalao. También comemos mucho marisco, cordero y verduras.

Soy María de la zona montañosa de los Pirineos. Somos muy conocidos en España por nuestros pimientos, tomates y cebollas.

Soy Marcelo de Guadalajara en el centro de España. Aquí comemos mucha carne: cerdo, cordero y ternera. Son conocidos nuestros quesos, como el delicioso queso manchego, uno de los mejores quesos del mundo.

Soy Ángel. Mi región es Andalucía en el sur de España. Cultivamos mucha fruta aquí. Esta zona es famosa por sus aceitunas y exportamos el aceite de oliva a países de todo el mundo. Quizás nuestro plato más famoso es el gazpacho, una sopa fría hecha de tomates y pepino. ¡Qué rico!

Me llamo Juan y soy de Barcelona en Cataluña. Lo más típico de allí son nuestros guisos de carne o pescado. También son conocidos los embutidos.

Hola! Soy Alicia y soy de Valencia en el este. Esta región es famosa por el arroz y sus platos típicos como la paella. ¡Deberías probarla!

1 ¿Por qué comen los españoles tanto pescado?
2 En el pasado, ¿por qué fue difícil la comunicación entre las regiones?
3 Según el artículo, ¿en qué regiones se come: **(a)** mucha verdura? **(b)** mucha carne? **(c)** mucho pescado?

6a ✏️ Completa lo siguiente eligiendo las palabras adecuadas de la lista de abajo.

¡Hola! _____ Ana. Soy de Lancashire en el _____ de Inglaterra. Mi región es famosa por sus productos lácteos, como el _____ . También comemos mucho _____ aquí porque estamos cerca de la costa atlántica. Nuestro plato más famoso es el Lancashire Hotpot. Es un _____ hecho de _____ y _____ .

> guiso   soy   pescado   norte
> queso   patatas   cordero

b 💬 Prepara una breve presentación sobre los platos típicos de tu región. Usa el ejemplo arriba para ayudarte.

7 📖 Lee la receta. Empareja las instrucciones con la imagen adecuada.

Ejemplo: a — Añade los tomates, guisantes, gambas y azafrán.

Paella Valenciana

Ingredientes
4 tazas de arroz de paella
8 tazas de caldo de pescado
8 langostinos
8 mejillones
200 gramos de gambas (50 gramos sin pelar)
200 gramos de guisantes (frescos o congelados)
2 tomates, pelados y trozeados
2 dientes de ajo picados
unos hilos de azafrán machacados
cuartos de limón
aceite de oliva para freír

Método
1 Fríe el ajo en la paellera.
2 Añade los tomates, guisantes, gambas y azafrán.
3 Cocínalo durante unos minutos.
4 Añade el arroz y el caldo.
5 Cuece durante aproximadamente veinte minutos.
6 Cuece el marisco durante unos minutos.
7 Decora con gambas y mejillones.
8 Decora la paella con cuartos de limón.
9 Sirve directamente de la paellera.

8a 📖 Lee las instrucciones para preparar la tortilla. Usando un diccionario para ayudarte, explica lo que significa cada palabra o frase en negrita en el texto.

Ejemplo: 1 pela — peel

Tortilla española

Ingredientes
4 huevos
½ kilo de patatas
una cebolla
un pimiento
aceite
sal y pimiento

Método
1 **Pela** las cebollas y las patatas.
2 **Pica** las cebollas en trozos no muy pequeños y ponlas a freír en una sartén con abundante aceite.
3 Mientras tanto pica las patatas en dados, sazónalas y añádelas a la sartén. **Corta** el pimiento y **fríe** todo a fuego medio, removiendo de vez en cuando, hasta que se dore todo un poco. Retíralo y escúrrelo.
4 **Prepara** un recipiente y **bate** los 4 huevos. **Añade** las patatas, cebollas y pimiento.
5 **Pon** un poco de aceite en una sartén y vierte la mezcla. **Cuaja** el huevo, primero a fuego vivo y después un poco más suave. **Da la vuelta** a la tortilla para que se dore por ambos lados y **sírvela** caliente con una ensalada.

¡ojo!

The *tú* imperative form is generally used to give recipe instructions.

-ar	-er	-ir
corta	cuece	sirve

Corta la carne.
Cut the meat.

Cuece el marisco durante 20 minutos.
Cook the shellfish for 20 minutes.

Sirve caliente.
Serve hot.

b Escribe una receta.

La comida rápida. ¿Cuáles conoces?

A pesar de la enorme expansión en los siglos XX y XXI de la industria que proporciona la comida rápida, todavía quedan muchas tradiciones interesantes con respecto a la comida y la merienda callejera. ¿Cuántos de estos conoces?

Tapas españolas

'Tapas' es como se denomina una gran variedad de platos que 'se pican' (se toman) normalmente en bares y cafeterías. Tradicionalmente se sirven acompañando a vinos y cañas para **reducir los efectos** del alcohol cuando se bebe con el estómago vacío. Las tapas pueden ser servidas frías, como aceitunas, jamón curado o queso, o calientes, como por ejemplo la tortilla, el pollo, el pescado o las patatas.

Como pueden ser apreciadas por **cualquiera** que las pruebe, hoy en día hay bares y restaurantes por todo el mundo donde se sirven las tapas. En muchos de esos lugares, **a pesar de** las tradiciones, se piden varias tapas diferentes para completar una comida o una cena entera. Algunos creen que las tapas tienen su origen en tiempos de Alfonso X. Como el Rey solo podía tomar porciones pequeñas de comida, solía preferir picar **cantidades muy escasas** con un buen vaso de vino.

Churros

Churros, **a menudo descritos como** 'el donut español', son cintas de masa fritas en aceite hirviendo. A menudo se venden de puestos que se encuentran por las calles. En España son muy populares como desayuno y por eso se sirven en bares y cafeterías.

Salchipapas

A todo el mundo le encantan los perros calientes, pero en Ecuador y Perú son muy especiales. ¡Una salchipapa es la comida rápida de Latinoamérica! Se preparan en el momento y se venden en la calle. **Proporcionan** una merienda deliciosa **compuesta de** lonchas de salchicha frita y servida con patatas fritas, huevo frito y salsa picante o mayonesa. ¡Exquisito!

México

México D. F. es una de las ciudades del mundo donde más puestos de comida rápida se encuentran. Hay uno **en cada esquina** y venden todo tipo de comida y plato rápido. Seguro que conoces los *tacos*, pero ¿**has oído hablar de** las tortas? Una torta es como un bocadillo mejicano **hecho con** ricos panecillos rellenos de todo tipo de ingrediente: aguacate, carne picada, pollo, pescado o judías. ¡Es un manjar que **no se debe perder**!

Colombia

Una comida rápida que se encuentra por zonas de Colombia, como Medellín, es la deliciosa torta *choclo* con queso. Básicamente es una torta de maíz frita rellena de queso. ¡Son deliciosas y muy baratas!

Por todas partes de América del Sur se encuentran puestos que venden zumos o 'jugos'. Como allí tienen tantas frutas exóticas, hay **un gran surtido de** sabores: maracuyá (de color amarilla), granadilla (de color naranja), papyuala, lulo (de color naranja), e higo. También es muy popular el zumo de papaya.

¡Hasta se venden postres! En Bogotá, por ejemplo, muy típicos son **raciones de** tarta de queso o vasitos de arroz con leche.

Chile – empanadas

Lo que más se ve por las calles en Chile son puestos de empanadas. Hechas de hojaldre, rellenas de muchos ingredientes diferentes, y fritas, son deliciosas y fáciles de servir. Se meten todo tipo de carne, queso, salsas, pescado – **ilo que haya!** Tienen nombres especiales también! El pino, por ejemplo, contiene carne picada, cebolla, pasas, aceitunas y trozos de huevo duro. Otra se llama *la mariscona*, y tiene marisco frito con un poco de espinacas.

a Copia las palabras y frases en negrita del texto. Encuentra los equivalentes en inglés en la lista abajo.

Ejemplo: **1** *sentirse los efectos* — feel the effects

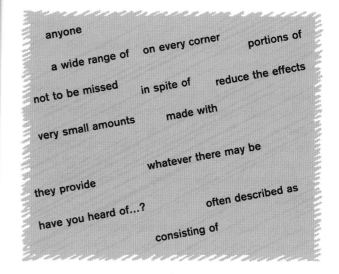

anyone

a wide range of   on every corner   portions of

not to be missed   in spite of   reduce the effects

very small amounts   made with

whatever there may be

they provide

have you heard of...?   often described as

consisting of

b Lee las frases siguientes y decide si son verdaderas (V) o falsas (F). Si son falsas, escribe une frase en español para corregirlas.

Ejemplo: **1** — *V*

1 *Las tapas son típicamente españolas.*
2 Las tapas son postres.
3 Las tapas son platos calientes.
4 Los churros se toman normalmente por las mañanas.
5 Las salchipapas se sirven en restaurantes muy elegantes.
6 Las puestas de comida en México solo venden tortas.
7 La torta *choclo* se prepara usando aceite.

10 Ahora busca comida típica callejera del mundo hispanohablante. Usa Internet y prepara una pequeña presentación sobre la información que has encontrado. Escribe una lista de páginas web útiles para tus compañeros.

Ejemplo:

En Guatemala se come mucho los rellenitos de plátano. Estos plátanos están fritos. Se preparan en casa para el desayuno o se compran en un puesto de la calle. Son muy fáciles de preparar y son deliciosos.

4 ¡Vivir a tope!

☑ Talk about youth issues
☑ Give opinions
☑ Use the subjunctive mood

1 📖 Lee el texto.

¿Eres un joven a quien le importa el mundo a su alrededor? ¿Tienes opiniones sobre los asuntos que afectan a los jóvenes hoy en día?

De momento estamos trabajando juntos para representar las opiniones de la juventud sobre los siguientes temas importantes:

- el terrorismo
- los malos tratos
- las oportunidades para jóvenes
- el medio ambiente
- la inmigración
- la seguridad ciudadana
- la delincuencia

¿Quieres mejorar tu mundo y ayudar a los demás? Si la respuesta es 'Sí', únete al Foro Juventud y ¡juntos haremos una diferencia!

Busca más información en nuestra página Web
www.osce.org

CULTURA

El Foro Juventud es la rama española del Foro Europeo de la Juventud, una organización que se dirige a fomentar la participación de los jóvenes en la formación de Europa y de la sociedad en que viven.

a 📖 ✏️ Estudia esta lista de temas y empareja la palabra o frase española con el inglés adecuado. Usa un diccionario para ayudarte.

el terrorismo	the environment
los malos tratos	immigration
oportunidades para jóvenes	terrorism
el medio ambiente	bullying/abuse
la inmigración	safety in the streets
la seguridad ciudadana	opportunities for young people
la delincuencia	crime and delinquency

b 📖 Lee lo que dicen estos jóvenes europeos y decide qué tema de la lista del texto les interesa.

Ejemplo: **1** *Marlene — el terrorismo*

Tengo miedo de un ataque terrorista.
Marlene (Alemania)

Me interesa proteger el planeta.
François (Francia)

En mi ciudad hay muchos problemas de delincuencia.
Callum (Reino Unido)

En mi pueblo hay demasiada gente de otros países.
Linda (Holanda)

Tengo problemas en el colegio con los alumnos mayores.
Alex (Polonia)

No sé qué podría hacer en el futuro.
Pietre (Austria)

Quiero salir sin tener miedo de que me pase algo.
Isolde (Dinamarca)

c  Practica este diálogo para saber lo que piensan tus amigos. Pregúntales qué temas de la lista son los más preocupantes.

> ¿Cuál crees que es más preocupante — el terrorismo o la delincuencia?

> Creo que el terrorismo es más preocupante que la delincuencia, pero menos que el problema del medio ambiente.

GRAMÁTICA

Giving opinions

If you want to say 'I don't think...', expressing an opinion that something will not happen, for example 'I don't think it will rain' or 'I doubt if there's a solution', you have to use the subjunctive. The subjunctive is not a tense but a 'mood' of the verb. It can be used in several tenses. The present tense of the subjunctive is formed as follows:

-ar verbs	-er verbs	-ir verbs
comprar	vender	vivir
compre	venda	viva
compres	vendas	vivas
compre	venda	viva
compremos	vendamos	vivamos
compréis	vendáis	viváis
compren	vendan	vivan

For example:

No creo que compre esa camisa.	I don't think he will buy that shirt.
Es improbable que vendamos nuestra casa.	It is unlikely we will sell our house.

Dudo que viva mucho mi hámster.
I doubt if my hamster will live very long.

There are a number of verbs that are irregular in the subjunctive form. These include *ser* and *estar*:

ser	estar
sea	esté
seas	estés
sea	esté
seamos	estemos
seáis	estéis
sean	estén

For example:

No creo que esté muy contento de momento.	I don't think he/she is very happy at the moment.
Dudo que sean ricos.	I doubt if they are rich.
No quiero que hagas eso.	I don't want you to do that.

Hay (there is/there are), from the verb *haber*, also has a subjunctive form, *haya*. For example:

No creo que haya suficiente comida para todos.	I don't think there will be enough food for everyone.
Es posible que haya nubes.	It's possible that it will be cloudy.

Read these grammar notes carefully, then work out how to say the following phrases and write them down:

Example: I don't think immigration is a big problem.
*No creo que la inmigración **sea** un gran problema.*

1 I don't think the environment is very important.
2 I don't think youth crime is a problem.
3 I doubt if we do enough to help the environment.
4 It's not likely there will be a lot of opportunities for young people.
5 I don't believe we buy enough recyclable things.
6 It's unlikely that we'll be living in the same kind of houses in the future.
7 I don't think the planet is in danger.
8 I doubt if it will rain.

2a 📖 Lee estos pósteres y empareja las frases abajo con el póster adecuado (a) o (b).

Ejemplo: *Trata del medio ambiente. — (a)*

1 Explica cómo proteger el mundo.
2 Da consejos sobre cómo evitar ataques personales.
3 Dice que debes mantener el contacto.
4 Dice que siempre tienes que tener compañía por las calles.
5 Quiere que ahorres energía.
6 Dice que tienes que dar buen ejemplo.
7 Tienes que presionar a la gente.
8 Dice que no te fíes de los desconocidos.
9 Aconseja que no vayas a sitios donde sería fácil cometer un crimen.
10 Te anima a promocionar la causa.

a

Ayúdenos a mejorar nuestro entorno

- Sea firme con la gente.

- Anímeles a respetar el mundo que es de todos.

- No deje que tiren basura.

- Haga que apaguen los aparatos electrónicos mientras no se usan.

- Sea ejemplar — una persona que evita usar el coche lo máximo posible.

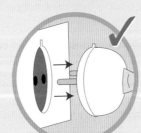

b

¿Sabes cuidarte en las calles?

Sigue estas reglas básicas y podrás salir sin miedo.

¡Que te lo pases muy bien!

- Cuéntales siempre a tus padres donde estás, con quién, cómo vas a volver y a qué hora.
- No salgas solo por la noche — vete por lo menos con otro amigo.
- No vayas a sitios aislados — quédate donde haya luz y gente.
- Vístete y compórtate apropiadamente a todas horas.
- No lleves mucho dinero contigo por la calle.
- Lleva tu teléfono móvil siempre y ten un plan previsto por si lo pierdes o te quedas sin crédito.

*No te olvides de las reglas
*Que todos lo pasemos bien
*¡Ten cuidado!

b Elige otro de los temas identificados por el Foro Juventud (ver ejercicio 1a) y prepara tu propio póster sobre él. Intenta usar el subjuntivo.

GRAMÁTICA

The imperative and present subjunctive forms

The imperative and the present subjunctive between them supply the Spanish commands (Do this!) and exhortative forms (Let's go! Let him try! May you be sorry!).

Informal (*tú/vosotros*) commands: the imperative form is used only in affirmative *tú/vosotros* commands.

Compra estos vaqueros.	Buy these jeans.
Aprended esta gramática.	Learn this grammar.

All negative commands use the subjunctive form.

No esperes más.	Don't wait any longer.
No desesperes.	Don't despair.

Formal (*usted*) commands: the subjunctive form is always used for formal commands, affirmative and negative.

Siga las instrucciones.	Follow the instructions.
No tire basura.	Don't throw rubbish.

The conjunction *que* generally introduces the exhortative forms in the third person (utterances with an implied 'Let them…')

Que venga ella si quiere.	Let her come if she wants to.
Que compren DVDs.	Let them buy DVDs.

Study the verb forms of the imperative in the singular then do the two tasks that follow it. If you are unsure of the imperative form of a verb, consult the verb tables at the back of the book.

Verb	Imperative (*tú*)	Negative Imperative (*tú*)	Imperative (*usted*), affirmative and negative
mirar (to look at)	*mira*	*no mires*	*mire/no mire*
ser (to be)	*sé*	*no seas*	*sea/no sea*
decidir (to decide)	*decide*	*no decidas*	*decida/no decida*
salir (to go out)	*sal*	*no salgas*	*salga/no salga*

Exercise A: choose the correct form of the singular imperative of the verbs in brackets, using the *tú* form.

Ejemplo: Por favor, _____ (hablar) más despacio.
Por favor, habla más despacio.

1 _____ (mirar) a aquella chica. Se parece a tu hermana.
2 Javier, ¡_____ (comer) más rápido!
3 _____ (salir) a las ocho si no te llamo antes.
4 Marga, ¡_____ (darme) el boli enseguida!
5 No me _____ (esperar) después de medianoche.
6 ¡_____ (hacer) tus deberes!
7 ¡No _____ (ser) tonta, María!
8 Por favor, _____ (venir) a las ocho en punto.

Exercise B: translate the sentences, using the appropriate form of the singular imperative.

Ejemplo: Look at the picture.   *Mira la imagen.*
Don't look at the sun.   *No mires el sol.*
Let him look behind him.   *Que mire hacia atrás.*

1 Don't be stupid.
2 Let her decide what she wants to do.
3 Get out of the room!
4 Look at the film.
5 Let it be a girl!
6 Decide quickly, please.
7 Don't go out alone.
8 Be responsible with your litter.
9 Don't decide the environment isn't important.
10 Let her look where she is going.

3 🎧 📖 Escucha el problema que menciona cada persona. Entonces lee las posibles soluciones. Empareja el problema (1–10) con la imagen (a–j) y con una solución escogida de la lista (i–x). Rellena la tabla.

Problema (1–10)	Imagen (a–j)	Solución (i–xi)
Ejemplo:	*g*	*i*
2		

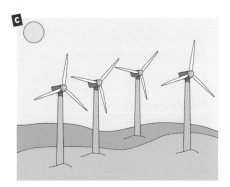

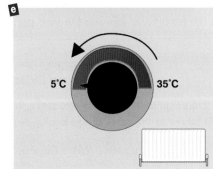

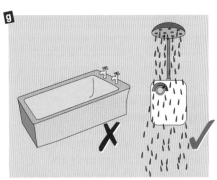

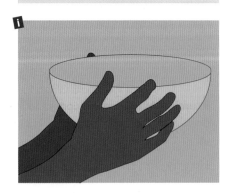

Soluciones

i
Lo que deberíamos hacer es pensar bien en cuanto gastamos. Podríamos ducharnos en vez de bañarnos y poner algo en la cisterna del wáter para reducir el volumen de agua.

ii
Debería haber más policías en la calle para evitar problemas, y mejor educación sobre cómo respetar a otras personas — cómo cuidarlas y tratarlas bien. Podríamos apreciar mucho más a los viejos y aprender de ellos. Son muy interesantes.

iii ¡La gente debería ser menos perezosa! Podríamos contaminar menos reduciendo el uso de vehículos que consumen gasolina o gasóleo. En cambio deberíamos andar más, usar el transporte público y sacar la bicicleta. ¡Sería mucho más sano también!

iv El gobierno debería dar más dinero a los científicos que investigan otros combustibles para proporcionar nuestra energía. Sin nuevas tecnologías no vamos a encontrar ninguna solución. Ahora se puede aprovechar el viento y el agua. ¡Hay que espabilarse!

v Si pudiéramos reciclar más, mejoraríamos nuestro medio ambiente. De compras, por ejemplo, podrías devolver tus bolsas de plástico al supermercado para que se reciclen. ¡Todo ayuda!

vi Hay que ocupar a los jóvenes. Si el gobierno hiciera más para animar a los jóvenes, estudiarían más y ayudarían a los demás. Muchos dicen que deberíamos empezar de nuevo el servicio militar.

vii Deberíamos seguir el ejemplo de varias religiones del mundo que toman como una obligación moral dar un porcentaje de nuestros bienes a los pobres. Podríamos fácilmente dar un poco cada mes a una institución de caridad, por ejemplo.

viii Podríamos malgastar menos y apreciar más lo que tenemos antes de tirar tanto. Sería muy fácil también comprar cosas de Comercio Justo para ayudar a los pobres. Me gustaría que nadie en este mundo tuviera hambre. ¡Ojalá que no fuera un sueño!

ix Deberíamos prohibir fumar en todos los lugares — dentro y fuera — y deberían poner más difícil el comprar alcohol, sobre todo para los jóvenes.

x Debería ser muy fácil apagar los aparatos cuando no están en uso. Se puede poner aislamiento en las paredes y los techos. ¿Y por qué no regulamos un poquito las temperaturas de la calefacción o el aire acondicionado?

GRAMÁTICA

The imperfect subjunctive and uses of the conditional

The imperfect subjunctive is a past tense that is used in the same circumstances as the present subjunctive:

*Me gustaría que nadie en este mundo **tuviera** hambre.*

I would like nobody in this world to go hungry.

The imperfect subjunctive is used frequently in subordinate clauses beginning with **si**, with the conditional being used in the main clause:

*Si **pudiéramos** reciclar más, **mejoraríamos** nuestro medio ambiente.*

If we could recycle more, we would improve our environment.

See the grammar summary on page 162 for the formation of the imperfect subjunctive.

Note that the conditional is used for possible actions. Check the formation of the conditional before you start the writing activity and note especially the verb endings.

*[Yo] **vendería** la casa.*	I would sell the house.
***Deberíamos** ahorrar energía.*	We should save energy.

4a Escribe al Foro Juventud sobre los problemas que existen donde vives y si puedes, ofrece soluciones. Usa los problemas y soluciones de arriba para ayudarte. Empieza tu carta así.

> Málaga 6 de enero
>
> Hola chicos del foro,
>
> Les estoy escribiendo para contarles lo que me preocupa de mi pueblo.
>
> En primer lugar ＿＿＿
>
> ＿＿＿ Yo creo que deberíamos ＿＿＿

b Ahora prepara una pequeña presentación de 2 a 3 minutos sobre uno de los temas identificados por el foro. Explica tus opiniones y cómo solucionarías el problema.

Ejemplo: ¡Hola! Me llamo Francisco y tengo dieciséis años.

Me interesa proteger el planeta.

Soy ecólogo.

El mundo está en peligro.

Paper 1: listening

Vas a oír una entrevista de la radio con José, un futbolista. Habla de cómo mantenerse en forma. Escúchala con atención y contesta a las preguntas **en español**. Habrá dos pausas durante la entrevista. Vas a oír la entrevista dos veces, pero antes tienes unos segundos para leer las preguntas.

1 ¿Cuántos años tiene José?

.... **[1]**

2 ¿Cómo es un día típico para un futbolista profesional?

.... **[1]**

3 ¿Cuánto tiempo tiene que entrenar?

.... **[1]**

[*PAUSA*]

4 ¿Cuántas horas debe dormir José?

.... **[1]**

5 ¿Cómo evita José el estrés?

.... **[1]**

6 ¿Cómo descansa José los fines de semana?

.... **[1]**

[*PAUSA*]

7 ¿Qué hay que comer todos los días, según José?

.... **[1]**

8 ¿Cómo se asegura José de llevar una dieta equilibrada?

.... **[1]**

9 ¿De qué bebidas habla?

.... **[1]**

[Total: 9]

Tips for success

- Remember to take time to read the questions carefully before answering, using the built-in pauses.
- There is frequently more than one way of expressing a correct answer.
- The questions follow the order of the audio recording.

 ## Paper 2: reading

This type of task requires careful reading of a complex passage. There are two types of question:

- Questions 1–6, which require answers in Spanish.
- Question 7, for which you have to understand the gist of part of the text, and choose the statement which summarises it best, out of 4 possibilities.

Lee este artículo sobre el medio ambiente y contesta a las preguntas **en español**.

Responsabilidad colectiva

A pesar de toda la publicidad sobre la importancia de cuidar el entorno en el que vivimos para salvar el medio ambiente, la mayoría de la gente opina, pero no actúa. Los gobiernos mundiales se han esforzado para educarnos sobre los efectos perjudiciales de la contaminación y lo que se puede hacer para disminuir el daño que produce, pero muchos seguimos ignorando la realidad. La única manera eficaz de seguir adelante con la campaña para salvar el mundo, es decidir responsabilizarse.

Por eso me animé mucho cuando descubrí lo que están haciendo unos chicos en un colegio cerca de donde vivo. Este grupo de jóvenes ha decidido hacer algo sorprendente.

Han puesto en práctica un proyecto que llaman *Vivir con sencillez*. Están intentando sobrevivir sin dinero durante un año y se reúnen todas las semanas para contar experiencias y compartir ideas.

Mikel, uno de los fundadores, solía gastar unos veinte euros a la semana en transporte público solo para ir al colegio. Cogió una bicicleta que encontró en la basura, la arregló y ahora va a todas partes en bicicleta gratis.

Otro chico, Joaquín, gastaba mucho dinero en la cafetería del colegio porque nunca tenía tiempo de prepararse el bocadillo para el recreo en casa. Estos jóvenes consiguieron permiso para preparar bocadillos en el patio durante los recreos. Si les falta algo que no pueden hacer, lo compran dando productos o ayudando, en vez de con dinero. Además, venden lo que les sobra en la cafetería, pero lo intercambian por alguna cosa, en vez de obtener dinero en efectivo. Así Joaquín trabaja preparando, cultivando y vendiendo productos, y ¡a cambio recibe bebidas gratis!

El lema de estos chicos es 'Nada es imposible si trabajamos juntos'. Son una inspiración y están atrayendo el interés de empresas y de la prensa. Me han devuelto mi fe en la humanidad.

Raúl del Bosque (63 años)

Lee estas preguntas y contéstalas en español.

1 ¿A qué problema social se refiere este artículo?

.... **[1]**

2 ¿Qué han intentado hacer los gobiernos?

.... **[1]**

3 ¿Cuál es el objetivo del grupo de jóvenes?

.... **[1]**

4 ¿Por qué Mikel ya no gasta veinte euros para ir al colegio?

.... **[1]**

5 ¿Qué hacen los jóvenes durante los recreos para conseguir su objetivo?

.... **[1]**

6 ¿Por qué Joaquín no tiene que pagar sus bebidas?

.... **[1]**

7 ¿Por qué Raúl se siente más animado? Indica tu respuesta colocando una X en la casilla correcta.

A		Porque unos jóvenes han ganado una competición.
B		Porque unos jóvenes están haciendo algo maravilloso.
C		Porque unos chicos se reúnen cada semana.
D		Porque unos chicos se están rebelando contra el gobierno.

[1]

[Total: 7]

Paper 3: speaking

The text below is an example of a good presentation about eating and healthy lifestyles. It is based around the photo prompt on the right.

🎧 Follow the text carefully as you listen to the recording. Notice how and when the interviewer steps in to ask additional relevant questions. The transcript is also annotated to point out inaccuracies you should try to avoid.

Sample student answer

Noun/adjectival agreements are important to get right, as they are here.

Hoy en día, con todos los métodos de comunicación y la tecnología que tenemos, nunca ha sido más polémico el asunto de cómo vivir una vida sana y féliz. Sin duda, es cada vez más difícil debido a la vida sedentaria que llevamos la mayoría. Además, como poca gente tiene tiempo para cocinar bien o pensando en qué es sano, la comida rápida sigue siendo la preferida. Es un problema serio, que preocupa mucho a los médicos y a los expertos porque saben que tal comportamiento consume recursos valiosos de nuestra seguridad social. Es imprescindible hacernos responsables de nuestra propia vida y encontrar una manera adecuada de buscar un equilibrio eficaz y sostenible. Por eso, hace mucho empecé a comer bien. Siempre intento comer tres comidas al día, preferiblemente a las mismas horas. Intento no condimentar las comidas demasiado y evito merendar cosas poco sanas.

It is important to remember where accents go. Here the accent puts the stress on the wrong syllable.

Watch out for nouns that you would logically expect to be masculine or feminine but which are not. Problema is masculine.

Good variety of verbs and adjectives used here.

Accurate use of past tense verbs. Using a variety of tenses is important.

¿Ah, sí? ¿Y qué comiste ayer, por ejemplo?

Pues desayuné muy bien, a las siete de la mañana. Tomé cereales, fruta y yogur, y a la hora del café, me tomé un vaso de leche con un bollo. Comí sobre las dos y me tomé una ensalada de atún, seguida de pollo con patatas y de postre, melón – y para beber, me tomé un zumo de naranja. Para cenar, a las ocho y media, me tomé una sopa de

Many repetitions of the verb *tomar*. Which alternatives could this candidate have used?

verduras y un bocadillo de jamón. Justo antes de acostarme, me tomé un vaso de leche caliente con unas galletas que había hecho mi padre. ¡Yo creo que eso ha sido un día bastante sano!

¿Así que para llevar una vida sana, solo hay que comer bien?
¡En absoluto! ¡También es muy importante hacer suficiente ejercicio! Dicen que debes conseguir que te lata el corazón a un ritmo más rápido de lo normal durante unos veinte minutos, por lo menos tres veces a la semana. Soy muy consciente de eso e intento ir en bicicleta al colegio todos los días y juego al baloncesto dos veces a la semana. Los fines de semana voy de paseo al campo con mi familia o con amigos.

Appropriate use of the subjunctive.

¿Y qué más es importante?
Por supuesto hay que tomar suficiente agua, sobre todo cuando haces ejercicio, y hay que dormir bien también. Además, según los expertos, el estrés es muy dañino para la salud. Todos reconocemos que la vida hoy en día produce mucho estrés, así que es importante tener maneras de combatirlo y tiempo para relajarte bien.

Good to see verb persons other than just first person.

¿Y qué haces tú para relajarte?
Intento acostarme pronto y tener así tiempo para leer un rato. Eso me relaja mucho. Me encanta hacer deporte y también me gusta dibujar y coser – esas cosas son mis pasatiempos principales. Me ayudan a pensar en cosas creativas y bonitas.

Accurate use of impersonal verbs throughout.

Practise with a partner. How would *you* answer each of the interviewer's questions? What would you include in a presentation about your lifestyle?

Paper 4: writing

Vas a describir tu rutina de compras. Escribe un correo electrónico a tu amigo/a por correspondencia que va a hacer un intercambio contigo y necesita saber dónde y cómo hacer compras en tu ciudad.

Menciona:
(a) cuándo y dónde compras comida
(b) dónde compras otras cosas y qué tipo de cosas sueles comprar
(c) por qué eliges esos sitios
(d) lo que hiciste y compraste la última vez que fuiste un día de compras

Debes escribir 130–140 palabras **en español**.

Tips for success
- Ensure that you cover all parts of the question.
- When you plan your answer, make sure that your ideas follow a logical sequence, and that you create a new paragraph for each new idea.
- Show that you are able to handle a range of tenses confidently by using verbs in the past, present and future.

Vocabulario

Parts of the body

la **boca**   mouth
el **brazo**   arm
la **cabeza**   head
el **codo**   elbow
el **corazón**   heart
el **cuello**   neck
el **dedo**   finger, toe
el **diente**/la **muela**   tooth
la **espalda**   back
el **estómago**   stomach
la **garganta**   throat
el **hombro**   shoulder
la **lengua**   tongue
la **mano**   hand
el **músculo**   muscle
la **nariz**   nose
el **oído**/la **oreja**   ear
el **ojo**   eye
el **pecho**   chest
el **pie**   foot
la **piel**   skin
la **pierna**   leg
la **rodilla**   knee

Problems and solutions

Estoy mareado/a.   I feel sick.
Me he cortado la mano.   I have cut my hand.
Me he cortado.   I have cut myself.
Me duele(n)…   …hurts.
No me siento bien.   I don't feel well.
Tengo el brazo roto/la pierna rota.   I have a broken arm/leg.
Tengo dolor de…   I have a/an…ache.
Tengo el tobillo torcido/la muñeca torcida.   I have a twisted ankle/wrist.
Tengo fiebre.   I have a temperature.
Tengo tos.   I have a cough.
Tengo un resfriado.   I have a cold.
Tengo una insolación.   I have sunstroke.
Tengo una picadura.   I have a bite.
Tengo una quemadura.   I have a burn.
el **comprimido**   pill, tablet
la **crema**   cream
el **jarabe**   syrup
la **pastilla**   tablet, pastille, pill
tomar   to take

Healthy lifestyles

beber mucha agua   to drink a lot of water
comer una dieta variada   to eat a varied diet
dormir bien   to sleep well
evitar el estrés   to avoid stress
hacer ejercicio   to do exercise
intentar   to try
mantener una vida sana   to maintain a healthy lifestyle

Shops

el **almacén**   shop, store
la **carnicería**   butcher's
el **centro comercial**   shopping centre
el **estanco**   tobacconist's
la **farmacia**   chemist's
la **frutería**   greengrocer's
la **joyería**   jeweller's
la **juguetería**   toy shop
la **librería**   bookshop
el **mercado**   market
la **panadería**   baker's
la **perfumería**   perfumery
la **pescadería**   fishmonger's
el **supermercado**   supermarket
la **tienda de música**   record/music shop
la **tienda de ropa**   clothes shop
la **tienda de ultramarinos**   grocer's
la **zapatería**   shoe shop

Food and drink

el **aceite**   oil
la **aceituna**   olive
el **agua** (f)   water
el **ajo**   garlic
el **arroz**   rice
el **atún**   tuna
el **azúcar**   sugar
el **bacalao**   cod
el **café**   coffee
la **carne**   meat
la **cebolla**   onion
el **cerdo**   pork
los **cereales**   cereals
la **comida basura**   junk food
la **comida rápida**   fast food
el **cordero**   lamb
el **champiñón**   mushroom
la **chuleta**   chop
el **dulce**   sweet
la **ensalada**   salad
los **espaguetis**   spaghetti
los **fideos**   noodles
el **filete**   steak
el **flan**   crème caramel
la **fresa**   strawberry
la **fruta**   fruit
la **galleta**   biscuit
las **gambas**   prawns
la **gaseosa**   fizzy drink
el **gazpacho**   chilled tomato soup
los **guisantes**   peas
la **hamburguesa**   hamburger
el **helado**   ice cream
las **hortalizas**   vegetables
el **huevo**   egg
el **jamón**   ham
las **judías verdes**   green beans
la **leche**   milk

la **lechuga**   lettuce
el **limón**   lemon
la **limonada**   lemonade
el **maíz**   corn
la **mantequilla**   butter
la **manzana**   apple
el **mejillón**   mussel
el **melocotón**   peach
la **merluza**   hake
la **naranja**   orange
la **nata**   cream
el **pan**   bread
el **pan tostado**   toasted bread
el **pastel**   cake
la **patata**   potato
las **patatas fritas**   chips, crisps
el **pavo**   turkey
el **pepino**   cucumber
la **pera**   pear
el **perrito caliente**   hot dog
el **pescado**   fish
el **pimiento**   pepper
la **piña**   pineapple
el **plátano**   banana
el **pollo**   chicken
el **pomelo**   grapefruit
el **queso**   cheese
la **sal**   salt
la **sardina**   sardine
la **sopa**   soup
las **tapas**   snacks
el **té**   tea
la **ternera**   veal
el **tomate**   tomato
la **tortilla de patatas**   Spanish omelette
la **tostada**   toast, piece of toast
las **verduras**   green vegetables
el **vino**   wine
el **yogur**   yoghurt
la **zanahoria**   carrot
el **zumo**   juice

Quantities

una barra de   a loaf of
una botella de   a bottle of
una caja de   a box of
un cartón de   a carton of
cien gramos de   100 grams of
una docena de   a dozen
un kilo de   a kilo of
una lata de   a tin of
medio kilo de   half a kilo of
un paquete de   a packet of
un trozo de   a slice of
un tubo de   a tube of
un vaso de   a glass of

Meals and meal times

al mediodía   at midday
beber   to drink

la **cena**   dinner/supper
cenar   to have dinner
comer   to eat
la **comida**   lunch; meal
desayunar   to have breakfast
el **desayuno**   breakfast
la **merienda**   snack, afternoon tea, picnic
por la mañana   in the morning
por la noche   at night
por la tarde   in the afternoon/evening
tomar   to have, take

Eating out
¡Que aproveche!   Enjoy your meal!
¡Salud!   Cheers!
la **cuchara**   spoon
el **cuchillo**   knife
El servicio está incluido.   Service is included.
en el rincón   in the corner
en la terraza   on the terrace
entonces   next, then
el **mantel**   tablecloth
Me falta(n)…   I need…
para empezar   to start…
el **plato**   plate
el **postre**   pudding, dessert
el **primer plato**   starter, first course
el **sacacorchos**   corkscrew
salir a cenar   to go out to eat
el **segundo plato**   main course, second course
la **servilleta**   napkin
el **tenedor**   knife
tener hambre   to be hungry
tener sed   to be thirsty

Traígame el menú, por favor.   Bring me the menu, please.
una mesa para dos   a table for two

The environment
ahorrar   to save
apagar   to switch/turn off
bañarse   to have a bath
la **basura**   rubbish
la **bolsa de plástico**   plastic bag
el **calentamiento global**   global warming
la **capa de ozono**   ozone layer
cerrar   to close
los **combustibles fósiles**   fossil fuels
consumir más/menos   to consume more/less
la **contaminación**   pollution
contaminar   to contaminate, pollute
el **contenedor de abono**   compost bin
los **desechos domésticos**   household waste
desenchufar   to unplug, turn off
devolver   to return
ducharse   to take a shower
encender   to switch/turn on
la **energía**   energy
estar en peligro   to be in danger
la **gasolina**   petrol
el **humo**   smoke
la **luz**   light
luchar contra/por   to fight against/for
malgastar   to waste
el **medio ambiente**   environment
el **papel**   paper
producir   to produce
prohibir   to forbid

proteger el planeta/el mundo   to protect the planet/world
reciclar   to recycle
el **reciclaje**   recycling
reducir   to reduce
respetar   to respect
reutilizar   to reuse
salvar   to save
la **selva**   forest
separar   to separate
ser ecológico/a   to be ecological
utilizar   to use
el **vidrio**   glass

Teenage concerns
abusar   to bully; to abuse
el **acoso escolar**   school bullying
los **ancianos**   old people
debemos   we should/must
la **delincuencia juvenil**   youth crime
el **desempleo**   unemployment
el **dinero**   money
el **estrés**   stress
Es necesario…   It is necessary to…
la **guerra**   war
los **inmigrantes**   immigrants
podemos   we can
recaudar dinero   to collect money
la **salud**   health
la **seguridad**   safety
los **sin techo**   homeless people
el **tabaco**   tobacco
el **Tercer Mundo**   Third World
el **terrorismo**   terrorism
tratar mejor   to treat better
la **violencia**   violence

Gramática

Nouns

Gender of nouns

As a general rule, nouns ending in -*o* are masculine and nouns ending in -*a* are feminine. However, there are some important exceptions:

el día	day
la mano	hand
el mapa	map
la moto	motorbike
el problema	problem
la radio	radio
el programa	programme
la modelo	(fashion) model
el tema	topic

The following groups of nouns are usually masculine:

- nouns ending in -*aje* or -*or*

el garaje	garage
el color	colour

- rivers, seas, mountains, fruit trees, colours, cars, days of the week and points of the compass

el Manzanares	the (river) Manzanares
el Mediterráneo	the Mediterranean
los Alpes	the Alps
el manzano	apple tree
el verde	green
el BMW	BMW
el domingo	Sunday
el norte	north

The following groups of nouns are usually feminine:

- nouns endings in: *ión*, -*dad*, -*tad*, -*triz*, -*tud*, -*umbre*, -*anza*, -*ie*

la región	region
la ciudad	town
la dificultad	difficulty
la actriz	actress
la inquietud	concern
la muchedumbre	crowd
la esperanza	hope
la serie	series

- letters of the alphabet

la eñe	the letter *ñ*

- islands and roads

las (islas) Canarias	the Canary Islands
la M50	the M50

Nouns ending in -*ista* have no separate masculine or feminine form:

el/la artista	artist
el/la periodista	journalist

Plurals

Spanish nouns form their plurals in various different ways:

- by adding -*s*, if the noun ends in a vowel, whether stressed or unstressed

el piso — los pisos	flat/s
la mano — las manos	hand/s
el café — los cafés	coffee/s

- by adding -*es*, if the noun ends in a consonant

el color — los colores	colour/s
el país — los países	country/-ies

- nouns ending in -*z* change the ending to -*ces*

la voz — las voces	voice/s

- nouns that have an accent on the last syllable lose the accent in the plural

la región — las regiones	region/s
el inglés — los ingleses	the English

- days of the week, except *sábado* and *domingo*, have the same form for singular and plural

el lunes — los lunes	Monday(s)
el sábado — los sábados	Saturday(s)

Articles

Definite article

The definite articles are *el/los* for the masculine and *la/las* for the feminine:

	Singular	Plural
Masculine	*el día*	*los días*
Feminine	*la chica*	*las chicas*

When the masculine singular definite article is preceded by *a* or *de*, the preposition combines with it to make one word:

*Vamos **al** parque.*
Let's go to the park. (*a* + *el* = al)

*Salieron **del** cine.*
They came out of the cinema. (*de* + *el* = del)

The other forms of the definite article, *la, los* and *las*, are unchanged after *a* and *de*.

The definite article is used in Spanish, but not in English, for:

- nouns used in a general sense

    No me gusta el chocolate.
    I don't like chocolate.

- languages, colours, days of the week (preceded by 'on' in English), the time, percentages, sports teams:

    El español es una lengua muy hermosa.
    Spanish is a beautiful language.

    Me gusta más el rojo que el amarillo.
    I like red better than yellow.

    El miércoles vamos a la piscina.
    On Wednesday we are going to the swimming pool.

    a las dos
    at 2 o'clock

    El 50% de los chicos tiene el pelo rubio.
    50% of the children have blond hair.

    el Real Madrid
    Real Madrid

- abstract nouns

    Todos buscamos la felicidad.
    We are all looking for happiness.

The definite article is omitted in Spanish, but used in English, for:

- the names of monarchs and popes with Roman numerals (when speaking):

    Alfonso XIII (Alfonso trece)
    Alfonso XIII (Alfonso the thirteenth)

- nouns that are in apposition

    José María Aznar, antiguo presidente de España
    José María Aznar, the former prime minister of Spain

Indefinite article

The indefinite articles are *un/unos* for the masculine and *una/unas* for the feminine:

	Singular (a/an)	Plural (some)
Masculine	*un piso*	*unos pisos*
Feminine	*una chica*	*unas chicas*

The indefinite article is omitted in Spanish where it is used in English:

- with occupations after *ser*

    Mi padre es enfermero.
    My father is a nurse.

- when the noun is in apposition

    Llegó Juan, amigo de mi padre.
    Juan, a friend of my father, arrived.

- with a number of common words, especially: *otro, qué* and *mil*

    El gamberrismo es otro problema.
    Hooliganism is another problem.

    ¡Qué milagro!
    What a miracle!

    Te he dicho mil veces.
    I've told you a thousand times.

The masculine definite and indefinite articles *el* and *un* replace the feminine forms *la* and *una* before feminine nouns in the singular that begin with stressed *a* or *ha*. These nouns remain feminine in gender:

Singular	Plural
el/un agua	*las/unas aguas*
el/un hambre	*las/unas hambres*

Lo + adjective

Lo is used as a neuter article and can act as a noun when followed by an adjective, e.g. *bueno, importante*:

Los exámenes han terminado y eso es lo bueno.
The exams are over and that's the good thing.

Lo importante es no perder el tren.
The important thing is not to miss the train.

Adjectives

Forms

Adjectives that end in -*o* (masculine) or -*a* (feminine) add -*s* for the plural:

	Singular	Plural
Masculine	*limpio*	*limpios*
Feminine	*limpia*	*limpias*

Gramática

Most adjectives that end in a vowel other than *-o/-a* or a consonant have the same form for masculine and feminine in the singular and plural. In the plural, *-s* is added to those ending in a vowel and *-es* to those ending in a consonant.

	Singular	Plural
Masculine	triste	tristes
Feminine	triste	tristes

	Singular	Plural
Masculine	azul	azules
Feminine	azul	azules

Adjectives ending in *-z* change the *z* to *c* in the plural:

	Singular	Plural
Masculine	feliz	felices
Feminine	feliz	felices

Adjectives denoting region or country that finish in a consonant normally have a feminine form ending in *-a*:

	Singular	Plural
Masculine	inglés	ingleses
Feminine	inglesa	inglesas

Adjectives ending in *–or* add *–a* for the feminine singular, *-es* for the masculine plural and *–as* for the feminine plural:

	Singular	Plural
Masculine	encantador	encantadores
Feminine	encantadora	encantadoras

Note: comparative adjectives ending in *-or* do not have a separate feminine form:

	Singular	Plural
Masculine	mejor	mejores
Feminine	mejor	mejores

When two nouns of different gender stand together, the adjective that qualifies them is masculine plural:

Eva y Jorge están contentos.
Eva and George are happy.

Position

Adjectives are normally placed after nouns:

una lengua difícil
a difficult language

Some common adjectives are often placed before the noun:

bueno
malo
pequeño
gran(de)

Cardinal and ordinal numbers and *último* are placed before the noun:

cien pasajeros
a hundred passengers

el quinto piso
the fifth floor

su última novela
his/her/your (formal) last/latest novel

Shortening (apocopation) of adjectives

Several common adjectives lose the final *-o* when they come before a masculine singular noun. This is called 'apocopation':

alguno — algún	any
primero — primer	first
bueno — buen	good
tercero — tercer	third
malo — mal	bad
uno — un	one, a
ninguno — ningún	no

Volveré algún día.	I'll come back some day.
Hace mal tiempo hoy.	The weather is bad today.

Grande shortens to *gran* before masculine and feminine singular nouns:

mi gran amiga, Paula my great friend, Paula

Comparison

Types of comparison

There are three basic types of comparison:
- of superiority (more...than) — *más...que*
- of inferiority (less...than) — *menos...que*
- of equality (as...as) — *tan(to)...como*

*Hace **más** frío en Escocia **que** en España.*
It's colder in Scotland than in Spain.

*Hace **menos** frío en España **que** en Escocia.*
It's less cold in Spain than in Scotland.

*Hace **tanto** calor en Madrid **como** en Caracas.*
It's as hot in Madrid as in Caracas.

Comparatives can be adjectives or adverbs.

Irregular adjectives of comparison

Certain common adjectives have special comparative forms:

Adjective	Comparative
bueno (good)	mejor (better)
malo (bad)	peor (worse)
mucho (much)	más (more)
poco (few)	menos (fewer, less)
grande (big, great)	mayor (bigger, greater)
pequeño (little)	menor (less)

Pedro tiene mejor apetito que Enrique.
Pedro has a better appetite than Enrique.

Irregular adverbs of comparison

Certain common adverbs have special comparative forms, which are invariable.

Adverb	Comparative
bien (well)	mejor (better)
mal (bad)	peor (worse)
más (more)	más (more)
poco (not much)	menos (less)

Mi hermano cocina mejor que mi hermana.
My brother cooks better than my sister.

Note: when a number comes after *más* it must be followed by *de* and not *que*:

Hay más de treinta alumnos en la clase.
There are more than 30 pupils in the class.

Superlatives

The way to express the idea of 'most' in Spanish is by placing the definite article before the noun being described and the comparative adjective after the noun:

La montaña más alta de España está en Canarias.
The highest mountain in Spain is in the Canaries.

Chile es el país más largo de América Latina.
Chile is the longest country in Latin America.

To express the idea of a quality possessed to an extreme degree, you can add *-ísimo* to the adjective:

Salamanca es una ciudad hermosísima.
Salamanca is a very beautiful city.

Chile es un país larguísimo.
Chile is an extremely long country.

Note that some *-ísimo* endings, as with the adjective *largo* in the example, require a spelling change to the last consonant of the adjective:

largo — larguísimo
rico — riquísimo
feliz — felicísimo

Demonstrative adjectives

There are three forms of demonstrative adjective in Spanish:

- *este, esta, estos, estas,* meaning 'this'
- *ese, esa, esos, esas,* meaning 'that' (near the listener)
- *aquel, aquella, aquellos, aquellas,* meaning 'that' (distant from both the speaker and the listener)

Masculine singular	Feminine singular	Masculine plural	Feminine plural
este chico (this boy)	esta chica (this girl)	estos chicos (these boys)	estas chicas (these girls)
ese chico (that boy)	esa chica (that girl)	esos chicos (those boys)	esas chicas (those girls)
aquel chico (that boy over there)	aquella chica (that girl over there)	aquellos chicos (those boys over there)	aquellas chicas (those girls over there)

Demonstrative pronouns

The demonstrative pronoun is distinguished from the demonstrative adjective by a written accent, e.g. *ése* ('that one'), *ese* ('that'). The accent is not now necessary, but it is still widely used.

Masculine singular	Feminine singular	Masculine plural	Feminine plural
éste (this (one))	ésta (this (one))	éstos (these (ones))	éstas (these (ones))
ése (that (one))	ésa (that (one))	ésos (those (ones))	ésas (those (ones))
aquél (that (one))	aquélla (that (one))	aquéllos (those (ones))	aquéllas (those (ones))

The neuter forms of the demonstrative pronouns are:

esto	this
eso	that
aquello	that

The neuter form refers to an indeterminate idea and not necessarily to a specific object:

¿Por qué no te gusta eso?
Why don't you like that?

Indefinites

Indefinites are words that refer to persons or things that are not specific. The following words are indefinites:

alguno/a/os/as	some, any
alguien	someone, anyone
algo	something, anything
cada	each, every
otro/a/os/as	(an)other
todo/a/os/as	all, any, every

Algún día visitaré Argentina.
Some day I'll visit Argentina.

Me llamaba cada 2 horas.
He used to ring me every 2 hours.

Alguien llamó a la puerta.
Somebody knocked at the door.

¿Has perdido algo?
Have you lost something?

No hay otra posibilidad.
There isn't another possibility.

Lo sabes todo.
You know it all.

Possessive adjectives

Singular	Plural
mi (my)	*mis* (my)
tu (your)	*tus* (your)
su (his, her, its, your (formal))	*sus* (his, her, its, your (formal))
vuestro/a (your)	*vuestros/as* (your)
su (their, your (formal))	*sus* (their, your (formal))

The possessive adjective agrees in number and gender with the noun that follows it:

Raúl nunca va al colegio con su hermana.
Raúl never goes to school with his sister.

Has dejado tus zapatillas en mi casa.
You've left your trainers at my house.

The possessive adjective *su(s)* can mean his/her/its/ their or your (formal):

Deme su pasaporte, señor.
Give me your passport, sir. (formal 'your')

Sabe que su pasaporte está caducado.
He/She knows that his/her passport is out of date.

Tu(s), *vuestro/a/os/as* or *su(s)* can all mean 'your', depending on whether the relationship with the person(s) addressed is familiar or formal:

Tus amigos han llegado, papá.
Your friends have arrived, dad.

Vuestro desayuno está listo, hijos.
Your breakfast is ready, children.

Por favor, abra su maleta, señora.
Open your suitcase, please, madam.

Possessive pronouns

Singular	Plural
mío/a (mine)	*míos/as* (mine)
tuyo/a (yours)	*tuyos/as* (yours)
suyo/a (his, hers, yours (formal))	*suyos/as* (his, hers, yours (formal))
nuestro/a (our)	*nuestros/as* (ours)
vuestro/a (yours)	*vuestros/as* (yours)
suyo/a (theirs, yours (formal))	*suyos/as* (theirs, yours (formal))

Possessive pronouns are used to replace nouns in order to avoid repetition. They agree in number and gender with the object possessed:

Ese boli, ¿es tuyo o mío?
Is that biro yours or mine?

Su coche nuevo no va tan rápido como el nuestro.
Their/your new car doesn't go as fast as ours.

Interrogative adjectives

The interrogative adjectives are:

- *¿qué?*   what?

  ¿De qué parte de España eres?
  What part of Spain are you from?

- *¿cuánto/a/os/as?*   how much/many?

  ¿Cuántos kilos de patatas deseas?
  How many kilos of potatoes do you want?

Interrogative pronouns

The interrogative pronouns are:

- *¿qué?*   what?

  ¿Qué te gustaría hacer esta noche?
  What would you like to do tonight?

- *¿cuál? ¿cuáles?*   which? what?
  (often for choosing between alternatives)

  ¿Cuál de los vestidos prefieres, el azul o el rojo?
  Which dress do you prefer, the blue one or the red one?

- *¿(de) quién/quiénes?*   who, (whose)?

  ¿De quién es esta bici?
  Whose bike is this?

- *¿cómo?*   how? what? why?

  ¿Cómo estás?
  How are you?

- *¿(a)dónde?*   where?

  ¿Adónde vamos este fin de semana?
  Where shall we go this weekend?

- *¿por qué?*   why?

  ¿Por qué no quieres salir con nosotros?
  Why don't you want to come out with us?

- *¿cuándo?*   when?

  ¿Cuándo nació tu hermano?
  When was your brother born?

- *¿cuánto?*   how much?

  ¿Cuánto vale?
  How much is it/How much does it cost?

Notes:
- Interrogative adjectives and pronouns always have a written accent.
- Direct questions in Spanish are preceded by an inverted question mark.

Exclamations

Some of the pronouns and adjectives used for questions are also used for exclamations:

- *¡cuánto(a/os/as)!*   how (much, many)!

  ¡Cuánto calor hace!
  How hot it is!

- *¡qué!*   what a...! how...!

  ¡Qué lástima!
  What a shame!

- *¡cómo!*   how! what!

  ¡Cómo me duele la cabeza!
  How my head aches!

Notes:
- Exclamation words always have a written accent.
- Exclamations are preceded by an inverted exclamation mark.

Relatives

Relatives are words like *que* and *cuyo*, which link two parts, or 'clauses', of a sentence:

- *que* (who, which, that) can be used as subject or object pronoun.

  El chico que está hablando con tu amigo es mi hermano.
  The boy who is speaking to your friend is my brother.

  La chica que ves en la plaza es mi hermana.
  The girl (that) you can see in the square is my sister.

- *el/la/los/las que* (who, which, that) is used mostly after prepositions.

  La casa en la que vivíamos está en las afueras de la ciudad.
  The house that we used to live in is on the outskirts of the town.

- *lo que* (what) refers to an idea rather than a specific noun.

  Haz lo que quieras.
  Do what you like.

- *quien(es)* (who, whom) is used only for people.

  La chica con quien trabajo se marchó ayer.
  The girl (that) I work with left yesterday.

- *cuyo/a/os/as* (whose) is an adjective that agrees in number and gender with the noun it qualifies.

  La chica cuya madre está en el hospital...
  The girl whose mother is in hospital...

Adverbs

Adverbs tell you *when* something is done (time), *how* it is done (manner) and *where* it is done (place).

Many adverbs are formed from the feminine of an adjective, by adding the suffix *-mente*:

Masculine adjective	Feminine adjective	Adverb
claro	*clara*	*claramente*
fácil	*fácil*	*fácilmente*
feliz	*feliz*	*felizmente*

Other common adverbs and adverbial phrases are:

- time

ahora	now
a menudo	frequently
antes	before
a veces	sometimes
después	later, afterwards
en seguida	at once, immediately
entonces	then, at that time
luego	then, later, soon
pronto	soon
siempre	always
tarde	late
temprano	early
todavía	still
ya	already, now

- manner

así	like this, thus
bien	well
de la misma manera	in the same way
de repente	suddenly
despacio, lentamente	slowly
mal	badly

- place

abajo	down, below
adelante	forward(s)
allí, allá	there
aquí, acá	here
arriba	above
atrás	back(wards)
cerca	near(by)
debajo	underneath
delante	in front
(a)dentro	inside
detrás	behind
encima	above, on top
en todas partes	everywhere
(a)fuera	outside
lejos	far

Note: when two *-mente* adverbs come together and are joined by *y*, the first one loses the *-mente* ending:

Trabajamos rápida y eficazmente.
We worked quickly and effectively.

Quantifiers

A number of adverbs, known as quantifiers, refer to the degree or amount to which something is (done). The most common quantifiers are:

- *bastante* enough; quite

  La película fue bastante buena.
  The film was quite good.

- *demasiado* too

  ¡Eres demasiado bueno!
  You are too good!

- *mucho* (very) much

  Va a hacer mucho más calor.
  It's going to get much hotter.

- *muy* very

  El partido fue muy emocionante.
  The match was very exciting.

- *(un) poco* (a) little

  Ese político es poco conocido.
  That politician is little known.

Personal pronouns

Subject pronouns

The subject pronouns are:

Singular	Plural
yo (I)	*nosotros/as* (we)
tú (you)	*vosotros/as* (you)
él (he, it)	*ellos* (they)
ella (she, it)	*ellas* (they)
usted (you (formal))	*ustedes* (you (formal))

Subject pronouns are used far less than in English. Usually the verb on its own is sufficient to express the meaning: *Habla español* means 'He/She speaks Spanish', without needing a subject pronoun to express 'he/she'.

You might include the subject pronoun, however, if you want to emphasise for some reason who it is who speaks Spanish:

Ella habla español, pero él no.
She speaks Spanish, but **he** doesn't.

Subject pronouns are also used standing on their own:

¿Hablas español?
Do you speak Spanish?

Yo no. Y tú?
No, I don't. Do you?

There are two forms of the subject pronoun for 'you':
- *tú* and *vosotros* for the familiar mode of address
- *usted* and *ustedes* for the formal mode of address

Note: *usted* and *ustedes* are always used with the third person form of the verb.

¿Conoce usted a mi profesor de español?
Do you know my Spanish teacher?

In the *tú* form this question would be:

¿Conoces a mi profesor de español?

Direct object pronouns

The direct object pronouns are:

Singular	Plural
me (me)	*nos* (us)
te (you)	*os* (you)
lo/le (him, it, you (formal masc.))	*los/les* (them (masc.), you (formal masc.))
la (her, it, you (formal fem.)	*las* (them (fem.), you (formal fem.))

Note that the third-person direct object pronouns *lo/le*, *la* ('him', 'her') and *los/les/las* ('them') are also used for 'you' (formal).

Lo/los and *le/les* are interchangeable:

Lo/le conozco bien.
I know him/it/you well.

La vi en Madrid.
I saw her/it/you in Madrid.

Los/les/las vi en Londres.
I saw them/you in London.

Direct object pronouns are usually placed before the verb:

Me vio ayer en la calle.
He saw me yesterday in the street.

They are always added to the end of the affirmative imperative:

¡Míralo!
Look at it!

They can be added to the end of an infinitive:

Quiero verlos en seguida.
I want to see them at once.

However, it is also possible to say:

Los quiero ver en seguida.

They are normally added to the end of a gerund:

Está escribiéndola.
He's writing it (e.g. a letter).

(Note that *escribiendo* has to have an accent to preserve the stress.)

However, it is also possible to say:

La está escribiendo.

Indirect object pronouns

Singular	Plural
me (to me)	*nos* (to us)
te (to you)	*os* (to you)
le (to him, her, it, you (formal))	*les* (to them, you (formal))

The direct object pronouns receive the action of the verb *directly*, whereas the indirect object pronouns receive it *indirectly*. In the sentence, 'We gave the ball to him', 'the ball' is the direct object and 'to him' is the indirect object: *Le dimos el balón.*

Me vas a decir la verdad.
You are going to tell (to) me the truth.

No te puedo recomendar aquel hotel.
I can't recommend that hotel to you.

Like direct object pronouns, indirect object pronouns are always added to the end of the affirmative imperative:

Tráigame la cuenta.
Bring (to) me the bill.

They can be added to the end of an infinitive:

Voy a decirle lo que pienso.
I'm going to tell (to) him what I think.

However, it is also possible to say:

Le voy a decir lo que pienso.

They are normally added to the end of a gerund:

Está escribiéndoles.
He's writing to them. (Note that escribiendo has to have an accent to preserve the stress.)

Gramática

However, it is also possible to say:

Les está escribiendo.

Order of object pronouns

In sentences that contain both a direct and an indirect object pronoun, the indirect one is always placed first:

Te lo daré mañana.
I'll give it to you tomorrow.

In the above sentence, *te* is the indirect object and *lo* the direct object pronoun.

The indirect object pronoun *le/les* changes to *se* before a third person direct object pronoun:

Se lo di.
I gave it to him/her/you/them.

A él, a ella, a usted, a ellos, a ellas, a ustedes may be added for clarity:

Se lo di a ella.
I gave it to her.

Disjunctive pronouns

Disjunctive pronouns are pronouns that are used after prepositions:

Singular	Plural
mí (me)	*nosotros/as* (us)
ti (you)	*vosotros/as* (you)
él (him, it)	*ellos* (them)
ella (her, it)	*ellas* (them)
usted (you (formal))	*ustedes* (you (formal))

Vamos a visitar el Prado con ellas.
We are going to visit the Prado with them.

Mí, ti and *sí* combine with the preposition *con* to make *conmigo* (with me), *contigo* (with you) and *consigo* (with him/her(self) etc.):

¿Por qué no le deja ir conmigo?
Why don't you let him go with me?

Reflexive pronouns

Reflexive pronouns refer back to the subject of the sentence.

Singular	Plural
me (myself)	*nos* (ourselves)
te (yourself)	*os* (yourselves)
se (himself, herself, yourself (formal))	*se* (themselves, yourselves (formal))

The reflexive pronoun normally precedes the verb but, like the object pronouns, it is added to the end of imperatives, gerunds and infinitives:

Se fue a Venezuela ayer.
He went to Venezuela yesterday.

¡Levántate!
Get up!

Está divirtiéndose.
She's enjoying herself.

Fueron a Las Vegas para casarse.
They went to Las Vegas to get married.

Verbs

Present tense

The present tense is formed by adding the highlighted endings to the stem of the infinitive:

- *-ar* verbs: *hablo, hablas, habla, hablamos, habláis, hablan*
- *-er* verbs: *como, comes, come, comemos, coméis, comen*
- *-ir* verbs: *escribo, escribes, escribe, escribimos, escribís, escriben*

The present tense is used for:

- something that exists at the time of speaking

  Hace frío en Soria.
  It's cold in Soria.

- describing a habit

  Nos reunimos en la discoteca todos los viernes.
  We meet at the disco every Friday.

- general statements

  Los Pirineos están en el norte de España.
  The Pyrenees are in the north of Spain.

- future intention

  ¿Vas a ver el partido?
  Are you going to see the match?

Note: some irregular verbs have a special form in the first person singular:

conocer	to know	*conozco, conoces, conoce…*
construir	to build	*construyo, construyes, construye…*
dar	to give	*doy, das, da…*
decir	to say	*digo, dices, dice…*
estar	to be	*estoy, estás, está…*
hacer	to do/make	*hago, haces, hace…*

ir	to go	*voy, vas, va…*
oír	to hear	*oigo, oyes, oye…*
poner	to put	*pongo, pones, pone…*
salir	to leave	*salgo, sales, sale…*
ser	to be	*soy, eres, es…*
tener	to have	*tengo, tienes, tiene…*
traer	to bring	*traigo, traes, trae…*
venir	to come	*vengo, vienes, viene…*

Note: some of these verbs have other irregularities.

Some verbs change the vowel of the stem in the first three persons of the singular and the third person plural (see also radical-changing verbs, pp. 165–67):

pensar	to think	*pienso, piensas, piensa, pensamos, pensáis, piensan*
encontrar	to find	*encuentro, encuentras, encuentra, encontramos, encontráis, encuentran*
pedir	to ask for	*pido, pides, pide, pedimos, pedís, piden*

Present continuous tense

The present continuous tense is formed by the present tense of verb *estar* plus the gerund. The gerund is the form of the verb that ends in *-ando* (*-ar* verbs) or *-iendo* (*-er* and *-ir* verbs):

This form of the present tense describes actions that are happening *now*:

> *Está hablando con Alex en su móvil.*
> She's talking to Alex on her mobile.

> *Estamos comiendo nuestro desayuno.*
> We're eating our breakfast.

Preterite tense

The preterite tense is formed by adding the highlighted endings to the stem of the infinitive:

- *-ar* verbs: *hablé, hablaste, habló, hablamos, hablasteis, hablaron*
- *-er* verbs: *comí, comiste, comió, comimos, comisteis, comieron*
- *-ir* verbs: *escribí, escribiste, escribió, escribimos, escribisteis, escribieron*

There are many irregular preterites, the most common being:

> *andar* — *anduve, anduviste, anduvo, anduvimos, anduvisteis, anduvieron*
> *conducir* — *conduje, condujiste, condujo, condujimos, condujisteis, condujeron*

> *dar* — *di, diste, dio, dimos, disteis, dieron*
> *decir* — *dije, dijiste, dijo, dijimos, dijisteis, dijeron*
> *estar* — *estuve, estuviste, estuvo, estuvimos, estuvisteis, estuvieron*
> *hacer* — *hice, hiciste, hizo, hicimos, hicisteis, hicieron*
> *ir* — *fui, fuiste, fue, fuimos, fuisteis, fueron*
> *poder* — *pude, pudiste, pudo, pudimos, pudisteis, pudieron*
> *poner* — *puse, pusiste, puso, pusimos, pusisteis, pusieron*
> *querer* — *quise, quisiste, quiso, quisimos, quisisteis, quisieron*
> *saber* — *supe, supiste, supo, supimos, supisteis, supieron*
> *ser* — *fui, fuiste, fue, fuimos, fuisteis, fueron*
> *tener* — *tuve, tuviste, tuvo, tuvimos, tuvisteis, tuvieron*
> *traer* — *traje, trajiste, trajo, trajimos, trajisteis, trajeron*
> *venir* — *vine, viniste, vino, vinimos, vinisteis, vinieron*
> *ver* — *vi, viste, vio, vimos, visteis, vieron*

Notes on the form of the preterite

- In *-ar* regular verbs, the first person plural has the same form in the preterite as in the present tense.
- The verbs *ir* and *ser* have exactly the same form in the preterite for all persons: *fui, fuiste, fue, fuimos, fuisteis, fueron*.
- The irregular preterite forms should be learned (see also the verb tables on pp. 171–79).

The preterite tense is used to express a *completed* action in the past that happened at a specific time:

> *El Rey de España fue a Argentina en mayo.*
> The King of Spain went to Argentina in May.

These actions are often a series of events within a specific period of time.

> *Ayer **fui** con Rosa al bar Manolo. Ella **tomó** una coca-cola y yo una cerveza. **Hablamos** de las vacaciones. Ella **dijo** que odiaba Benidorm y no quería ir allí otra vez. ¡No nos **pusimos** de acuerdo! Luego **llegó** Roberto. Le **pregunté** qué pensaba. Él **respondió** que no sabía. ¡Qué lata!*

> Yesterday I went to Manolo's bar with Rosa. She had a coke and I had a beer. We spoke about the holidays. She said she hated Benidorm and didn't want to go there again. We didn't agree! Then Roberto arrived. I asked him what he thought. He said he didn't know. What a pain!

Note: students of Spanish who are also studying French often use the Spanish perfect tense (*he hablado*) when they should use the preterite (*hablé*). This is because they don't realise that the French perfect tense (*j'ai parlé* etc.) is similar in its use to the Spanish preterite tense (*hablé* etc.). Thus, 'I spoke to her' in Spanish would normally be '*Hablé con ella*', and not '*He hablado con ella*'.

Gramática

Imperfect tense

The imperfect tense is formed by adding the highlighted endings to the stem of the infinitive:

- -ar verbs: *habl**aba**, habl**abas**, habl**aba**, habl**ábamos**, habl**abais**, habl**aban***
- -er verbs: *com**ía**, com**ías**, com**ía**, com**íamos**, com**íais**, com**ían***
- -ir verbs: *escrib**ía**, escrib**ías**, escrib**ía**, escrib**íamos**, escrib**íais**, escrib**ían***

Three verbs are irregular in the imperfect tense:

ir — iba, ibas, iba, íbamos, ibais, iban
ser — era, eras, era, éramos, erais, eran
ver — veía, veías, veía, veíamos, veíais, veían

The imperfect tense is used for:

- actions that happened regularly in the past, i.e. what we **used to** do

Mi abuela siempre estaba sentada al lado del fuego.
My grandma always sat by the fire.

Íbamos a la playa todos los días.
We went/used to go to the beach every day.

- descriptions in the past

José Carlos era un hombre alto.
José Carlos was a tall man.

Imperfect continuous tense

The imperfect continuous tense is formed by the imperfect tense of the verb *estar* plus the gerund. The gerund is the form of the verb that ends in -*ando* (-*ar* verbs) or -*iendo* (-*er* and -*ir* verbs).

This form of the imperfect tense describes actions that were happening at that time, as in the English sentence:

Estaba hablando con Alex en su móvil.
He was talking to Alex on his mobile.

Estábamos andando en la playa.
We were walking on the beach.

Future tense

The future tense is formed by adding the highlighted endings to the infinitive of the verb:

- -ar verbs: *hablar**é**, hablar**ás**, hablar**á**, hablar**emos**, hablar**éis**, hablar**án***
- -er verbs: *comer**é**, comer**ás**, comer**á**, comer**emos**, comer**éis**, comer**án***
- -ir verbs: *escribir**é**, escribir**ás**, escribir**á**, escribir**emos**, escribir**éis**, escribir**án***

A number of common verbs have an irregular future stem. The most important of these are:

decir — **diré** etc
hacer — **haré** etc.
poder — **podré** etc
poner — **pondré** etc.
querer — **querré** etc.
saber — **sabré** etc.
salir — **saldré** etc.
tener — **tendré** etc.
venir — **vendré** etc.

The future tense expresses what *will* happen:

Volverán de Segovia a las dos.
They'll return from Segovia at 2 o'clock.

Hablaré con ella mañana.
I'll speak to her tomorrow.

Immediate future

The immediate future is formed using *ir a* and the infinitive of the verb. It is often used to express future intention, especially in colloquial Spanish. This form is often interchangeable with the future (see the section above).

¿Vas a verle?
Are you going to see her?

Voy a buscar pan.
I'm going to get some bread.

Conditional tense

The conditional tense is formed by adding the highlighted endings to the infinitive of the verb:

- -ar verbs: *hablar**ía**, hablar**ías**, hablar**ía**, hablar**íamos**, hablar**íais**, hablar**ían***
- -er verbs: *comer**ía**, comer**ías**, comer**ía**, comer**íamos**, comer**íais**, comer**ían***
- -ir verbs: *escribir**ía**, escribir**ías**, escribir**ía**, escribir**íamos**, escribir**íais**, escribir**ían***

A number of common verbs have an irregular form in the conditional. These are the same verbs as those that have an irregular future, i.e. *decir* (*diría* etc.), *hacer* (*haría* etc.), *poder* (*podría*) etc. (See the section above on the future tense.)

The conditional tense expresses what **would** happen:

¿Te gustaría pasar el día en el campo?
Would you like to spend the day in the country?

¿Qué preferirías hacer, ir al cine o a la discoteca?
What would you prefer to do, go to the cinema or the disco?

The conditional is also used to make polite requests:

Por favor, ¿podría darme un folleto?
Could you please give me a leaflet?

Perfect tense

The perfect tense is a compound tense, formed from the auxiliary verb *haber* plus the past participle of the verb (*hablado, comido, escrito* etc.).

he *hablado/comido/escrito*
has *hablado/comido/escrito*
ha *hablado/comido/escrito,*
hemos *hablado/comido/escrito*
habéis *hablado/comido/escrito*
han *hablado/comido/escrito*

The perfect tense is used to connect past time with present time. It describes actions that have begun in the past and are continuing and/or have an effect now:

He empezado a estudiar italiano.
I've started to study Italian (and I am continuing to study Italian now).

The perfect tense is also used to express the very recent past, especially events that happened today:

Esta mañana me he levantado a las 7.30.
I got up this morning at 7.30.

Note: there are a number of irregular past participles of common verbs, which should be learned. These are the most common:

abrir	to open	*abierto*	opened
decir	to say	*dicho*	said
escribir	to write	*escrito*	written
hacer	to do/make	*hecho*	done/made
morir	to die	*muerto*	died
poner	to put	*puesto*	put
romper	to break	*roto*	broken
ver	to see	*visto*	seen
volver	to return	*vuelto*	returned

When used as part of the perfect tense, the past participle never agrees in number or gender with the subject of the sentence:

Hemos tenido buena suerte.
We've been lucky (i.e. We've had good luck).

Tu hermana ha ganado el concurso, ¿no?
Your sister has won the competition, hasn't she?

Pluperfect tense

The pluperfect tense is formed from the imperfect tense of *haber* and the past participle of the verb (*hablado, comido, escrito*).

había *hablado/comido/escrito*
habías *hablado/comido/escrito*
había *hablado/comido/escrito,*
habíamos *hablado/comido/escrito*
habíais *hablado/comido/escrito*
habían *hablado/comido/escrito*

This tense expresses what had happened before another action in the past:

La fiesta ya había comenzado cuando llegó Jaime.
The party had already started when Jaime arrived.

Subjunctive

The subjunctive is one of three moods of the verb (the others are the indicative and the imperative). The subjunctive is used in four tenses: the present, the imperfect, the perfect and the pluperfect. All four tenses of the subjunctive are widely used.

It is important to be able to use the present subjunctive and to be able to recognise the imperfect subjunctive.

Present subjunctive

The present subjunctive is formed by adding the highlighted endings to the stem of the infinitive:
- *-ar* verbs: *hable, hables, hable, hablemos, habléis, hablen*
- *-er* verbs: *coma, comas, coma, comamos, comáis, coman*
- *-ir* verbs: *escriba, escribas, escriba, escribamos, escribáis, escriban*

The endings of *-ar* verbs are the same as the present indicative endings of *-er* verbs, and those of *-er* and *-ir* verbs are the same as the present indicative endings of *-ar* verbs, with the exception of the first person singular.

The present subjunctive of most irregular verbs is formed by removing the final *-o* from the end of the first person singular of the present indicative and adding the endings listed above. Most irregular verbs keep the final consonant of the first person singular for all persons. For example:

hacer — haga, hagas, haga, hagamos, hagáis, hagan.

See verb tables on pp. 171–79 for more irregular subjunctives.

Gramática

Imperfect subjunctive

The imperfect subjunctive is formed by removing the ending of the third person plural of the preterite tense and adding the highlighted endings:

- -ar verbs: either *hablara, hablaras, hablara, habláramos, hablarais, hablaran*

  or *hablase, hablases, hablase, hablásemos, hablaseis, hablasen*

- -er verbs: either *comiera, comieras, comiera, comiéramos, comierais, comieran*

  or *comiese, comieses, comiese, comiésemos, comieseis, comiesen*

- -ir verbs: either *escribiera, escribieras, escribiera, escribiéramos, escribierais, escribieran*

  or *escribiese, escribieses, escribiese, escribiésemos, escribieseis, escribiesen*

The -ara/ase and -iera/iese endings are interchangeable.

Perfect subjunctive

The perfect subjunctive is formed from the present subjunctive of *haber* plus the past participle, e.g. *haya hablado, hayas hablado, haya hablado* etc.

Pluperfect subjunctive

The pluperfect subjunctive is formed from the imperfect subjunctive of *haber* plus the past participle, e.g. *hubiera/iese hablado, hubieras/ieses hablado, hubiera/iese hablado* etc.

Uses of the subjunctive

The subjunctive is used in three main areas: subordinate clauses, main clauses and conditional sentences.

Important uses of the subjunctive are:

- after conjunctions of time, such as *cuando* and *mientras*, when expressing the future

  Cuando tenga yo 18 años voy a dar una fiesta enorme.
  When I'm 18 I'm going to have a huge party.

  Hugo tendrá que buscar trabajo temporal mientras viaje por Latinoamérica.
  Hugo will have to look for temporary work while he travels round Latin America

- after verbs of wishing, command, request and emotion

  Laura quiere que le acompañes al cine.
  Laura wants you to go with her to the cinema.

Espero que me escribas pronto.
I hope you will write to me soon.

Te digo que no salgas esta noche.
I'm telling you not to go out tonight.

Pídele que me compre las entradas.
Ask him to buy me the tickets.

- to express purpose, after *para que*

  Te daré la llave para que puedas entrar en el piso.
  I'll give you the key so that you can get into the flat.

- to express possibility, probability and necessity

  Es posible que la selección española gane la copa.
  It's possible that the Spanish team will win the cup.

  No es necesario que ellos vayan a la estación con nosotros.
  It's not necessary for them to go to the station with us.

- to express permission and prohibition

  ¡Déjale que venga!
  Let him come!

- after verbs of saying and thinking used in the negative

  No creo que los estudiantes encuentren fácil el trabajo.
  I don't think the students will find the work easy.

- to express the formal imperative and the negative form of the familiar imperative (for the imperative see the next section)

Imperatives

The imperative mood is for instructions and commands.

Affirmative commands

For regular verbs, the **informal** *tú* imperative is formed by removing the last letter, s, from the second person singular of the present indicative:

hablas — habla
comes — come
escribes — escribe

There are nine irregular forms, which have to be learned:

Verb	Tú imperative
decir (to say)	*di*
hacer (to do)	*haz*
ir (to go)	*ve*
oír (to hear)	*oye*
poner (to put)	*pon*
salir (to go out)	*sal*
ser (to be)	*sé*
tener (to have)	*ten*
venir (to come)	*ven*

Escríbeme pronto.
Write to me soon.

Pon el libro en la mesa.
Put the book on the table.

The *vosotros* imperative is formed by replacing the final -*r* of the infinitive with -*d*. Note that the final -*d* is omitted from reflexive forms:

Volved conmigo, amigos.
Come back with me, friends.

¡Levantaos!
Get up!

In the **formal** *usted/ustedes* form, both the singular and the plural are the same as the third person (*usted/ustedes*) of the present subjunctive.

Por favor, firme aquí.
Sign here please.

Dígame lo que ocurre.
Tell me what is happening.

Perdonen, señoras.
Excuse me, ladies.

Negative commands
Negative familiar commands use the second person (*tú/vosotros*) of the present subjunctive:

¡No hables así!
Don't speak like that!

¡No salgas!
Don't go out!

No me lo digáis.
Don't tell me.

Negative *usted/ustedes* commands, like the affirmative ones, use the third person of the present subjunctive:

¡No me diga!
You don't say!

No se molesten.
Don't get upset.

Note: *que* + the subjunctive may be used for wishes and commands. *Que* is sometimes omitted:

(Que) vayan todos.
Let them all go.

¡(Que) viva el Rey!
Long live the King!

Passive
A passive sentence has the same meaning as an active one, but the parts of the sentence are in a different order. For example, 'My handbag was stolen by a thief' is a passive sentence, which can also be expressed actively as 'A thief stole my handbag'.

In a passive sentence, there is normally an agent, usually preceded by the preposition *por*. However, the agent may be omitted from the sentence, as in:

La carta fue escrita ayer.
The letter was written yesterday.

The passive is formed from *ser* plus the past participle, which agrees in number and gender with the subject of the sentence:

El acuerdo fue firmado por el presidente.
The agreement was signed by the president.

La novela será publicada mañana.
The novel will be published tomorrow.

Gerund
The gerund expresses the idea of the *duration* of the action of the verb.

To form the gerund, add -*ando* to the stem of -*ar* verbs and -*iendo* to the stem of -*er* and -*ir* verbs. The gerund is invariable in form.

hablar — hablando
comer — comiendo
escribir — ecribiendo

The gerund is used for actions that take place at the same time as the main verb:

Van corriendo por la calle.
They go running along the street.

It is used for the continuous form of the verb:

Estaban mirando el cielo para ver si iba a llover.
They were looking at the sky to see if it was going to rain.

Continuar, seguir and *llevar* are followed by the gerund to emphasise the duration of the verb:

Por favor, sigue hablando.
Carry on talking, please.

Llevamos 3 años viviendo en Barcelona.
We've been living in Barcelona for 3 years.

Note: don't confuse the English present participle ending in *–ing* (e.g. 'eating') with the Spanish gerund. The English *-ing* form after a preposition is translated by an infinitive:

Después de terminar mis deberes, me acosté.
After finishing my homework, I went to bed.

Ser and estar

These two verbs both mean 'to be', but they are used in different circumstances.

Ser refers to characteristics that are 'inherent' to a person, thing or idea, such as identity, permanent features, occupation, time:

Soy gallego.
I'm Galician.

Madrid es la capital de España.
Madrid is the capital of Spain.

Es policía.
He's a policeman.

Son las nueve y media.
It's half past nine.

Estar refers to a temporary state or to where a person or thing is, whether temporarily or permanently:

Estamos contentos.
We're happy (but this is a momentary feeling).

Málaga está en el sur de España.
Malaga is in the south of Spain.

Ser and estar with adjectives

Some adjectives are always used with *ser*, others always with *estar*:

Ser		Estar	
(in)justo/a	(un)fair	*bien/mal/fatal*	good/bad/terrible
(in)necesario/a	(un)necessary	*de buen/mal humor*	in a good/mad mood
(in)conveniente	(in)appropriate	*enfadado/a*	angry
importante	important	*enfermo/a*	ill
inteligente	intelligent	*ocupado/a*	busy

Some adjectives can be used with either *ser* or *estar*, but their meaning is different. *Ser* meanings always reflect permanent characteristics; *estar* meanings refer to temporary states. The most common of these adjectives are:

Adjective	Used with *ser*	Used with *estar*
aburrido	boring	bored
listo	clever	ready
malo	bad, evil	ill
nervioso	nervous (disposition)	nervous (temporarily)
triste	sad (disposition)	sad (temporarily)

Impersonal verbs

Verbs such as *gustar, encantar, costar, doler, faltar, hacer falta, interesar* and *molestar* are used with a special construction that is the reverse of the English one. The sentence:

Me gusta la dieta mediterránea.
I like the Mediterranean diet.

can be broken down literally in English as follows:

Indirect object	Third person verb	Subject
Me To me	*gusta* is pleasing	*la dieta mediterránea* the Mediterranean diet

If the subject is plural, the verb must also be plural, as in:

Le gustan los tomates.
He likes tomatoes. (Literally 'To him are pleasing the tomatoes.')

Frequently, the person concerned is emphasised by adding *a* plus a personal pronoun:

A mí me gustan los tomates.
I like tomatoes.

The same construction can be seen in the following examples:

¿Te duele la cabeza?
Have you got a headache?

Les encanta la playa.
They love the beach.

Me costó un dineral.
It cost me a bomb.

¿A ti te molesta que venga Julio?
Are you bothered that Julio's coming?

Reflexive verbs

In Spanish, reflexive verbs are always accompanied by a reflexive pronoun, which changes according to the subject of the verb. For example:

levantarse	to get up
me levanto	I get up
te levantas	you get up
se levanta	he/she/it/you (formal) gets up
nos levantamos	we get up
os levantáis	you get up
se levantan	they/you (formal) get up

Reflexive verbs often do not have a reflexive pronoun when translated into English, for example: *acostarse* to go to bed; *afeitarse* to shave; *casarse* to marry.

Infinitives

Many common verbs are followed by a preposition, usually either *a, de, en, con, para* or *por*, before an infinitive. Some of the most common of these verbs are given below.

Verb + *a* + infinitive

acercarse a	to get near to
aprender a	to learn to
ayudar a	to help to
comenzar a	to begin to
decidirse a	to decide to
empezar a	to begin to
enseñar a	to teach to
invitar a	to invite to
ir a	to go to
volver a	to (do) again

Por favor, ayúdame a preparar la cena.
Help me to prepare dinner, please.

Comenzaron a entrar a las 9.00.
They started to go in at 9.00.

Verb + *de* + infinitive

acabar de	to finish (doing); to have just
acordarse de	to remember
alegrarse de	to be pleased about
olvidarse de	to forget to
terminar de	to stop (doing)
tratar de	to try to

Me alegro de saber eso.
I'm pleased to know that.

¡Trata de hacerlo!
Try to do it!

Verb + *en* + infinitive

dudar en	to hesitate to
insistir en	to insist on (doing)
interesarse en	to be interested in (doing)
tardar en	to take time in (doing)

El tren tardaba mucho en salir.
The train was very late departing.

Verb + *con* + infinitive

amenazar con	to threaten to
contentarse con	to be happy to
soñar con	to dream of (doing)

Sueña con ser piloto. He dreams about being a pilot.

Verb + *para* + infinitive

prepararse para	to prepare oneself to
faltar para	to have time/distance to go

Se está preparando para hacer el examen.
He's preparing to take the exam.

Falta poco para llegar a Zaragoza.
It's not far to Zaragoza.

Verb + *por* + infinitive

comenzar por	to begin by (doing)
empezar por	to begin by (doing)
luchar por	to fight/struggle to

Comenzamos la tarde por comer tapas.
We started the evening by eating tapas.

Three special constructions with the infinitive

- *Al* + the infinitive is used with the meaning 'when…', referring to an action that happens at the same time as that of the main verb:

  Al llegar a la estación vio que el tren había salido.
  When he got to the station he saw that the train had left.

- *Volver* followed by *a* + the infinitive means 'to do something again':

  No he vuelto a verle.
  I haven't seen him again.

- *Acabar* followed by *de* + the infinitive means 'to have just (done something)':

  Acaban de volver.
  They have just come back.

Radical-changing verbs

Radical-changing verbs are so called because they make changes to the 'root' or stem of the verb. Many Spanish verbs are of this type.

For example, in the verb *pensar* (to think) the stem is *pens-* (the infinitive without the -*ar* ending). In this verb, the -*e* of the stem changes to –*ie*; 'I think' is *pienso*.

Radical changes affect -*ar*, -*er* and -*ir* verbs. It is not easy to predict whether a given verb will have a stem change or not, so the radical-changing verbs have to be learned.

Conjugation of radical-changing verbs

In the present indicative tense of -*ar* and -*er* verbs, the main vowel of the stem splits into two when it is stressed. The vowel changes from *e* to *ie* and *o* to *ue*

Gramática

in the first, second and third persons singular and the third person plural:

cerrar (to close)	encontrar (to find)	perder (to lose)	volver (to return)
cierro	encuentro	pierdo	vuelvo
cierras	encuentras	pierdes	vuelves
cierra	encuentra	pierde	vuelve
cerramos	encontramos	perdemos	volvemos
cerráis	encontráis	perdéis	volvéis
cierran	encuentran	pierden	vuelven

The stem also changes in the *tú* (familiar) form of the imperative:

cierra

encuentra

pierde

vuelve

Other common *-ar* and *-er* verbs that follow the same pattern are:

e > ie:

-ar verbs	-er verbs
calentar (to heat)	defender (to defend)
comenzar (to begin)	encender (to switch on, to light)
despertar (to wake)	entender (to understand)
empezar (to begin)	querer (to wish, to want)
*nevar (to snow)	
pensar (to think)	
recomendar (to recommend)	
sentarse (to sit down)	

*nevar is used only in the third person singular

o > ue

-ar verbs	-er verbs
acordarse de (to remember)	doler (to hurt)
acostarse (to go to bed)	*llover (to rain)
contar (to count, to tell)	mover (to move)
costar (to cost)	poder (to be able)
probar (to prove, taste, try (on))	soler (to do habitually)
recordar (to remember)	torcer (to turn, twist)
soñar (to dream)	
volar (to fly)	

*llover is used only in the third person singular

Note: *jugar* (to play), with stem vowel *u*, follows the same pattern as verbs with stem vowel *o*: *juego, juegas, juega, jugamos, jugáis, juegan.*

-ir verbs

There are three types of radical-changing -ir verbs:

- those that change the stem vowel in the present tense from *e* to *i*, such as *pedir* (to ask for)
- those that change the stem vowel in the present tense from *e* to *ie*, such as *sentir* (to feel, be sorry)
- those that change the stem vowel in the present tense from *o* to *ue*, such as *dormir* (to sleep)

In the present indicative, the changes take place in the first, second and third persons singular and the third person plural, when the stress falls on the stem:

e > i	e > ie	o > ue
pedir	sentir	dormir
pido	siento	duermo
pides	sientes	duermes
pide	siente	duerme
pedimos	sentimos	dormimos
pedís	sentís	dormís
piden	sienten	duermen

In the stem of the preterite, in the third persons singular and plural, *e* changes to *i* and *o* changes to *u*:

pedí	sentí	dormí
pediste	sentiste	dormiste
pidió	sintió	durmió
pedimos	sentimos	dormimos
pedisteis	sentisteis	dormisteis
pidieron	sintieron	durmieron

The stem also changes in the *tú* (familiar) form of the imperative, following the pattern of the present indicative:

pide

siente

duerme

In the gerund, the stem changes from *e > i* or *o > u*:

pidiendo

sintiendo

durmiendo

Other common verbs which follow the *e > i* pattern are:

conseguir	to succeed
corregir	to correct
despedir	to dismiss, say goodbye to
elegir	to choose
impedir	to prevent
medir	to measure
reír	to laugh (río, ríes, ríe...)
reñir	to quarrel
repetir	to repeat
seguir	to follow
sonreír	to smile (sonrío, sonríes, sonríe...)
vestir	to dress

Other common verbs that follow the *e > ie* pattern are:

convertir	to convert
divertir	to entertain
herir	to wound
mentir	to lie
preferir	to prefer
referir	to refer

The only verbs to follow the *o > ue* pattern are:

dormir	to sleep
morir	to die

Spelling changes in verbs

Some Spanish verbs make spelling changes in order to comply with the rules of Spanish pronunciation. These changes are of two types and affect:

- the consonant immediately before the verb ending, which changes in order to keep the correct sound
- the use of the accent, which is needed in order to keep the required stress on a vowel

Changes to the spelling of the final consonant:

For *-ar* verbs, these changes occur before the vowel *-e*:

- *c > qu*   *buscar*   to look for

present subjunctive: *busque, busques, busque* etc.
preterite: *busqué, buscaste* etc.

- *g > gu*   *llegar*   to arrive

present subjunctive: *llegue, llegues, llegue* etc.
preterite: *llegué, llegaste* etc.

- *z > c*   *empezar*   to begin

present subjunctive: *empiece, empieces, empiece* etc.
preterite: *empecé, empezaste* etc.

For *-er* and *-ir* verbs, these changes occur before the vowel *-o* in the first person singular of the present indicative and before *-a* in the present subjunctive:

- *c > z*   *vencer*   to conquer

present indicative: *venzo, vences* etc.
present subjunctive: *venza, venzas, venza* etc.

- *g > j*   *coger*   to take, catch

present indicative: *cojo, coges* etc.
present subjunctive: *coja, cojas* etc.

- *gu > g*   *seguir*   to follow

present indicative: *sigo, sigues* etc.
present subjunctive: *siga, sigas, siga* etc.

Addition of an accent in order to keep the correct stress

Verbs ending in *-uar* and *-iar* do not have an accent in their infinitive form but they add an accent in the first, second and third persons singular and in the third person plural of the present indicative, the present subjunctive and in the *tú* form of the imperative:

continuar (to continue)		
Present indicative	**Present subjunctive**	**Imperative**
continúo	*continúe*	
continúas	*continúes*	*continúa*
continúa	*continúe*	
continuamos	*continuemos*	
continuáis	*continuéis*	
continúan	*continúen*	

enviar (to send)		
Present indicative	**Present subjunctive**	**Imperative**
envío	*envíe*	
envías	*envíes*	*envía*
envía	*envíe*	
enviamos	*enviemos*	
enviáis	*enviéis*	
envían	*envíen*	

Negatives

It is usual in Spanish for the negative to be expressed by two words (with the exception of *no* meaning 'not'). All the negatives below can, however, be expressed either:

- as two words, with *no* before the verb and the negative word after it, or
- as one word placed before the verb, eliminating the need for *no*

For example, 'They say that it never snows in Malaga' can be translated as:

*Dicen que **no** nieva **nunca** en Málaga.*

or

*Dicen que **nunca** nieva en Málaga.*

Negative	Example
no	*No viene.* (He isn't coming.)
nunca	*No llueve nunca.* (It never rains.)
jamás	*No voy a volver jamás.* (I'm never going to come back.)
tampoco	*Tampoco lo sabían ellos.* (They didn't know either.)
ni...ni...	*Ayer no vinieron ni Carlos ni Pepe.* (Neither Carlos nor Pepe came yesterday.)
nada	*No sabe nada.* (He doesn't know anything.)
nadie	*No hay nadie aquí.* (There is nobody here.)
ninguno	*No hay ninguna persona en la calle.* (There is no one in the street.)

Prepositions

a

a translates the English word 'at' when it refers to time or rate:

a la una
at one o'clock

Están viajando a solo 20 kilómetros por hora.
They are only travelling at 20 kph.

de

de means 'of', indicating possession, and 'from', indicating origin. It can also mean 'by', 'about' and 'in':

Están hablando de ti.
They are talking about you.

Vienen de Almagro.
They are coming from Almagro.

en

en means 'in' and 'at' of location:

en casa
at home

Estaba esperando en la estación.
He was waiting at the station.

enfrente de and frente a

These two prepositional phrases mean 'opposite':

La oficina de turismo está enfrente de/frente a la catedral.
The tourist office is opposite the cathedral.

para

para means 'for' and '(in order) to' in the sense of destination or purpose:

Tomamos una botella de agua fría para el viaje.
We're taking a bottle of cold water for the journey.

Voy a utilizar mi tarjeta de crédito para pagar el hotel.
I'm going to use my credit card to pay for the hotel.

por

por is used for cause and origin. The English equivalents of *por* are 'by', 'through', 'on behalf of' and 'because of':

Lo compré por Internet.
I bought it through the internet.

Hablaremos por teléfono.
We'll speak on the phone.

Salió por la puerta principal.
He went out by the main door.

Contesté por él.
I answered on his behalf.

por is also used to introduce the agent in passive sentences (see p. 163):

Aquel poema fue escrito por García Lorca.
That poem was written by García Lorca.

sobre

sobre means 'on (top of)', 'above' or 'over':

El avión voló sobre mi casa.
The plane flew over my house

Tus postales están sobre la mesa.
Your postcards are on the table.

sobre is also used to indicate an approximate time or number:

Llegarán sobre las nueve.
They'll arrive around 9 o'clock.

Conjunctions

Conjunctions are words that link phrases and sentences. Examples of conjunctions are:

y	and
o	or
pero	but
porque	because
cuando	when

Quiero ir al cine pero mi madre no me deja salir.
I want to go to the cinema but my mother won't let me go out.

Ha venido porque quiere hablar con el profesor.
He's come because he wants to speak to the teacher.

Note: *y* becomes *e* before 'i' and 'hi':

Pedro es serio e inteligente.
Pedro is serious and intelligent.

o becomes *u* before 'o' and 'ho':

siete u ocho
seven or eight

Numbers

Cardinal numbers

The numbers that are used for counting are called cardinal numbers:

1	*uno/una*
2	*dos*
3	*tres*
4	*cuatro*
5	*cinco*
6	*seis*
7	*siete*
8	*ocho*
9	*nueve*
10	*diez*
11	*once*
12	*doce*
13	*trece*
14	*catorce*
15	*quince*
16	*dieciséis*
17	*diecisiete*
18	*dieciocho*
19	*diecinueve*
20	*veinte*
21	*veintiuno/una*
22	*veintidós*
23	*veintitrés*
24	*veinticuatro*
25	*veinticinco*
26	*veintiséis*
27	*veintisiete*
28	*veintiocho*
29	*veintinueve*
30	*treinta*
31	*treinta y uno*
32	*treinta y dos*
40	*cuarenta*
50	*cincuenta*
60	*sesenta*
70	*setenta*
80	*ochenta*
90	*noventa*
100	*cien(to)*
101	*ciento uno/una*
102	*ciento dos*
153	*ciento cincuenta y dos*
200	*doscientos/as*
300	*trescientos/as*
400	*cuatrocientos/as*
500	*quinientos/as*
600	*seiscientos/as*
700	*setecientos/as*
800	*ochocientos/as*
900	*novecientos/as*
1000	*mil*
1001	*mil uno/una*
4.005	*cuatro mil cinco*
7.238	*siete mil doscientos treinta y ocho*
1.000.000	*un millón*
9.000.000	*nueve millones*

Notes:

- Numbers up to 30 are written as one word.
- *uno* becomes *un* before a masculine singular noun:

  un billete
  one ticket

  cuarenta y un años
  forty-one years

- Cardinal numbers containing *un(o)* and multiples of *ciento* have a masculine and a feminine form; other numbers do not:

  trescientas libras
  three hundred pounds

- *Ciento* is shortened to *cien* before a noun or an adjective but not before another number, except *mil*:

  cien kilómetros
  a hundred kilometres

  ciento veinte litros
  a hundred and twenty litres

- There is no indefinite article before *cien* and *mil*, unlike the English 'a hundred' and 'a thousand':

  mil euros
  a thousand euros

- *Un millón* (a million) is preceded by the indefinite article, as in English, and is followed by *de*:

  un millón de habitantes
  a million inhabitants

- Numbers over a thousand are frequently written with a dot after the figure for a thousand. This sometimes happens with dates:

  20.301   20,301

  2.009   2009

Gramática

Ordinal numbers

Ordinal numbers indicate the order or sequence of things (1st, 2nd, 3rd, 4th, etc.):

1st	1°/1ª	primero/a
2nd	2°/2ª	segundo/a
3rd	3°/3ª	tercero/a
4th	4°/4ª	cuarto/a
5th	5°/5ª	quinto/a
6th	6°/6ª	sexto/a
7th	7°/7ª	séptimo/a
8th	8°/8ª	octavo/a
9th	9°/9ª	noveno/a
10th	10°/10ª	décimo/a

Ordinal numbers agree with the noun in number and gender:

las primeras horas de la mañana
the first hours of the morning

Primero and *tercero* drop the final *-o* before a masculine singular noun:

el primer día de la primavera
the first day of spring

el tercer piso
the third floor

Ordinal numbers are normally used up to 10, after which cardinal numbers are used:

Carlos V (read '*quinto*')
Charles V (the fifth)

but

el siglo XXI (read '*veintiuno*')
the twenty-first century

Time, dates and years

Clock time

Cardinal numbers are used to tell the time. With *la una*, the singular of *ser* is used; the plural is used with all other times:

¿Qué hora es?
What time is it?

Es la una y media.
It's half past one.

Son las ocho y media.
It's half-past eight.

Note that the 24-hour clock is used for timetables:

El tren salió a las 20.45.
The train left at 8.45 p.m.

The phrases '*de la mañana*' (a.m.) and '*de la tarde/noche*' (p.m.) are often placed after the number:

las seis de la mañana
6 a.m.

las diez y cuarto de la noche
10.15 p.m.

Dates

For dates, cardinal numbers are used except for the first of the month, where the ordinal number is used:

el 4 de julio
4th July

el primero de enero
1st January

Note that when writing the date it is usual to insert *de* before the month and year:

el 3 de marzo de 1995
3rd March 1995

Years

In Spanish, years are expressed by listing thousands, hundreds, tens and units.

mil novecientos cincuenta y nueve
nineteen hundred and fifty nine

dos mil diez
two thousand and ten

Time expressions

The idea of 'for' with a period of time can be expressed by using *desde hace* plus the time expression:

Vivimos en Méjico desde hace 3 años.
We've lived in Mexico for 3 years.

or *llevar* followed by the gerund:

Llevamos 3 años viviendo en Méjico.

Note that this construction involves a change of tense from the English perfect to the Spanish present. Similarly, the pluperfect tense in English is translated by the imperfect tense in Spanish:

Vivíamos en Méjico desde hacía 3 años
or
Llevábamos 3 años viviendo en Méjico.
We had lived in Mexico for 3 years.

Verb tables

Regular verbs

hablar		**Gerund:** *hablando*	**Past principle:** *hablado*
Imperative familiar	**Present indicative**	**Imperfect indicative**	**Preterite**
habla	hablo	hablaba	hablé
hablad	hablas	hablabas	hablaste
	habla	hablaba	habló
	hablamos	hablábamos	hablamos
	habláis	hablabais	hablasteis
	hablan	hablaban	hablaron
Future	**Conditional**	**Present subjunctive**	**Imperfect subjunctive**
hablaré	hablaría	hable	hablara/ase
hablarás	hablarías	hables	hablaras/ases
hablará	hablaría	hable	hablara/ase
hablaremos	hablaríamos	hablemos	habláramos/ásemos
hablaréis	hablaríais	habléis	hablarais/aseis
hablarán	hablarían	hablen	hablaran/asen

comer		**Gerund:** *comiendo*	**Past principle:** *comido*
Imperative familiar	**Present indicative**	**Imperfect indicative**	**Preterite**
come	como	comía	comí
comed	comes	comías	comiste
	come	comía	comió
	comemos	comíamos	comimos
	coméis	comíais	comisteis
	comen	comían	comieron
Future	**Conditional**	**Present subjunctive**	**Imperfect subjunctive**
comeré	comería	coma	comiera/ese
comerás	comerías	comas	comieras/eses
comerá	comería	coma	comiera/ese
comeremos	comeríamos	comamos	comiéramos/ésemos
comeréis	comeríais	comáis	comierais/eseis
comerán	comerían	coman	comieran/esen

escribir		**Gerund:** *escribiendo*	**Past principle:** *escrito*
Imperative familiar	**Present indicative**	**Imperfect indicative**	**Preterite**
escribe	escribo	escribía	escribí
escribid	escribes	escribías	escribiste
	escribe	escribía	escribió
	escribimos	escribíamos	escribimos
	escribís	escribíais	escribisteis
	escriben	escribían	escribieron
Future	**Conditional**	**Present subjunctive**	**Imperfect subjunctive**
escribiré	escribiría	escriba	escribiera/ese
escribirás	escribirías	escribas	escribieras/eses
escribirá	escribiría	escriba	escribiera/ese
escribiremos	escribiríamos	escribamos	escribiéramos/ésemos
escribiréis	escribiríais	escribáis	escribierais/eseis
escribirán	escribirían	escriban	escribieran/esen

Common irregular verbs

conocer		**Gerund:** *conociendo*	**Past principle:** *conocido*
Imperative familiar	**Present indicative**	**Imperfect indicative**	**Preterite**
conoce	conozco	conocía	conocí
conoced	conoces	conocías	conociste
	conoce	conocía	conoció
	conocemos	conocíamos	conocimos
	conocéis	conociáis	conocisteis
	conocen	conocían	conocieron
Future	**Conditional**	**Present subjunctive**	**Imperfect subjunctive**
conoceré	conocería	conozca	conociera/ese
conocerás	conocerías	conozcas	conocieras/eses
conocerá	conocería	conozca	conociera/ese
conoceremos	conoceríamos	conozcamos	conociéramos/ésemos
conoceréis	conoceríais	conozcáis	conocierais/eseis
conocerán	conocerían	conozcan	conocieran/esen

dar		**Gerund:** *dando*	**Past principle:** *dado*
Imperative familiar	**Present indicative**	**Imperfect indicative**	**Preterite**
da	doy	daba	di
dad	das	dabas	diste
	da	daba	dio
	damos	dábamos	dimos
	dais	dabais	disteis
	dan	daban	dieron
Future	**Conditional**	**Present subjunctive**	**Imperfect subjunctive**
daré	daría	dé	diera/ese
darás	darías	des	dieras/eses
dará	daría	dé	diera/ese
daremos	daríamos	demos	diéramos/ésemos
daréis	daríais	deis	dierais/eseis
darán	darían	den	dieran/esen

decir		**Gerund:** *diciendo*	**Past principle:** *dicho*
Imperative familiar	**Present indicative**	**Imperfect indicative**	**Preterite**
di	digo	decía	dije
decid	dices	decías	dijiste
	dice	decía	dijo
	decimos	decíamos	dijimos
	decís	decíais	dijisteis
	dicen	decían	dijeron
Future	**Conditional**	**Present subjunctive**	**Imperfect subjunctive**
diré	diría	diga	dijera/ese
dirás	dirías	digas	dijeras/eses
dirá	diría	diga	dijera/ese
diremos	diríamos	digamos	dijéramos/ésemos
diréis	diríais	digáis	dijerais/eseis
dirán	dirían	digan	dijeran/esen

estar

estar		Gerund: *estando*	Past principle: *estado*
Imperative familiar	**Present indicative**	**Imperfect indicative**	**Preterite**
está	estoy	estaba	estuve
estad	estás	estabas	estuviste
	está	estaba	estuvo
	estamos	estábamos	estuvimos
	estáis	estabais	estuvisteis
	están	estaban	estuvieron

Future	**Conditional**	**Present subjunctive**	**Imperfect subjunctive**
estaré	estaría	esté	estuviera/ese
estarás	estarías	estés	estuvieras/eses
estará	estaría	esté	estuviera/ese
estaremos	estaríamos	estemos	estuviéramos/ésemos
estaréis	estaríais	estéis	estuvierais/eseis
estarán	estarían	estén	estuvieran/esen

haber (auxilary verb)

haber (auxilary verb)		Gerund: *habiendo*	Past principle: *habido*
Imperative familiar	**Present indicative**	**Imperfect indicative**	**Preterite**
Imperative not used	he	había	hube
	has	habías	hubiste
	ha	había	hubo
	hemos	habíamos	hubimos
	habéis	habíais	hubisteis
	han	habían	hubieron

Future	**Conditional**	**Present subjunctive**	**Imperfect subjunctive**
habré	habría	haya	hubiera/ese
habrás	habrías	hayas	hubieras/eses
habrá	habría	haya	hubiera/ese
habremos	habríamos	hayamos	hubiéramos/ésemos
habréis	habríais	hayáis	hubierais/eseis
habrán	habrían	hayan	hubieran/esen

hacer

hacer		Gerund: *haciendo*	Past principle: *hecho*
Imperative familiar	**Present indicative**	**Imperfect indicative**	**Preterite**
haz	hago	hacía	hice
haced	haces	hacías	hiciste
	hace	hacía	hizo
	hacemos	hacíamos	hicimos
	hacéis	hacíais	hicisteis
	hacen	hacían	hicieron

Future	**Conditional**	**Present subjunctive**	**Imperfect subjunctive**
haré	haría	haga	hiciera/ese
harás	harías	hagas	hicieras/eses
hará	haría	haga	hiciera/ese
haremos	haríamos	hagamos	hiciéramos/ésemos
haréis	haríais	hagáis	hicierais/eseis
harán	harían	hagan	hicieran/esen

Verb tables

ir		Gerund: *yendo*	Past principle: *ido*
Imperative familiar	**Present indicative**	**Imperfect indicative**	**Preterite**
ve	voy	iba	fui
id	vas	ibas	fuiste
	va	iba	fue
	vamos	íbamos	fuimos
	vais	ibais	fuisteis
	van	iban	fueron

Future	**Conditional**	**Present subjunctive**	**Imperfect subjunctive**
iré	iría	vaya	fuera/se
irás	irías	vayas	fueras/eses
irá	iría	vaya	fuera/ese
iremos	iríamos	vayamos	fuéramos/ésemos
iréis	iríais	vayáis	fuerais/eseis
irán	irían	vayan	fueran/esen

leer		Gerund: *leyendo*	Past principle: *leído*
Imperative familiar	**Present indicative**	**Imperfect indicative**	**Preterite**
lee	leo	leía	leí
leed	lees	leías	leíste
	lee	leía	leyó
	leemos	leíamos	leímos
	leéis	leíais	leísteis
	leen	leían	leyeron

Future	**Conditional**	**Present subjunctive**	**Imperfect subjunctive**
leeré	leería	lea	leyera/ese
leerás	leerías	leas	leyeras/eses
leerá	leería	lea	leyera/ese
leeremos	leeríamos	leamos	leyéramos/ésemos
leeréis	leeríais	leáis	leyerais/eseis
leerán	leerían	lean	leyeran/esen

oír		Gerund: *oyendo*	Past principle: *oído*
Imperative familiar	**Present indicative**	**Imperfect indicative**	**Preterite**
oye	oigo	oía	oí
oíd	oyes	oías	oíste
	oye	oía	oyó
	oímos	oíamos	oímos
	oís	oíais	oísteis
	oyen	oían	oyeron

Future	**Conditional**	**Present subjunctive**	**Imperfect subjunctive**
oiré	oiría	oiga	oyera/ese
oirás	oirías	oigas	oyeras/eses
oirá	oiría	oiga	oyera/ese
oiremos	oiríamos	oigamos	oyéramos/ésemos
oiréis	oiríais	oigáis	oyerais/eseis
oirán	oirían	oigan	oyeran/esen

pedir

		Gerund: *pidiendo*	Past principle: *pedido*

Imperative familiar	Present indicative	Imperfect indicative	Preterite
pide *pedid*	*pido* *pides* *pide* *pedimos* *pedís* *piden*	*pedía* *pedías* *pedía* *pedíamos* *pedíais* *pedían*	*pedí* *pediste* *pidió* *pedimos* *pedisteis* *pidieron*

Future	Conditional	Present subjunctive	Imperfect subjunctive
pediré *pedirás* *pedirá* *pediremos* *pediréis* *pedirán*	*pediría* *pedirías* *pediría* *pediríamos* *pediríais* *pedirían*	*pida* *pidas* *pida* *pidamos* *pidáis* *pidan*	*pidiera/ese* *pidieras/eses* *pidiera/ese* *pidiéramos/ésemos* *pidierais/eseis* *pidieran/esen*

poder

		Gerund: *pudiendo*	Past principle: *podido*

Imperative familiar	Present indicative	Imperfect indicative	Preterite
Imperative not used	*puedo* *puedes* *puede* *podemos* *podéis* *pueden*	*podía* *podías* *podía* *podíamos* *podíais* *podían*	*pude* *pudiste* *pudo* *pudimos* *pudisteis* *pudieron*

Future	Conditional	Present subjunctive	Imperfect subjunctive
podré *podrás* *podrá* *podremos* *podréis* *podrán*	*podría* *podrías* *podría* *podríamos* *podríais* *podrían*	*pueda* *puedas* *pueda* *podamos* *podáis* *puedan*	*pudiera/ese* *pudieras/eses* *pudiera/ese* *pudiéramos/ésemos* *pudierais/eseis* *pudieran/esen*

poner

		Gerund: *poniendo*	Past principle: *puesto*

Imperative familiar	Present indicative	Imperfect indicative	Preterite
pon *poned*	*pongo* *pones* *pone* *ponemos* *ponéis* *ponen*	*ponía* *ponías* *ponía* *poníamos* *poníais* *ponían*	*puse* *pusiste* *puso* *pusimos* *pusisteis* *pusieron*

Future	Conditional	Present subjunctive	Imperfect subjunctive
pondré *pondrás* *pondrá* *pondremos* *pondréis* *pondrán*	*pondría* *pondrías* *pondría* *pondríamos* *pondríais* *pondrían*	*ponga* *pongas* *ponga* *pongamos* *pongáis* *pongan*	*pusiera/ese* *pusieras/eses* *pusiera/ese* *pusiéramos/ésemos* *pusierais/eseis* *pusieran/esen*

Verb tables

querer
Gerund: *queriendo*   **Past principle:** *querido*

Imperative familiar	Present indicative	Imperfect indicative	Preterite
quiere	quiero	quería	quise
quered	quieres	querías	quisiste
	quiere	quería	quiso
	queremos	queríamos	quisimos
	queréis	queríais	quisisteis
	quieren	querían	quisieron

Future	Conditional	Present subjunctive	Imperfect subjunctive
querré	querría	quiera	quisiera/ese
querrás	querrías	quieras	quisieras/eses
querrá	querría	quiera	quisiera/ese
querremos	querríamos	queramos	quisiéramos/ésemos
querréis	querríais	queráis	quisierais/eseis
querrán	querrían	quieran	quisieran/esen

saber
Gerund: *sabiendo*   **Past principle:** *sabido*

Imperative familiar	Present indicative	Imperfect indicative	Preterite
sabe	sé	sabía	supe
sabed	sabes	sabías	supiste
	sabe	sabía	supo
	sabemos	sabíamos	supimos
	sabéis	sabíais	supisteis
	saben	sabían	supieron

Future	Conditional	Present subjunctive	Imperfect subjunctive
sabré	sabría	sepa	supiera/ese
sabrás	sabrías	sepas	supieras/eses
sabrá	sabría	sepa	supiera/ese
sabremos	sabríamos	sepamos	supiéramos/ésemos
sabréis	sabríais	sepáis	supierais/eseis
sabrán	sabrían	sepan	supieran/esen

salir
Gerund: *saliendo*   **Past principle:** *salido*

Imperative familiar	Present indicative	Imperfect indicative	Preterite
sal	salgo	salía	salí
salid	sales	salías	saliste
	sale	salía	salió
	salimos	salíamos	salimos
	salís	salíais	salisteis
	salen	salían	salieron

Future	Conditional	Present subjunctive	Imperfect subjunctive
saldré	saldría	salga	saliera/ese
saldrás	saldrías	salgas	salieras/eses
saldrá	saldría	salga	saliera/ese
saldremos	saldríamos	salgamos	saliéramos/ésemos
saldréis	saldríais	salgáis	salierais/eseis
saldrán	saldrían	salgan	salieran/esen

seguir

Gerund: *siguiendo* **Past principle:** *seguido*

Imperative familiar	Present indicative	Imperfect indicative	Preterite
sigue	sigo	seguía	seguí
seguid	sigues	seguías	seguiste
	sigue	seguía	siguió
	seguimos	seguíamos	seguimos
	seguís	seguíais	seguisteis
	siguen	seguían	siguieron

Future	Conditional	Present subjunctive	Imperfect subjunctive
seguiré	seguiría	siga	siguiera/ese
seguirás	seguirías	sigas	siguieras/eses
seguirá	seguiría	siga	siguiera/ese
seguiremos	seguiríamos	sigamos	siguiéramos/ésemos
seguiréis	seguiríais	sigáis	siguierais/eseis
seguirán	seguirían	sigan	siguieran/esen

sentir

Gerund: *sintiendo* **Past principle:** *sentido*

Imperative familiar	Present indicative	Imperfect indicative	Preterite
siente	siento	sentía	sentí
sentid	sientes	sentías	sentiste
	siente	sentía	sintió
	sentimos	sentíamos	sentimos
	sentís	sentíais	sentisteis
	sienten	sentían	sintieron

Future	Conditional	Present subjunctive	Imperfect subjunctive
sentiré	sentiría	sienta	sintiera/ese
sentirás	sentirías	sientas	sintieras/eses
sentirá	sentiría	sienta	sintiera/ese
sentiremos	sentiríamos	sintamos	sintiéramos/ésemos
sentiréis	sentiríais	sintáis	sintierais/eseis
sentirán	sentirían	sientan	sintieran/esen

ser

Gerund: *siendo* **Past principle:** *sido*

Imperative familiar	Present indicative	Imperfect indicative	Preterite
sé	soy	era	fui
sed	eres	eras	fuiste
	es	era	fue
	somos	éramos	fuimos
	sois	erais	fuisteis
	son	eran	fueron

Future	Conditional	Present subjunctive	Imperfect subjunctive
seré	sería	sea	fuera/ese
serás	serías	seas	fueras/eses
será	sería	sea	fuera/ese
seremos	seríamos	seamos	fuéramos/ésemos
seréis	seríais	seáis	fuerais/eseis
serán	serían	sean	fueran/esen

Verb tables

tener
Gerund: *teniendo* **Past principle:** *tenido*

Imperative familiar	Present indicative	Imperfect indicative	Preterite
ten	tengo	tenía	tuve
tened	tienes	tenías	tuviste
	tiene	tenía	tuvo
	tenemos	teníamos	tuvimos
	tenéis	teníais	tuvisteis
	tienen	tenían	tuvieron

Future	Conditional	Present subjunctive	Imperfect subjunctive
tendré	tendría	tenga	tuviera/ese
tendrás	tendrías	tengas	tuvieras/eses
tendrá	tendría	tenga	tuviera/ese
tendremos	tendríamos	tengamos	tuviéramos/ésemos
tendréis	tendríais	tengáis	tuvierais/eseis
tendrán	tendrían	tengan	tuvieran/esen

traer
Gerund: *trayendo* **Past principle:** *traído*

Imperative familiar	Present indicative	Imperfect indicative	Preterite
trae	traigo	traía	traje
traed	traes	traías	trajiste
	trae	traía	trajo
	traemos	traíamos	trajimos
	traéis	traíais	trajisteis
	traen	traían	trajeron

Future	Conditional	Present subjunctive	Imperfect subjunctive
traeré	traería	traiga	trajera/ese
traerás	traerías	traigas	trajeras/eses
traerá	traería	traiga	trajera/ese
traeremos	traeríamos	traigamos	trajéramos/ésemos
traeréis	traeríais	traigáis	trajerais/eseis
traerán	traerían	traigan	trajeran/esen

venir
Gerund: *viniendo* **Past principle:** *venido*

Imperative familiar	Present indicative	Imperfect indicative	Preterite
ven	vengo	venía	vine
venid	vienes	venías	viniste
	viene	venía	vino
	venimos	veníamos	vinimos
	venís	veníais	vinisteis
	vienen	venían	vinieron

Future	Conditional	Present subjunctive	Imperfect subjunctive
vendré	vendría	venga	viniera/ese
vendrás	vendrías	vengas	vinieras/eses
vendrá	vendría	venga	viniera/ese
vendremos	vendríamos	vengamos	viniéramos/ésemos
vendréis	vendríais	vengáis	vinierais/eseis
vendrán	vendrían	vengan	vinieran/esen

ver

Gerund: *viendo* **Past principle:** *visto*

Imperative familiar	Present indicative	Imperfect indicative	Preterite
ve	veo	veía	vi
ved	ves	veías	viste
	ve	veía	vio
	vemos	veíamos	vimos
	veis	veíais	visteis
	ven	veían	vieron

Future	Conditional	Present subjunctive	Imperfect subjunctive
veré	vería	vea	viera/ese
verás	verías	veas	vieras/eses
verá	vería	vea	viera/ese
veremos	veríamos	veamos	viéramos/ésemos
veréis	veríais	veáis	vierais/eseis
verán	verían	vean	vieran/esen

volver

Gerund: *volviendo* **Past principle:** *vuelto*

Imperative familiar	Present indicative	Imperfect indicative	Preterite
vuelve	vuelvo	volvía	volví
volved	vuelves	volvías	volviste
	vuelve	volvía	volvió
	volvemos	volvíamos	volvimos
	volvéis	volvíais	volvisteis
	vuelven	volvían	volvieron

Future	Conditional	Present subjunctive	Imperfect subjunctive
volveré	volvería	vuelva	volviera/ese
volverás	volverías	vuelvas	volvieras/eses
volverá	volvería	vuelva	volviera/ese
volveremos	volveríamos	volvamos	volviéramos/ésemos
volveréis	volveríais	volváis	volvierais/eseis
volverán	volverían	vuelvan	volvieran/esen

Vocabulario

The following abbreviations are used in this section:

(*coll.*) colloquial
(*f*) feminine
(*pl*) plural
(*LA*) Latin America
(*Sp*) Spain

A

a (su) alcance within (their) reach
a causa de because of
a comienzos de at the beginning of
a diario daily
a eso de around
a finales de at the end of
a la derecha to the right
a la izquierda to the left
a la semana per week, weekly
al aire libre in the open air
al contrario on the contrary
al día siguiente the next day
al final de at the end of
al lado de next to
al lado del mar by the seaside
al mismo tiempo at the same time
a lo alto de at the top of
a lo largo de along, throughout
a lo mejor maybe
a menudo often
a partir de from, starting on
a pesar de in spite of
¿a qué hora? at what time?
a toda hora at all times
a través de across
a veces sometimes
abajo below, down(stairs)
el **abanico** fan
abierto/a open
el/la **abogado/a** lawyer
el **abrazo** hug
el **abrigo** coat
abril April
abrir to open

el/la **abuelo/a** grandfather/ grandmother
aburrido/a boring, bored
aburrirse to get bored
abusar to bully; to abuse
acá here
acabar to finish
acabar de to have just
el **acantilado** cliff
el **accidente** accident
la **acción** action
el **aceite de oliva** olive oil
el **aceite** oil
la **aceituna** olive
aceptar to accept
acerca de about
acercarse a to near, to approach
acompañar to go with, to accompany
aconsejar to advise
el **acontecimiento** event
acordarse de to remember
el **acoso escolar** school bullying
acostarse to go to bed
la **actitud** attitude
la **actividad** activity
las **actividades deportivas** sporting activities
las **actividades extraescolares** extra-curricular activities
activo/a active
el **actor** actor
el **actor secundario** supporting actor
la **actriz** actress
actuar to act
adecuado/a suitable, appropriate
además moreover

además de as well as
adentro inside, within
admitir to admit
el/la **adolescente** teenager
¿adónde? where to?
adoptar to adopt
el **adulto** adult
aeróbico/a aerobic
el **aeropuerto** airport
afeitarse to shave
afortunado/a fortunate
afuera outside
la **agencia de viajes** travel agency
agosto August
agradable pleasant
agradecer to thank
agresivo/a aggressive
el/la **agricultor/a** farmer
el **agua** (*f*) **bendita** holy water
el **agua** (*f*) **con gas** fizzy/ sparkling water
el **agua** (*f*) **esterilizada** sterilised water
el **agua** (*f*) **mineral** mineral water
el **aguacate** avocado
aguantar to put up with, to bear
ahí there
ahora now
ahorrar to save
el **aire** air
el **aire acondicionado** air conditioning
aislado/a isolated
aislante insulating
el **ajedrez** chess
el **ajo** garlic
alargado/a extended, long
el **albañil** builder
el **albergue juvenil** youth hostel

alcanzar to reach

la **aldea** village

alegre happy, cheerful

la **alegría** happiness, merriment

Alemania Germany

el **alemán** German (language/subject)

alemán/alemana German

la alergia allergy

alérgico/a allergic

algo something, anything

algo así something like this/that

¿algo más? anything else?

el **algodón** cotton

alguien someone

algún, alguno/a some, any

algunas veces sometimes

alimentar to feed

el **alimento** food

allí there

el **almacén** shop, store

la **almendra** almond

el **alojamiento** accommodation, lodging

el **alpinismo** mountain/rock climbing

alojarse to lodge, to stay

alquilar to hire, to rent

alrededor de around

los **alrededores** outskirts

alterar to alter

alto/a tall

la **altura** height

alucinante fantastic, amazing

el/la **alumno/a** pupil

el **ama** (f) **de casa** housewife

amable kind, friendly

amar to love

amarillo/a yellow

la **ambición** ambition

ambicioso/a ambitious

el **ambiente** atmosphere, environment

ambos/as both

la **amenaza** threat

amenazar to threaten

América Latina Latin America

el/la **amigo/a** friend

la **amistad** friendship

el/la **amo/a de casa** housewife/househusband

amplio/a roomy, spacious

ancho/a wide

anciano/a old

los **ancianos** old people

andando on foot, walking

andar to walk

el **andén** platform

el/la **anfitrión/anfitriona** host(ess)

el **anillo** ring

animado/a lively

el **animal salvaje** wild animal

animar to encourage

anoche last night

anteayer the day before yesterday

la **antena** aerial

antes (de) before

anticuado/a old-fashioned

las **antigüedades** antiques

antiguo/a former; ancient

antipático/a unpleasant; unkind

el **anuncio** advertisement

añadir to add

el **año** year

apagar to switch/turn off

el **aparador** sideboard

el **aparato** machine

el **aparcamiento** parking

aparcar to park

aparecer to appear

la **apariencia** appearance

el **apartamento** flat, apartment

aparte de apart from

el **apellido** surname

apenas scarcely

apetecer to appeal, to fancy

aprender (a) to learn (to)

el **aprendizaje** apprenticeship

aprobar to pass (examinations)

apropiado/a appropriate

aprovechar to use, to make use of

aproximadamente about, approximately

apuntar to note

el **apunte** note

aquí here

árabe Arabic

la **araña** spider

el **árbol** tree

archivar to file

archivo file

el **área** (f) area

la **arena** sand

Argentina Argentina

el **argumento** argument

el **armario** wardrobe; cupboard

el **arpa** (f) harp

el/la **arqueólogo/a** archaeologist

el/la **arquitecto/a** architect

arquitectónico/a architectural

arreglar to arrange, to put right, to tidy

arriba above, up(stairs)

la **arroba** @

el **arroz** rice

el **arte dramático** drama

las **artes marciales** martial arts

la **artesanía** crafts

el **artículo** article

el/la **artista** artist

la **asamblea** assembly

asar to roast

el **ascensor** lift

asegurar to assure

el **aseo** toilet

asequible achievable

así thus

así que and so

el **asiento** seat

el/la **asesor/a** consultant

la **asignatura** (school) subject

asistir a to attend

la **aspiradora** vacuum cleaner

el **asunto** topic

asustar to frighten

el **ataque** attack
atar to tie
aterrizar to land
el **ático** attic
el **atletismo** athletics
atracar to mug
la **atracción** attraction
el **atraco** mugging
atrevido/a daring
atropellar to knock down
el **atún** tuna
el **aula** (*f*) classroom
aumentar to increase
el **aumento** increase
aun even
aún still, yet
aunque although
Austria Austria
el **autobús** bus
el **autocar** coach
la **autopista** motorway
las **autoridades** authorities
el/la **auxiliar de vuelo** flight
attendant
el **avance** advance
el **ave** (*f*) bird
la **aventura** adventure
la **avería** breakdown
averiguar to find out
el **avión** plane
el **aviso** warning
la **avispa** wasp
ayer yesterday
la **ayuda** help
ayudar to help
el **ayuntamiento** town hall
el/la **azafato/a** flight attendant
el **azafrán** saffron
el **azúcar** sugar
azul blue

B

el **bacalao** cod
bailar to dance
el **baile** dance
bajar to go down

bajo beneath, under
bajo/a low, short
el **bádminton** badminton
el **baile** dance
el **balcón** balcony
el **baloncesto** basketball
el **balonmano** handball
el **banco** bank
la **banda sonora** soundtrack
la **bandera** flag
bañarse to have a bath; to
bathe
bañarse en el mar to swim
in the sea
la **bañera** bath
el **baño** bath(room)
barato/a cheap
la **barba** beard
la **barbacoa** barbecue
el **barco** boat
la **barra** loaf
barrer el suelo to sweep the
floor
el **barrio** neighbourhood, area
¡basta! (that's) enough!
bastante quite, enough, a little
bit
bastar to be enough
la **basura** rubbish
el **basurero** bin
la **batalla** battle
la **batería** drumkit
el/la **bebé** baby
beber to drink
la **bebida** drink
el **béisbol** baseball
el **belén** crib
Bélgica Belgium
la **belleza** beauty
bello/a beautiful
el **beneficio** benefit
besar to kiss
el **beso** kiss
la **biblioteca** library
la **bicicleta, bici** (*coll.*) bicycle,
bike
bien educado/a
well-mannered, polite

los **bienes** goods, possessions
el **bienestar** well-being
bienvenido/a welcome
el **bigote** moustache
el **billar** billiards
el **billete** ticket (travel)
el **billete de ida y
vuelta** return ticket
el **billete sencillo** single ticket
la **biología** biology
el/la **bisabuelo/a**
great-grandfather/
great-grandmother
el **bistec** steak
blanco/a white
el **bloc** pad
el **bloque** block
la **blusa** blouse
bobo/a silly
la **boca** mouth
el **bocadillo** sandwich
la **boda** wedding
la **bodega** wine cellar; winery
la **bola de nieve** snowball
la **bolera** bowling alley
el **bolígrafo, boli** (*coll.*) biro
el **bollo** bread roll
la **bolsa** bag
la **bolsa de plástico** plastic
bag
el **bolsillo** pocket
el **bolso** handbag
el/la **bombero/a** firefighter
bonito/a pretty
el **bono de lotería** lottery ticket
borrar to delete
el **bosque** wood
la **bota** boot
el **bote** can, tin
la **botella** bottle
el **botiquín** first-aid kit
el **botón** button
el **boxeo** boxing
el **brazo** arm
Brasil Brazil
breve brief, short
brevemente briefly
brindar to drink a toast

el **bricolaje** DIY

británico/a British

bronceado/a tanned

broncearse to get brown

el **buceo** (scuba)diving

buenísimo/a very good

bueno/a good

el **buen tiempo** good weather

¡buen viaje! have a good journey!

la **bufanda** scarf

buscar to look for

buscar un trabajo to look for a job

la **búsqueda** search

la **butaca** seat, armchair

el **buzón** post-box

C

el **caballo** horse

la **cabeza** head

la **cabina** booth

la **cacerola** saucepan

cada each

cada día each/every day

cada vez más more and more

la **cadena** chain, channel

caer to fall

la **caída** fall

el **café** coffee

la **cafetería** café, coffee shop

la **caja** box; till

el/la **cajero/a** cashier

el **cajero automático** cash point

la **cala** cove

los **calamares** squid

los **calcetines** socks

la **calculadora** calculator

el **caldo** soup, broth

la **calefacción** heating

el **calentamiento global** global warming

la **calidad** quality

cálido/a hot (climate)

caliente hot

callado/a quiet

callarse to be quiet

la **calle** street

callejero/a (of the) street

el **calor** heat

caluroso/a hot, warm

calvo/a bald

la **cama** bed

la **cámara** camera

la **camaradería** camaraderie

el/la **camarero/a** waiter/waitress

cambiar to change

cambiarse to get changed

el **cambio** bureau de change

el **camino** road

el **camión** lorry

la **camisa** shirt

la **camiseta** T-shirt

la **campana** bell

el/la **campeón/ campeona** champion

el **camping** campsite

el **campo** the country(side)

el **campo de deportes** sports field

Canadá Canada

el **canario** canary

la **canción** song

el/la **canguro** babysitter

cansado/a tired

cansar to tire

el/la **cantante** singer

cantar to sing

la **cantidad** amount, quantity

cantidad de a lot of

la **cantina** canteen

la **capacidad** capacity

la **capa de ozono** ozone layer

la **capa polar** polar ice-cap

capaz capable

la **capital** capital (city)

la **cara** face

el **caracol** snail

el **carácter** character

caracterizarse por to be characterised by

el **caramelo** sweet

la **caravana** caravan

el **carbón** carbon; coal

la **cárcel** prison

la **caridad** charity

el **cariño** affection

cariñoso/a affectionate, loving

la **carne** meat

la **carnicería** butcher's

caro/a expensive

la **carpeta** folder

el/la **carpintero/a** carpenter, joiner

la **carrera** career; race

la **carretera** (main) road, highway

la **carta** letter

el/la **cartero/a** postman/ postwoman

el **cartón** carton; cardboard

la **casa** house

la **casa de mis sueños** dream house

casado/a married

casarse to get married

el **casco** helmet

casi almost

el **caso** case

castaño/a brown, chestnut (colour)

castigar to punish

el **castigo** detention; punishment

el **castillo** castle

la **catarata** waterfall

catastrófico/a catastrophic

el **catarro** cold

la **catedral** cathedral

católico/a catholic

la **caza** hunting

la **cebolla** onion

la **celebración** celebration

celebrar to celebrate

los **celos** jealousy

celoso/a jealous

la **cena** evening meal, dinner

cenar to have dinner

el **centímetro** centimetre

céntrico/a central

el **centro**   centre

el **centro comercial**   shopping centre

cepillarse los dientes   to brush one´s teeth

la **cerámica**   ceramics

cerca de   near (to)

cercano/a   near

el **cerdo**   pig; pork

los **cereales**   cereals

la **cerilla**   match

cerrar   to shut, to close (down)

la **cerveza**   beer

el **chalet**   house, cottage, bungalow

el **champán**   champagne

el **champiñón**   mushroom

el **champú**   shampoo

el **chantaje**   blackmail

la **chaqueta**   jacket

chatear   to chat

el/la **chico/a**   boy/girl

el **chicle**   chewing-gum

Chile   Chile

la **chinchilla**   chinchilla

Chipre   Cyprus

el **chófer**   driver

el **chubasco**   shower (of rain)

la **chuleta**   chop

el **ciclismo**   cycling

ciego/a   blind

el **cielo**   sky, heaven

cien(to)   a hundred

la **ciencia ficción**   science fiction

las **ciencias**   science

el/la **científico/a**   scientist

cierto/a   certain, true

la **cifra**   figure

el **cine**   cinema

el/la **cineasta**   film director

la **cinta**   ribbon, tape

la **cintura**   waist

el **cinturón**   belt

el/la **cirujano/a**   surgeon

la **cita**   date, appointment

la **ciudad**   town; city

la **civilización**   civilisation

claro/a   clear, light

la **clase**   class; lesson

el **clavo**   clove; nail

el/la **cliente**   customer

el **clima**   climate

el **club de jóvenes**   youth club

la **cobaya**   guinea pig

cocer   to cook

el **coche**   car

el **coche de carreras**   racing car

la **cocina**   kitchen; cooking; cooker

cocinar   to cook

el/la **cocinero/a**   cook, chef

el **codo**   elbow

coger   to take; to catch

coger recados   to take messages

cogerse un año sabático   to take a year out

coger un tren   to catch a train

coleccionar   to collect

el/la **colega**   colleague

el **colegio, cole** (*coll.*)   school (often independent)

el **colegio de primaria**   primary school

el **colegio de secundaria**   secondary school

el **collar**   necklace

colocar   to place

Colombia   Colombia

los **combustibles fósiles**   fossil fuels

la **comedia**   comedy

el **comedor**   dining room; canteen

comenzar (a)   to begin (to)

comer   to eat

el **Comercio Justo**   Fair Trade

cometer un crimen   to commit a crime

la **comida**   food; lunch-time meal

la **comida basura**   junk food

la **comida rápida**   fast food

la **comisaría**   police station

como   like, as, since

como es debido   properly, as it should be done

la **cómoda**   chest of drawers

cómodo/a   convenient, comfortable

el/la **compañero/a**   companion

la **compañía**   company

el **compartimiento**   compartment

compartir   to share

el **compás**   compass

los **complementos**   accessories

completar   to complete

el **comportamiento**   behaviour

comportarse   to behave

comprar   to buy

comprensivo/a   understanding

el **comprimido**   pill, tablet

común   common

la **computadora** (*LA*)   computer

las **comunicaciones**   communications

comunicar   to communicate

la **comunidad**   community

con   with

con respecto a   with respect to, concerning

con vistas al mar   with views of the sea

la **concentración**   concentration

concentrarse   to concentrate

el **concierto**   concert

el **concurso**   competition; game show

conducir   to drive, to lead

la **conducta**   behaviour

el/la **conductor/a**   driver

el **conejo**   rabbit

la **confianza**   confidence, trust

el **conflicto**   conflict

el **congelador**   freezer

los **congelados** frozen products

conocer to know (a person/ place etc.)

conocido/a (well) known

los **conocimientos** knowledge

conquistar to overcome, to conquer

la **consecuencia** consequence, result

conseguir to obtain

el **consejo** (piece of) advice

consistir en to consist of

constipado/a having a cold

construir to build

consumir energía to consume energy

el/la **contable** accountant

el **contacto** contact

la **contaminación** pollution

contaminado/a polluted

contaminar to contaminate, pollute

contar to tell; to narrate; to count

contar con to rely on

contener to contain

el **contenedor de abono** compost bin

los **contenidos** contents

contento/a happy, content

el **contestador automático** answer machine

contestar to answer

(en) **contra (de)** against

la **contraseña** password

el **contrato** contract

contribuir to contribute

convencer to convince

convenir to suit

la **conversación** conversation

convertirse en to turn into

la **copa** glass, drink

la **copia** copy

el **corazón** heart

la **corbata** tie

el **cordero** lamb

la **corneta** cornet

el **coro** choir

la **correa** lead (dog's)

correcto/a correct

el **corrector líquido** correcting fluid

corregir to correct

el **correo** mail

el **correo electrónico** e-mail

Correos post office

correr to run

la **corrida de toros** bullfight

cortar to cut

cortés courteous, polite

la **cortesía** politeness

corto/a short

el **cortometraje** short film

la **cosa** thing

la **costa** coast

costero/a coastal

la **costumbre** custom

cotidiano/a daily

crear to create

creativo/a creative

crecer to grow

creciente growing

el **crecimiento** growth

los **créditos** credits

la **creencia** belief

crear to create

creer to believe, to think

creído/a conceited

la **crema** cream

la **crema antiséptica** antiseptic cream

la **crema de sol** sun cream

el **críquet** cricket

el **crimen** crime

el **cristal** glass

cristiano/a Christian

la **crítica de cine** film review

el **cruce** crossroads

cruzar to cross

el **cuaderno** exercise book

cuadrado/a square

¿cuál? which?, what?

la **cualidad** quality

las **cualificaciones** qualifications

cualquiera anyone

el **cuarto** quarter; room

el **cuarto de baño** bathroom

cubierto/a covered

la **cuchara** spoon

el **cuchillo** knife

el **cuello** neck

la **cuenta** bill

la **cuerda** rope, cord

el **cuero** leather

el **cuerpo** the body

cuesta mucho it costs a lot

¡cuidado! careful!

cuidadoso/a careful

cuidar to look after

la **culpa** fault

cultivar to grow

la **cultura** culture

el **cumpleaños** birthday

cumplir to fulfil

el/la **cuñado/a** brother-in-law/ sister-in-law

el **curso** course; school year

da vergüenza it's a disgrace

dado que since, given that

dañar to harm, to damage

el **daño** harm, damage

la **danza** dance

dar to give

dar a to overlook

dar de comer to feed

dar la lata to tell (someone) off

dar las gracias to thank

dar miedo to frighten

dar un paseo to go for a walk

los **dardos** darts

darse cuenta de to realise

darse prisa to hurry

de acuerdo OK, agreed

de buen/mal humor in a good/bad mood

de moda fashionable

de momento at present

de nada don't mention it

de nuevo again

de paso by the way

de pie standing up

de primera/segunda clase first/second class

de prisa quickly, in a hurry

¿de qué color? what/which colour?

¿de quién? whose?

de repente suddenly

de talla media medium size

de todos modos in any case, anyway

de veras really

de vez en cuando from time to time

debajo de below, beneath

deber to have to, to owe

los **deberes** homework

decidir to decide

decir to say

la **decisión** decision

el **dedo** finger; toe

dejar to let, to leave

dejar el colegio to leave school

delante de in front of

delgado/a thin, slim

delicioso/a delicious

la **delincuencia juvenil** youth crime

los **demás** others, other people

demasiado/a too much, too many

demostrar to show, to demonstrate

el/la **dentista** dentist

dentro (de) inside

el **departamento** department

depender de to depend on

el/la **dependiente/a** shop assistant

el **deporte** sport

los **deportes acuáticos** water sports

el/la **deportista** sportsperson

deportivo/a sporty

derecho/a straight, right

derribar to knock down, to demolish

desafortunadamente unfortunately

desagradable unpleasant

desarrollarse to develop

el **desastre** disaster

desayunar to have breakfast

el **desayuno** breakfast

descansar to rest, relax

el **descanso** break

la **descongelación** melting

el/la **desconocido/a** stranger

describir to describe

descubrir to discover, to reveal

descuidarse to neglect, to be careless

desde from

desde...hasta... from...to...

desde luego of course

desear to want, to wish

los **desechos domésticos** household waste

el **desempleo** unemployment

desenchufar to unplug, turn off

el **desorden** disorder

desordenado/a untidy, messy

el **despacho** office, study

despacio slowly

despectivo/a derogatory

despegar to take off (aeroplane)

el **despertador** alarm clock

despertarse to wake up

despistado/a forgetful

después (de) after

el **destino** destination

destruir to destroy

el **detalle** detail

detener to arrest

detenerse to stop

detestar to detest

detrás (de) behind

devolver to give back, return

el **día** day

el **Día de la Madre** Mother's Day

el **día escolar** school day

el **día festivo** holiday

el **diario** newspaper

diario/a daily

dibujar to draw

el **dibujo** art

el **dibujo animado** cartoon

el **diccionario** dictionary

diciembre December

el **diente** tooth

la **dieta equilibrada** balanced diet

la **diferencia** difference

diferente different

difícil difficult

la **dificultad** difficulty

dígame hello (on telephone)

Dinamarca Denmark

el **dinero** money

la **dirección** direction; address

el/la **director/a** headteacher

el/la **director/a de cine** film director

el **disco** CD, disk

el **disco duro** hard disk

la **discoteca** club; disco

la **discriminación** discrimination

discutir to argue

el/la **diseñador/a** designer

el **diseño** design

los **disfraces** dressing-up clothes

el **disfraz** disguise, costume

disfrazar to disguise

disfrutar to enjoy

disminuir to diminish, to lessen

disponible available

dispuesto/a ready

distinto/a different

distraer to distract

distraerse to get distracted

la **diversión**   fun, entertainment

divertido/a   funny, entertaining

dividir   to divide

divorciado/a   divorced

doblar   to bend, fold

doble   double

la **docena**   dozen

el **documental**   documentary

doler   to hurt

el **dolor**   pain

el **domicilio**   residence, abode

el **domingo**   (on) Sunday

donde   where

dorarse   to turn golden brown

dormir   to sleep

dormirse   to go to sleep

el **dormitorio**   bedroom

el **drama**   drama

la **ducha**   shower

ducharse   to have a shower

dudar   to doubt

el/la **dueño/a**   owner

dulce   sweet

los **dulces**   sweets

el **dúplex**   maisonette

durante   during, for

durar   to last

duro/a   hard

E

e   and (before *i* and *hi*)

echar   to put on, to show (programme, film); to throw

echar la siesta   to have a siesta

ecológico/a   ecological

el/la **ecólogo/a**   ecologist

el/la **economista**   economist

la **edad**   age

el **edificio**   building

la **educación**   education

la **educación cívica**   PHSE

la **educación física**   physical education

los **efectos especiales**   special effects

eficaz   effective

egoísta   selfish

el **ejemplar**   copy

el **ejemplo**   example

el **ejercicio**   exercise

la **elección**   choice

el/la **electricista**   electrician

elegante   smart

elegir   to choose

elevado/a   high

embarazada   pregnant

el **embutido**   sausage

la **emoción**   excitement, emotion

emocionante   exciting

la **empanada**   pasty

emparejar   to match, to pair

empezar (a)   to begin (to)

el/la **empleado/a**   employee

el/la **empleado/a temporal**   temporary employee

el **empleo**   job

la **empresa**   company, business

el/la **empresario/a**   employer

en bicicleta   by bicycle

en coche   by car

en el centro de   in the centre of

en el extranjero   abroad

en el fondo   at the bottom, deep down

¡enhorabuena!   congratulations!

en las afueras   in the outskirts

en paro   out of work

en realidad   in fact

enseguida, en seguida   at once

en vivo   live (e.g. music)

enamorarse de   to fall in love with

encantado/a   pleased to meet you, enchanted

el **encanto**   charm

encender   to light, to turn/switch on

enchufado/a   connected

el **encierro**   running of the bulls festival

encima de   on (top of)

encontrar   to find

encontrarse   to be found/situated

la **encuesta**   survey

el/la **enemigo/a**   enemy

la **energía**   energy

enero   January

enfadarse   to get angry

la **enfermedad**   illness

el/la **enfermero/a**   nurse

el/la **enfermo/a**   sick person

enfrente (de)   opposite

el **enlace**   link

enorme   enormous

la **ensalada**   salad

ensayar   to rehearse

la **enseñanza**   teaching

enseñar (a)   to teach (to); to show

ensimismado/a   engrossed, absorbed

entender   to understand

enterarse de   to find out

entero/a   entire, whole

enterrar   to bury

entonces   then

el **entorno**   environment

la **entrada**   entrance; ticket (film etc.)

entrar   to go in, to enter

entre   between

el **entrenador**   trainer

el **entrenamiento**   training, exercise

entrenarse   to train

entretenido/a   entertaining, enjoyable

la **entrevista**   interview

el/la **entusiasta**   enthusiast

enviar   to send

el **equipaje**   luggage

el **equipo** team

equivocado/a wrong

la **equitación** horse riding

la **escalera** staircase, stairs

escapar to escape

el **escaparate** shop window

escaso/a scarce

la **escena** scene

escoger to choose

esconder to hide

escribir to write

el/la **escritor/a** writer

escuchar to listen (to)

la **escuela** school

la **escultura** sculpture

es decir that is

la **esgrima** fencing

el **espacio** space

los **espaguetis** spaghetti

la **espalda** back

España Spain

el **español** Spanish (language/ subject)

español/española Spanish

especializado/a specialised

especialmente especially

el/la **espectador/a** spectator

el **espejo** mirror

esperar to hope; to expect; to wait for

las **espinacas** spinach

el/la **esposo/a** husband; wife

el **esquí** skiing

el **esquí acuático** water-skiing

esquiar to ski

la **esquina** corner

esta mañana this morning

esta tarde this afternoon

estable stable

la **estación** season; station

la **estación de trenes** railway station

la **estación de autobuses** bus station

el **estadio** stadium

los **Estados Unidos** USA

la **estancia** stay

el **estanco** tobacconist's

la **estantería** bookcase

estar to be

estar a favor de to be in favour of

estar al teléfono to be on the phone/taking a call

estar contento/a to be happy/contented

estar de acuerdo to agree

estar de broma to be joking

estar de moda to be fashionable

estar de pie to be standing up

estar de prisa to be in a hurry

estar en contra de to be against

estar en forma to keep fit

estar harto/a to be fed up

estar mareado/a to feel sick

el **este** east

el **estilo** style

Estimado señor Dear Sir

estirar to stretch

el **estómago** stomach

estrecho/a narrow

la **estrella** star

la **estrella de cine** film star

el **estrés** stress

estresante stressful

estricto/a strict

estropear to break, to damage

el **estuche** pencil case

el/la **estudiante** student

estudiar to study

el **estudio** study

estudioso/a studious

¡estupendo! great!

estúpido/a stupid

la **evaluación** assessment

evitar to avoid

exacto/a exact, accurate

exagerado/a excessive, extravagant

el **examen**, *pl.* **exámenes** examination

excepto except

la **excusa** excuse

el **éxito** success

exitoso/a successful

la **experiencia** experience

explicar to explain

la **exposición** exhibition

extenderse to extend

extranjero/a foreign

extraño/a strange

extraordinario/a extraordinary

los **extras** extras

extrovertido/a extrovert

F

la **fábrica** factory

la **fábrica de galletas** biscuit factory

fácil easy

la **facultad** faculty

la **falda** skirt

las **Fallas** Fallas (fiesta in Valencia)

el **fallo** defect, fault

falso/a false

la **falta** fault, error

faltar to be lacking/missing

la **fama** fame

la **familia** family

el/la **familiar** family member

famoso/a famous

el/la **farmacéutico/a** chemist, pharmacist

la **farmacia** chemist's

fatal terrible, badly

favorito/a favourite

febrero February

la **fecha de nacimiento** date of birth

la **felicidad** happiness

feliz happy

¡feliz cumpleaños! happy birthday!

¡fenomenal! fantastic!

feo/a ugly

la **feria** festival, fair

la **Feria de Abril**   Feria (fiesta in Seville)

el **ferrocarril**   railway

fiarse de   to trust

la **fibra**   fibre

los **fideos**   noodles

la **fiesta**   party; festival; holiday

el **filete**   steak

el **fin**   end

el **fin de semana**   weekend

finalmente   finally

las **finanzas**   finance

la **física**   physics

físicamente   physically

físico/a   physical

el **flan**   crème caramel

la **flauta**   flute

el **flamenco**   type of dance

la **flor**   flower

la **florería**   florist

la **floristería**   florist

el **folleto**   brochure

el/la **fontanero/a**   plumber

el **footing**   jogging

la **formación**   training

el **formulario**   from

la **foto**   photo

el **francés**   French (language/subject)

francés/francesa   French

Francia   France

la **frase**   sentence

frecuente   frequent

el **fregadero**   kitchen sink

fregar   to wash, to scrub, to mop

fregar los platos   to wash the dishes

freír   to fry

la **fresa**   strawberry

fresco/a   fresh

frío/a   cold

frito/a   fried

la **frontera**   border, frontier

la **fruta**   fruit

la **frutería**   fruit shop

el **fuego**   fire

los **fuegos artificiales**   fireworks

la **fuente**   fountain

fuera (de)   outside

fuera de (su) alcance   out of (one's) reach

fuerte   strong

la **fuerza**   strength

fundado/a   funded

furioso/a   furious, violent

el **fútbol**   football

el **futbolín**   table football

el/la **futbolista**   footballer

el **futuro**   future

G

las **gafas**   glasses

las **gafas de sol**   sun glasses

Gales   Wales

la **galleta**   biscuit

la **gama**   range

las **gambas**   prawns

ganar   to win, to earn

ganar dinero   to earn money

la **ganga**   bargain

el **garaje**   garage

la **garganta**   throat

la **gasolina**   petrol

la **gaseosa**   fizzy drink

gastar   to spend

gastar dinero   to spend money

el **gato**   cat

el **gazpacho**   chilled tomato soup

el/la **gemelo/a**   twin

generoso/a   generous

¡genial!   great!

la **gente**   people

la **geografía**   geography

el **gerbo**   gerbil

la **gimnasia**   gymnastics

el **gimnasio**   gymnasium

el **golf**   golf

la **goma**   rubber

gordo/a   fat

la **gorra**   cap

gracias a   thanks to

graciosamente   funnily

gracioso/a   funny

el **grado**   degree

el **gramo**   gramme

grande   big

los **grandes almacenes**   department store

la **granja**   farm

el **granjero**   farmer

la **grapadora**   stapler

la **grasa**   fat

gratis   free

grave   serious

Grecia   Greece

gris   grey

gritar   to shout

grosero/a   rude

grueso/a   thick

el **grupo**   group

el **guante**   glove

guapo/a   good-looking

guardar   to keep, to save (document)

el **guardarropa**   cloakroom

guay (*coll.*)   cool

la **guerra**   war

la **guía**   guidebook

el/la **guía**   guide

el/la **guionista**   scriptwriter

el **guisante**   pea

el **guiso**   stew

la **guitarra**   guitar

gustar   to like

el **gusto**   taste

H

haber   to have (auxiliary verb)

hábil   skilful

la habilidad   skill

la habitación   room

el/la **habitante**   inhabitant

hablador/a   talkative

hablar   to speak, to talk

hace (una semana)   (a week) ago

hace buen tiempo the weather is good
hace frío it's cold
hace sol it's sunny
hace viento it's windy
hacer to do, to make
hacer bricolaje to do DIY
hacer caso a to take notice of
hacer de canguro to babysit
hacer deporte to play sports
hacer el café to make the coffee
hacer falta to need
hacer la cama to make the bed
hacer la compra to go shopping
hacer las prácticas de trabajo to do work experience
hacer los deberes to do homework
hacer surf to go surfing
hacer transbordo (en) to change (e.g. trains)
hacer un aprendizaje to do an apprenticeship
hacer vela to go sailing
hacerse to become
hacia towards
hacia atrás back(wards)
hacia delante forwards
la **halterofilia** weightlifting
el **hambre** (*f*) hunger
la **hamburguesa** hamburger
el **hámster** hamster
hasta until; up to; even
hasta luego bye
hay there is, there are
el **helado** ice cream
el **hemisferio** hemisphere
la **herencia** heritage
el/la **hermanastro/a** stepbrother/ stepsister
el/la **hermano/a mayor** older brother/sister

el/la **hermano/a menor** younger brother/sister
los **hermanos** brothers and sisters
hermoso/a beautiful
la **hermosura** beauty
el **héroe** hero
la **heroína** heroine; heroin
hervir to boil
el **hielo** ice
el **higo** fig
el/la **hijastro/a** stepson/ stepdaughter
el **hijo único/la hija única** only child
el **hipermercado** hypermarket
hispanohablante Spanish-speaking
la **historia** story, history
histórico/a historic(al)
el **hockey** hockey
el **hogar** home
la **hoguera** bonfire
el **hojaldre** puff pastry
el **hombre** man
el **hombre de negocios** businessman
el **hombro** shoulder
hondo/a deep
honesto/a honest
honrado/a honest
la **hora** time, hour
la **hora de comer** lunch time
la **hora de llegar** time of arrival
la **hora de salir** time of departure
el **horario** timetable
el **horno** oven
horroroso/a dreadful
las **hortalizas/ verduras** vegetables
el **hospital** hospital
la **hostelería** hotel business
hoy today
hoy en día nowadays

el **huevo** egg
húmedo/a wet
el **humo** smoke
Hungría Hungary

la **idea** idea
el **idioma** language
la **iglesia** church
igual equal
la **igualdad** equality
ilegal illegal
la **imagen**, *pl.* **imágenes** image, picture, photo
la **imaginación** imagination
imaginar to imagine
impaciente impatient
el **imperdible** safety pin
importante important
imposible impossible
imprescindible essential, indispensable
impresionante impressive
improbable unlikely
incendio fire
incluido/a included
incluir to include
incluso even
incómodo/a uncomfortable, inconvenient
increíble incredible
indicar to indicate
la **industria** industry
industrial industrial
inequívoco/a unequivocal
la **infancia** childhood
la **información** information
la **informática** ICT
la **información** information
el **informativo** news programme
el/la **ingeniero/a** engineer
Inglaterra England
el **inglés** English (language/ subject)
inglés/inglesa English

injusto/a   unjust, unfair
inmediatamente   immediately
la inmigración   immigration
el/la inmigrante   immigrant
insistir   to insist
la insolación   sunstroke
insoportable   unbearable
inspirar   to inspire
las instalaciones   facilities
el instituto   high school
inteligente   intelligent
intentar   to try
el interés   interest
interesante   interesting
interesarse en/por   to be
    interested in
interior   interior, internal
(el/la) Internet   internet
interrumpir   to interrupt
la inundación   flood
inútil   useless
el invierno   winter
invitar   to invite
ir   to go
ir a la universidad   to go to
    university
ir al extranjero   to go abroad
ir a reuniones   to go to
    meetings
ir de compras   to go
    shopping
ir de excursion   to go hiking;
    to go on a trip
ir de viaje   to go travelling
ir en monopatín   to go
    skateboarding
ir de paseo   to go for a walk
Irlanda   Ireland
irse   to go away
irse de juerga   to live it up
isla   island
Islandia   Iceland
Italia   Italy
el italiano   Italian (language/
    subject)

J

el jabón   soap
jamás   never, ever
el jamón   ham
el jarabe   syrup
el jardín   garden
la jardinería   gardening
el jefe/la jefa   boss
el jerbo   gerbil
la jornada   working day
el/la joven   young (person)
los jóvenes   young people
la joyería   jeweller's
jubilado/a   retired
la judía   bean
las judías verdes   green beans
el juego   game
los juegos de azar   games of
    chance
el jueves   (on) Thursday
el/la jugador/a   player
jugar   to play
el juguete   toy
la juguetería   toy shop
julio   July
junio   June
juntarse   to gather, to come
    together
junto con   together with
justo/a   fair, right
la juventud   youth
juzgar   to judge

K

el kárate   karate
el kilo   kilo
el kilómetro   kilometre

L

el laboratorio   laboratory
los lácteos   dairy products
el lago   lake

la lagartija   small lizard
el lagarto   lizard
la lágrima   tear
la lámpara   lamp
la lana   wool
el lapicero   pencil
el lápiz   pencil
el lápiz de color   coloured
    pencil
largo/a   long
la lata   tin
el latín   Latin (language/
    subject)
latinoamericano/a   Latin
    American
los lavabos   toilets
la lavadora   washing machine
el lavaplatos   dishwasher
lavar el pelo   to wash hair
lavar el coche   to wash the
    car
lavar(se)   to wash, to clean
leal   loyal, faithful
la leche   milk
la lechuga   lettuce
el/la lector/a   reader
la lectura   reading
leer   to read
las legumbres   pulse
lejos   far
la lengua   language; tongue
lento/a   slow
la letra   letter
levantarse   to get up
la libertad   freedom
libre   free
la librería   bookshop
el libro   book
el libro de texto   textbook
la licenciatura   degree
ligeramente   lightly
ligero/a   light
el límite   limit
el limón   lemon
la limonada   lemonade
limpiar   to clean
limpiar los cristales   to clean
    the windows

limpiar el polvo to do the dusting
la **limpieza** cleaning
limpio/a clean
la **limusina** limousine
la **linterna** torch
liso/a smooth, straight (hair)
listo/a ready, clever
la **literatura** literature
el **litro** litre
la **llamada** telephone call
llamarse to be called
la **llave** key
llegar to get (to a place), to arrive
llenar to fill
lleno/a de full of
llevar to wear; to take (e.g. by car)
llevar una vida dura to lead a hard life
llevar uniforme to wear a uniform
llorar to cry
llover to rain
la **lluvia** rain
lo bueno de the good thing about
lo malo de the bad thing about
lo mejor the best thing
lo peor the worst thing
lo siento I'm sorry
lo único the only thing
el **local** premises
loco/a mad
la **locura** madness
lograr to gain, to succeed (in)
el **logro** success, achievement
la **loncha** slice
el **loro** parrot
la **lucha** struggle; wrestling
luchar (contra) to struggle (against)
luego then, next
el **lugar** place
los **lugares de interés** places of interest

la **luna** moon
el **lunes** (on) Monday
Luxemburgo Luxembourg
la **luz** light

M

la **madera** wood
la **madrastra** stepmother
la **madre** mother
el/la **madrileño/a** citizen of Madrid
la **madrugada** the early hours of the morning
mágico/a magic
el **maíz** corn, maize
majo/a good-looking, nice, lovely
mal badly
el **mal tiempo** bad weather
maleducado/a badly behaved
la **maleta** suitcase
el **maletín** (*Sp*) briefcase
malgastar to waste
el **malgasto** waste
malo/a bad
los **malos tratos** physical abuse
el **maltrato** abuse
mañana morning; tomorrow
mandar to send
mandar un fax to send a fax
la **manera** way, manner
la **mano** hand
el **mantel** tablecloth
mantener to maintain, to keep
mantenerse en forma to keep fit
mantenerse sano to keep healthy
la **mantequilla** butter
la **manzana** apple; block (of houses)
el **mapa** map
el **maquillaje** make-up

maquillarse to put on one's make-up
la **máquina** machine
el **mar** sea
la **maravilla** wonder
maravilloso/a marvellous
marcar un gol to score a goal
mareado/a sick, dizzy
el **marido** husband
el/la **marinero/a** sailor
el **marisco** shellfish
marrón brown
marrón claro/a light brown
marrón oscuro/a dark brown
Marruecos Morocco
el **martes** (on) Tuesday
marzo March
más more
más adelante further on
más de more than (followed by a number)
más...que more...than
la **masa** dough
la **mascota** pet
masticar to chew
matar to kill
las **matemáticas** maths
el **matrimonio** marriage
mayo May
mayor larger; older
la **mayoría** majority
la **mayoría de la gente** most people
la **mayoría del tiempo** most of the time
el/la **mecánico/a** mechanic
el **mechero** cigarette lighter
la **media** stocking
la **medianoche** midnight
(la) **media pensión** half board
el/la **médico/a** doctor
medio half, mid
el **medio ambiente** environment
el **mediodía** midday
los **medios (de comunicación)** media
medir to measure

Méjico, México Mexico

el **mejillón** mussel

mejor better

mejorar to improve

el **melocotón** peach

mencionar to mention

menor smaller; younger

menos less, except

menos…que less…than

el **mensaje** message

el **mensaje de texto** sms, text message

la **mente** mind

mentir to lie

la **mentira** lie

mentiroso/a lying, false

el **mercadillo** street market

el **mercado** market

la **merienda** snack, afternoon tea, picnic

el **mérito** merit

la **merluza** hake

el **mes** month

la **mesa** table

mestizo/a mixed race

meter goles to score goals

meter to put

el **método** method

el **metro** metre; underground

la **mezcla** mixture

mezclar to mix

el **microondas** microwave

el **miedo** fear

mientras (que) while

el **miércoles** (on) Wednesday

mil a thousand

el **minuto** minute

la **misa** mass

mismo/a same; (one)self

la **mitad** half

la **mochila** school bag, backpack

la **moda** fashion

el/la **modelo** model

el **modo de transporte** means of transport

el **modo de vivir** way of life

¡**mola mazo!** fantastic!

molestar to bother, to annoy, to upset

el **momento** moment

la **moneda** coin; currency

el **monedero** purse

la **montaña** mountain

montañoso/a mountainous

montar a caballo to ride a horse

montar en bici to go for a bike ride

moreno/a dark

morir to die

morir de hambre to die of hunger

mostrar to show

la **moto** motorbike

mover to move

el **móvil** mobile phone

el/la **muchacho/a** boy/girl

la **muchedumbre** crowd

mucho/a much, a lot

mucho gusto pleased to meet you

mudarse to move house

mudo/a dumb

los **muebles** furniture

la **muela** tooth

muerto/a de hambre starving

la **mujer** woman; wife

la **mujer de negocios** businesswoman

mundial worldwide

el **mundo** world

la **muñeca** doll

el **músculo** muscle

el **museo** museum

el **museo de arte** art gallery

la **música** music

musulmán/ musulmana Moslem

muy very

N

nacer to be born

el **nacimiento** birth

la **nación** nation

la **nacionalidad** nationality

nada nothing, anything

nadar to swim

nadie no one, anyone

la **naranja** orange

la **nariz** nose

la **nata** fresh cream

la **natación** swimming

naturalmente naturally

navegar to navigate

navegar por/en Internet to surf the internet

Navidad(es) Christmas

navideño/a (of) Christmas

necesario/a necessary

necesitar to need

negro/a black

nervioso/a nervous

nevar to snow

la **nevera** fridge

ni…ni… neither…nor…

ni siquiera not even

la **niebla** fog

el/la **nieto/a** grandson/grand-daughter

la **nieve** snow

ningún, ninguno/a no

el/la **niño/niña** boy/girl

el **nivel** level

no importa it doesn't matter

no obstante nevertheless

la **noche** night

la **Nochebuena** Christmas Eve

el **nombre** name

el **nombre de pila** first name

el **noreste** northeast

la **norma** rule

el **noroeste** northwest

el **norte** north

la **nota** note; mark

las **noticias** news

Vocabulario

la **novia** girlfriend; bride

noviembre November

el **novio** boyfriend; bridegroom

nublado/a cloudy

la **nuera** daughter-in-law

Nueva Zelanda New Zealand

la **nuez** nut, walnut

nunca never

O

o or

obediente obedient

objetos perdidos lost property

obligar to oblige

obligatorio/a obligatory, compulsory

la **obra de teatro** play

el/la **obrero/a** labourer

obtener to obtain, to get

obvio/a obvious

el **océano** ocean

ocho días a week

el **ocio** leisure

octubre October

ocupado/a busy, engaged

ocurrir to happen

odiar to hate

el **oeste** west

ofender to offend

la **oficina** office

la **oficina de turismo** tourist office

el/la **oficinista** office worker

ofrecer to offer

el **oído** ear

oír to hear

ojalá if only

el **ojo** eye

oler to smell

el **olor** smell

olvidarse de to forget

ondulado/a wavy

opinar to have an opinion

la **opinión** opinion

la **oportunidad** opportunity

optimista optimistic

el **ordenador** (*Sp*) computer

la **oreja** ear

organizar to organise

orgulloso/a proud

el **origen** origin

originarse to originate

el **oro** gold

la **orquesta** orchestra

oscuro/a dark

el **otoño** autumn

otro/a other

otra vez again

el/la **oyente** listener

P

la **paciencia** patience

paciente patient

padecer to suffer

el **padrastro** step-father

los **padres** parents

el **padrino** godfather

pagar to pay

la **página** page

la **página web** webpage

el **país** country

el **paisaje** countryside

los **Paises Bajos** the Netherlands

el **pájaro** bird

la **palabra** word

el **palacio** palace

pálido/a pale

el **pan** bread

la **panadería** baker's

el **panecillo** roll

los **pantalones** trousers

el **pan toastado** toasted bread

el **pañuelo de papel** paper handkerchief

el **papagayo** parrot

el **papel** paper

el **papel (de cine)** role

el **papel higiénico** toilet paper

la **papelería** stationer's

el **paquete** packet

para for, in order to/that

la **parada de autobús** bus stop

el **parador** (*Sp*) state-run hotel

el **paraguas** umbrella

parar to stop

parece mentira que I can't believe that, it's unbelievable

parecer to appear, to seem

parecido/a similar

la **pared** wall

la **pareja** partner, pair

los **parientes** relatives

el **parque** park

el **parque de atracciones** amusement park

el **parque temático** theme park

la **parte** part

el **partido** match (e.g. football)

el **patrimonio** patrimony

la **pasa** raisin

el **pasado** past

pasado/a de moda outdated, old-fashioned

el/la **pasajero/a** passenger

el **pasaporte** passport

pasar to happen

pasar de largo to go straight past

pasar la aspiradora to hoover

pasarlo bomba to have a great time

el **pasatiempo** hobby, pastime

la **Pascua** Easter

pasear el perro to walk the dog

pasearse to go for a stroll

el **paseo** walk

el **pasillo** corridor

la **pasta de dientes** toothpaste

el **pastel** cake

la **pastelería** cake shop

la **pastilla** tablet, pastille, pill

la **patata** potato

las **patatas fritas** chips; crisps

el **patín** skate

el **patinaje** skating

patinar to skate

patinar sobre ruedas to roller-skate

el **patio** patio; playground

el **pavo** turkey

la **paz** peace

la **peca** freckle

el **pedazo** piece

pediatra pediatric

pedir to ask for

pegar to strike, to hit; to stick

el **pegamento** glue

peinarse to comb one's hair

pelar to peel

pelear(se) to fight

la **película** film

la **película de acción** action film

la **película de amor** romantic film

la **película de aventura** adventure film

la **película de ciencia ficción** science-fiction film

la **película de espionaje** spy film

la **película de fantasía** fantasy film

la **película de guerra** war film

la **película del Oeste** Western

la **película de terror** horror film

la **película de vaqueros** western

la **película histórica** historical film

la **película musical** musical

la **película policíaca** detective/ crime film

la **película romántica** romantic film

el **peligro** danger

peligroso/a dangerous

pelirrojo/a red-haired

el **pelo** hair

la **peluquería** hairdresser's

el/la **peluquero/a** hairdresser

la **pena** pity, sorrow, shame

el **pendiente** earring

la **península** peninsula

la **pensamiento** thought

pensar to think, to intend

pensativo/a thoughtful

la **pensión** cheap hotel

(la) **pensión completa** full board

el **pepino** cucumber

pequeño/a little, small

los **pequeños** little children

la **pera** pear

perder to miss; to lose

la **pérdida** loss

la **pérdida de tiempo** waste of time

perdido/a lost

perdón excuse me

perdonar to forgive

perezoso/a lazy

perfecto/a perfect

la **perfumería** perfumery

el **perico** parakeet

el **periódico** newspaper

el/la **periodista** journalist

el **permiso** permission

permitir to allow, to permit

peor worse

el **perro** dog

el **perro caliente** hot dog

perseguir to pursue

la **persona** person

la **personalidad** personality

pertenecer to belong

Perú Peru

la **pesadilla** nightmare

pesado/a boring, tedious

pesar to weigh

las **pesas** weight-training

la **pesca** fishing

la **pescadería** fishmonger's

el **pescado** fish (to eat)

pesimista pessimistic

el **peso** weight

el **pez** fish (in water)

el **pez dorado** goldfish

el **piano** piano

picado/a chopped

la **picadura** bite

picar to sting; to prick; to nibble

a **pie** on foot

el **pie** foot

la **piel** skin

la **pierna** leg

la **pila** battery

pillar (coll.) to catch

el **piloto** pilot

el **pimiento** pepper

la **piña** pineapple

pintar to paint

pintoresco/a picturesque

las **pinzas** tweezers

el **piragüismo** canoeing

el **piropo** compliment

la **piscina** swimming pool

el **piso** flat; floor

la **pista** track; slope

la **pista de hielo/de patinaje** ice rink

la **pista de tenis** tennis court

la **pistola** baguette

planchar la ropa to iron clothes

planear to plan

el **planeta** planet

el **plano** plan

la **planta** floor, storey

la **planta baja** ground floor

el **plástico** plastic

el **plátano** banana

los **platillos** cymbals

el **plato** plate, dish

la **playa** beach

la **plaza** square, place

la **plaza de toros** bullring

la **plaza mayor** main square

la **pluma** fountain pen

pobre poor

la **pobreza** poverty

pocas veces seldom, rarely

poco/a little, not much

un **poco** a little

poco a poco gradually

poco interestante uninteresting, dull

pocos/as few

poder to be able

el/la **policía** policeman/woman

el **polideportivo** sports centre

el/la **político/a** politician

el **pollo** chicken

Vocabulario

Polonia Poland
el **pomelo** grapefruit
poner to put on, to show (programme, film)
poner la mesa to lay the table
ponerse to put on (clothes)
ponerse de acuerdo to agree
poquito a little bit
por by, because of, along
por cierto certainly
por día each/per day
por eso therefore
por la mañana in the morning
por la noche in the evening/ at night
por la tarde in the afternoon/ evening
por lo menos at least
por medio de by means of
por otra parte on the other hand
por otro lado on the other hand
por parte de (mi madre etc.) on (my mother's etc.) side
por supuesto of course
por todas partes everywhere
por una parte on the one hand
por un lado on the one hand
el **porcentaje** percentage
porque because
el **portafolio** (LA) briefcase
el/la **portero/a** caretaker
¿por qué? why?
posible possible
la **posibilidad** possibility
la **posición** position
la **postal** postcard
el **póster** poster
el **postre** pudding, dessert
el **pozo** well
la **práctica de trabajo** work experience

practicar to practise
práctico/a practical
el **precio** price, cost
precioso/a beautiful, lovely
la **precipitación** rainfall
precipitarse to rush
la **preferencia** preference
preferible preferable
preferir to prefer
preguntar to ask (a question)
el **prejuicio** prejudice
premiado/a prize-winning
el **premio** prize
la **prensa** press
la **preocupación** worry
preocupado/a anxious
preocupante worrying
preocuparse por to worry about
prepararse para to prepare for
el/la **presentador/a** presenter
la **primavera** spring
primero/a first
el/la **primo/a** cousin
principal main, principal
principalmente mainly
el **principio** beginning
probar to try, to taste
el **problema** problem
la **procesión** procession
producir to produce
el **producto** product
el **productor** producer
la **profesión** job, profession
el/la **profesor/a, profe** (coll.) teacher
profundo/a deep, profound
el **programa** program(me)
la **programación** viewing guide
prohibir to forbid
prometer to promise
el **pronóstico** weather forecast
pronto soon
propio/a own
proporcionar to give, to provide
la **protección** protection

proteger to protect
provocar to cause
próximo/a next
la **prueba** test, proof
la **publicidad** publicity; advertising
público/a public
pueblerino/a rustic
el **pueblo** small town; village
el **puente** bridge
la **puerta** door
la **puerta de embarque** departure gate
el **puerto** port, harbour
pues then, well
el **puesto** stall
la **pulgada** inch
el **pulso** pulse

Q

quedarse to stay, to remain
quedarse en el cole to stay on at school
quedarse en la cama to stay in bed
la **queja** complaint
quejarse to complain
la **quemadura** burn
quemar to burn
querer to wish, to want, to love
querer decir to mean
querido/a dear
el **queso** cheese
¡Que aproveche! Enjoy your meal!, Bon appetit!
¡Qué pena! What a shame!
¿Qué pasa? What's happening?
¿Qué tal? How are you/ things?
quien who, whom
la **química** chemistry
quince días a fortnight
las **quinielas** football pools
el **quiosco** kiosk
quitar to take away

quitar la mesa to clear the table

quizás perhaps

R

la **ración** portion, helping

la **radio** radio

la **rana** frog

rápidamente quickly

rápido/a rapid, quick

raro/a strange

el **rasgo** trait

el **rato** time, while

la **rata** rat

el **ratón** mouse

la **razón** reason

razonable reasonable

recaudar dinero to collect money

la **recepción** reception

el/la **recepcionista** receptionist

rechazar to reject

recibir to receive

recibir una llamada to receive a call

el **recibo** receipt

reciclable recyclable

reciclar to recycle

recién hecho/a just made/ done

reciente recent

el **recipiente** container

recomendar to recommend

reconocer to recognise

recordar to remember

el **recreo** break

el **recuerdo** souvenir, memory

los **recursos** resources

la **red** network, web

redondo/a round

reducir to reduce

el **refresco** soft drink

la **regla** rule, ruler

el **regalo** present

regar las plantas to water the plants

el **régimen**, *pl.*
  regímenes diet; regime

la **región** region

la **regla** ruler

regresar to return

regresar a casa to go home

el **regreso** return

la **reina** queen

el **Reino Unido** United Kingdom

reír to laugh

reírse de to laugh at, to mock

la **relación** relation, relationship

relajarse to relax

el **relámpago** lightning

la **religión** religion

religioso/a religious

rellenar to fill

el **reloj** clock, watch

el **remedio** cure, remedy

remover to stir

remunerar to remunerate

el **rendimiento escolar** school performance

repartir el correo to deliver the post

el **reparto** cast

repasar to revise

repentino/a sudden

repetir to repeat

repetitivo/a repetitive

el **reportaje** report

el/la **reportero/a** reporter

requerir to require

la **reserva** reservation

reservar to book, to reserve

respetar to respect

la **respiración** breathing

respirar to breathe

resplandeciente radiant, shining

responder to respond, to answer

la **responsabilidad** responsibility

responsable responsible

la **respuesta** reply, response

el **resultado** result

el **retraso** delay

el **retrete** toilet

la **reunión** meeting

reunirse to meet (up)

reutilizar to reuse

la **revista** magazine

el **rey** king

los **Reyes Magos** Magi, Three Kings

rico/a rich, tasty (of food)

el **riesgo** risk

el **rincón** corner

el **río** river

la **risa** laughter

rizado/a curly

robar to steal

el **robo** robbery

rodeado/a de surrounded by

la **rodilla** knee

el **rollo** bore

romántico/a romantic

la **ropa** clothes

la **ropa de moda** fashionable clothes

rosa pink

roto/a broken

el **rotulador** felt-tip pen; marker pen

rubio/a blond(e)

el **rugby** rugby

el **ruido** noise

ruidoso/a noisy

rural rural

la **ruta** route

la **rutina** routine

S

el **sábado** (on) Saturday

saber to know

el **sabor** taste

sabroso/a tasty

el **sacapuntas** pencil sharpener

sacar to take out

el **sacacorchos** corkscrew

sacar la basura to take out the rubbish

sacar fotos to take photos

Vocabulario

el **saco de dormir**   sleeping bag

la **sal**   salt

la **sala**   room

la **sala de espera**   waiting room

la **sala de estar**   living room

la **sala de profesores**   staff room

la **salchicha**   sausage

la **salida**   exit; departure

salir   to go out

salir de casa   to leave the house

el **salón**   lounge, living room

saltar   to jump

el **salto**   jump

la **salud**   health

¡Salud!   Cheers!

saludable   healthy

saludar   to greet

el **saludo**   greeting

salvar   to save

salvo   except

la **sangre**   blood

sano/a   healthy

San Valentín   Valentine's day

la **sardina**   sardine

la **sartén**   frying pan

satisfecho/a   satisfied

el **saxofón**   saxophone

secarse   to get dry

la **sección**   department (in store), section

seco/a   dry

el/la **secretario/a**   secretary

la **seda**   silk

seguir   to continue, to follow

seguir estudiando   to carry on studying

según   according to

segundo/a   second

la **seguridad**   safety, security

seguro/a   sure

el **sello**   stamp

la **selva**   forest

el **semáforo**   traffic light

la **semana**   week

la **semana pasada**   last week

la **semana que viene**   next week

(la) **Semana Santa**   Holy Week

semejante   similar

la **señal**   signal, sign

señalar   to point out

sencillo/a   simple; single (ticket)

sensible   sensitive

sentado/a   seated

sentarse   to sit down

el **sentido común**   common sense

el **sentido del humor**   sense of humour

el **sentimiento**   feeling

sentir   to feel

separar   to separate

separado/a   separated

septiembre   September

la **sequía**   drought

ser   to be

ser aficionado/a a   to be keen on

ser ecológico/a   to be ecological

ser licenciado/a   to have a degree

serio/a   serious

la **serpiente**   snake

el **servicio**   toilet, washroom

la **servilleta**   serviette, napkin

servir   to serve

severo/a   strict

si   if

siempre   always

la **sierra**   mountain range

el **siglo**   century

significar   to mean, to signify

significativo/a   significant

siguiente   following, next

la **silla**   chair

el **sillón**   armchair

el **símbolo**   symbol

simpático/a   nice, kind

sin   without

sincero/a   sincere

sin duda   without doubt

sin embargo   however

sino   but

los **sin techo**   homeless people

el **sistema**   system

el **sitio**   place, site, pitch

la **situación**   situation

situarse   to be situated

sobre   on, about (of time)

sobre todo   especially

sobrevivir   to survive

el/la **sobrino/a**   nephew/niece

el/la **socio/a**   member

el **socorro**   help

el **sofá**   sofa

el **sol**   sun

solamente   only

soler   to do as a habit/usually

solicitar un puesto   to apply for a job

solo/a   alone, on one's own

solo   only

soltero/a   single, unmarried

la **sombra**   shadow

el **sombrero**   hat

el **sonido**   sound

sonriente   smiling

la **sonrisa**   smile

soñar (con)   to dream (about/of)

la **sopa**   soup

sordo/a   deaf

sorprendentemente   surprisingly

la **sorpresa**   surprise

el **sótano**   basement

suave   mild

suavemente   gently, smoothly

la **subida**   rise

subir   to rise, to go up

los **subtítulos**   subtitles

sucio/a   dirty

Sudáfrica   South Africa

Suecia   Sweden

el/la **suegro/a**   father-in-law/mother-in-law

el **sueldo**   salary

el **suelo**   ground

el **sueño** sleep, dream
suficiente enough, suffcient
sufrir to suffer
la **sugerencia** suggestion
sugerir to suggest
Suiza Switzerland
superar to overcome
superguapo/a very good-looking
el **supermercado** supermarket
suponer to suppose
el **sur** south
el **sureste** southeast
surfear Internet to surf the internet
surgir to arise
el **suroeste** southwest
el **surtido** selection, range
suspender un examen to fail an exam
sustituir to substitute

T

la **talla** size
el **taller** workshop
tal vez perhaps
el **tamaño** size
también also
el **tambor** drum
tampoco neither
tan...como as...as
tanto/a...como as/so much...as
la **taquilla** box office, ticket office
tardar (en) to be late
tarde late
la **tarea** task
la **tarea de casa** household task/chore
la **tarjeta** card
la **tarjeta móvil** mobile card
la **tarta** tart, cake
el **taxi** taxi
la **taza** cup(ful)
el **té** tea

el **teatro** theatre; drama
el **tebeo** comic
el **techo** roof
el **teclado** keyboard
el/la **técnico/a** technician
la **tecnología** technology
la **tela** fabric, cloth
el **telediario** news
telefonear to telephone
el **(telefóno) móvil** mobile phone
la **telenovela** soap opera
el **televisor** television set
el **tema** topic, theme
temer to fear, to be afraid
el **temor** fear
la **temperatura** temperature
la **temporada** season
temporal temporary
temprano/a early
el **tenedor** fork
tener to have
tener celos to be jealous
tener cuidado to be careful
tener dolor de cabeza to have a headache
tener dolor de muelas to have toothache
tener éxito to be successful
tener fiebre to have a temperature/fever
tener ganas de to want to
tener hambre to be hungry
tener lugar to take place
tener miedo to be afraid
tener que to have to
tener razón to be right
tener sed to be thirsty
tener sueño to be sleepy
tener suerte to be lucky
tener tos to have a cough
tener una insolación to have sunstroke
tener una picadura to have a bite
tener una quemadura to have a burn
tener un resfriado to have a cold

el **tenis** tennis
el **tenis de mesa** table tennis, ping pong
la **terapia** therapy
el **Tercer Mundo** Third World
tercero/a third
terminar to finish
el **termómetro** thermometer
la **ternera** veal
la **terraza** terrace, balcony
el **terrorismo** terrorism
el **tiempo** weather; time
el **tiempo libre** free time
la **tienda** shop; tent
la **tienda de música** record/ music shop
la **tienda de ropa** clothes shop
la **tienda de ultramarinos** greengrocer's
la **tierra** land
las **tijeras** scissors
tímido/a shy
la **tinta** ink
el/la **tío/a** uncle/aunt
típico/a typical
el **tipo** type, kind
tirar to throw away
la **tirita** plaster
el **tiro con arco** archery
los **titulares** headlines
el **título** title; qualification
la **toalla** towel
el **tobillo** ankle
tocar to play (an instrument); to touch
todo/a all
todavía still
todo el mundo everybody
todo el rato all the time
todos los días each/every day
tomar to take
tomar el aire fresco to take in the fresh air
tomar el sol to sunbathe
el **tomate** tomato
tonto/a stupid, crazy
torcer to turn, to twist
el/la **torero/a** bullfighter

la **tormenta**   storm
la **tortilla**   omelette
la **tortilla de patatas**   Spanish
      omelette
la **tortuga**   tortoise
la **tos**   cough
la **tostada**   toast, piece of toast
trabajador/a   hardworking
trabajar   to work
el **trabajo de mis sueños**   my
      dream job
la **tradición**   tradition
tradicional   traditional
traer   to bring, to get, to fetch
el **tráfico**   traffic
tragar   to swallow
el **traje**   dress, suit
tranquilo/a   calm
el **tratamiento**   treatment
tratar de   to be about
tratar mejor   to treat better
travieso/a   naughty
la **trayectoria**   route
el **tren**   train
el **tren de**
      cercanías   suburban/
      commuter train
el **trimestre**   term
triste   sad
el **trombón**   trombone
la **trompeta**   trumpet
trozear   to cut into pieces
el **trozo**   slice, piece
el **trueno**   thunder
el **tubo**   tube
el **túnel**   tunnel
el **turismo**   tourism
el/la **turista**   tourist
turístico/a   tourist
el **turrón** (*Sp*)   nougat
el/la **tutor/a**   tutor
la **tutoría**   tutorial

U

u   or (before *o* and *ho*)
último/a   last
los **ultramarinos**   groceries
una vez   once
único/a   only
el **uniforme**   uniform
unir   to join
la **universidad**   university
usar   to use
útil   useful
utilizar   to use
la **uva**   grape

V

la **vaca**   cow
las **vacaciones**   holidays
vaciar el lavavajillas   to
      empty the dishwasher
vacío/a   empty
vago/a   lazy
vale   OK
vale la pena   it's worth while
valiente   brave
valioso/a   useful
el **valle**   valley
el **valor**   value
los **vaqueros**   jeans
la **variedad**   variety
el **vaso**   glass
el/la **vecino/a**   neighbour
la **vela**   candle; sailing
vencer   to beat, conquer
la **venda**   bandage
el **vendaval**   gale
vender   to sell
Venezuela   Venezuela
venir   to come

la **venta**   sale
la **ventaja**   advantage
la **ventana**   window
ver   to see
ver la televisión   to watch
      television
el **verano**   summer
la **verbena**   open-air celebration,
      festival
la **verdad**   truth
verdaderamente   really, truly
verdadero/a   true
verde   green
las **verduras**   green vegetables
verter   to pour (out)
el **vestido**   dress
vestirse   to dress/get dressed
el/la **veterinario/a**   vet
la **vez**   time
viajar   to travel
el **viaje**   journey, trip
el/la **viajero/a**   traveller
vibrar   to vibrate
la **vida**   life
el **videoclub**   video-rental shop
los **videojuegos**   video games
el **vidrio**   glass
viejo/a   old
el **viento**   wind
el **viernes**   (on) Friday
el **villancico**   Christmas carol
el **vino**   wine
la **violencia**   violence
el **violín**   violin
visitar   to visit
la **víspera**   night before
la **vista**   view
vistas al mar   sea views
viudo/a   widowed
la **vivienda**   dwelling
vivir   to live

vivir a tope   to live life to
the full

vivo/a   bright, vivid

volar   to fly

el **volcán**   volcano

el **voleibol**   volleyball

voltear   to turn over

el **volumen**   volume

voluntario/a   voluntary
worker

volver   to return

volver a + *infinitive*   to (do)
again

la **voz**   voice

el **vuelo**   flight

la **vuelta**   return

W

el **windsurf**   windsurfing

Y

ya   now, already

ya no   no longer

ya que   since

el **yerno**   son-in-law

el **yogur**   yogurt

Z

la **zanahoria**   carrot

la **zapatería**   shoe shop

la **zapatilla**   slipper

las **zapatillas (de
deporte)**   trainers

el **zapato**   shoe

la **zona**   area, region

el **zumo**   juice